Deadly Affair

Deadly Affair

Nicholas Davies

BLAKE'S
TRUE
CRIME
LIBRARY

Published by Blake Publishing Ltd,
3 Bramber Court, 2 Bramber Road,
London W14 9PB, England

First published in 1999

ISBN 1 85782 3583

British Library Cataloguing-in-Publication Data:
A catalogue record for this book is available
from the British Library.

Typeset by t2

Printed in Finland by WSOY

1 3 5 7 9 10 8 6 4 2

Contents

Dear Reader,

Few can say that they have never felt the surges of sexual jealousy; it is commonplace enough. So it is all the more terrifying when we hear of the devastating effect it can have on the minds of those who are not psychologically prepared to deal with it.

The immediacy of the story that unfolds within the pages of this book is one that will shock you to the very core. It is the true story of a classic love triangle that culminated in one of the most gruesome murders in living memory. The author has spoken to the people at the very heart of the scenario, and the result is not only a brilliantly realised resumé of the horrifc events surrounding this crime, but also an important psychological portayal of the mind of a killer besotted by overpowering jealousy.

If this book makes you uncomfortable, then well it might. It is a reminder of what can happen when things go too far ...

Adam Parfitt
Editor
Blake's True Crime Library

Penny

★ ★ ★

Penny McAllister ran up the steps to her parents' home, calling out to them as she pushed open the door. She would be home for the weekend, away from the security alerts of Northern Ireland but also away from the man she loved, her husband, Duncan.

Norma and Desmond Squire greeted Penny with smiles and hugs. Despite six years of married life, she remained close to her parents, and they still missed their beloved, bright daughter of whom they had always been so proud. Over a cup of coffee Penny chatted away to them, telling them her latest news and gossip and all about her life as an army officer's wife amid the Troubles.

Norma asked particularly about Penny's husband, a Duncan McAllister, a captain in the Royal Signals Regiment, stationed with the 3rd Infantry Brigade Headquarters at Armagh in Northern Ireland. 'Oh, he's fine, he's great,' she replied, 'but he's working so hard.'

Throughout that weekend of partying Norma waited patiently, and with some anxiety, to see whether her daughter would mention 'the other woman', the young army private Penny had spoken of just once before in a telephone conversation two months previously.

That weekend, however, Penny never said a word about the young woman who had become the major problem in her life, the woman who would not leave her husband alone. And Norma, too, said nothing. She hoped her daughter's 'problem' had gone away.

Penny had flown home to celebrate the twenty-first birthday of Mandy, her brother Nick's girlfriend whom she had never met. She had heard so much about her that she wanted to be at home for the family celebrations. Penny was doubly interested to meet Mandy because she believed her brother might marry her and Penny wanted to get to know her future sister-in-law.

Throughout that weekend the family talked of their happy times together in England, Gibraltar and Germany where her father Desmond had been a posted overseas teaching children of army personnel in schools run by SCEA, the Services Children's Education Authority.

In many ways Penny had had an idyllic early life, growing up in a family where love was of paramount importance. Norma has always been convinced that Penny had been conceived on a hillside in Wordsworth country, as she and Desmond lazed together on the rolling downs above Lake Windermere one summer's afternoon.

'It was simply a wonderful romantic day,' Norma explained. 'Heaven-sent. I know some women believe it impossible to know precisely when their babies are conceived, but others, like me, believe sometimes one does know exactly the moment. I am convinced that Penny was conceived on that beautiful hillside overlooking Lake Windermere. It was so very romantic.' Penny was born nine months later, in May 1966.

Norma would say later, 'I am sure it was one of those extraordinary, unbelievable, coincidences that occur in life. Penny was conceived in the open air and she would die in the open air.'

Norma and Desmond met while singing in an Operatic Society in Bracknell New Town, Berkshire. She was married when just eighteen, the same age her mother married and the same age at which Penny, too, would eventually marry.

Norma's early life with Desmond was tough. He taught at Priestwood Primary School, Berkshire, and they had great difficulty making ends meet. He recalled, 'We were so poor. I can remember calling round to Norma's parents at the end of every month because we just didn't have any money left for food. They would give us whatever food we needed. Without their help we would have found it impossible to cope.

'Worse still,' he joked, 'I can even remember having to raid Penny's piggy bank to get the money for the bus fare to her parents' home on the odd occasion. We really were that poor. At that time I was earning £50 a month and having to pay £20 a month rent. I saved money by cycling everywhere. But at the end of every month we were broke. It was fortunate, Norma's parents were so kind.'

Meanwhile, baby Penny stole all their attention. Bright, lively, chubby and always alert, Penny would stay awake for hours at night and Norma and Desmond would take it in turns to rock their baby to sleep, sometimes for hours at a time.

Norma commented, 'Penny was truly a wonderful baby but, I must confess, we did spoil her, though not materially because we couldn't afford to. We thought she was pretty, of course, but she wasn't amazingly so. She walked at ten months and started reading at an early age. And we encouraged her as much as we could in everything she tackled.'

In order to break out of their church-mouse existence, Desmond applied to the Ministry of Defence for an overseas teaching job and was posted to Gibraltar in January 1969, just seven months after their second child, Nicholas, was born.

Norma recalled, 'It was extraordinary. Both Penny and Nick were born on the same day, 23 May. In that way I know that whatever happens I will never forget Penny. She will always be in our minds.'

As a child, Penny suffered from asthma and the warm sunshine of Gibraltar helped her overcome the problem. It would never recur.

After the years of struggle Gibraltar was fun, the family forged close ties in those years. Norma took a job, hosting the Rock's weekly television show *Midweek*. She would say, later, 'Sometimes I would have to take both Penny and Nick to the studio because I couldn't aways arrange a babysitter. I can still remember them playing under my desk in the studio while the programe was in full swing. Of course it proved quite difficult to concentrate; I was so worried that one of them would suddenly stand up or shout or cry. Yet somehow they didn't.'

Three years later the family moved to Germany, and spent the first two years at Fallingbostel near Hanover, before moving in 1974 to Soltau, only fifteen miles away. Four years later they would move to Lippstadt where Desmond became acting headmaster of King's School, and where Penny was destined to meet her future husband, Duncan McAllister.

Norma recalls, 'Despite the tragedy that has wrecked our lives I keep recalling those idyllic years the family were together. We were all so very happy because we grew so close to one another. I think it was serving in foreign countries, sometimes in closed garrison towns, that helped to keep the family together as a unit.

'Neither Penny nor Nick wanted to rush off on a their own. They seemed to want to stay together with us and, of course, it was wonderful for Desmond and me.'

From an early age Penny attended school and until eleven years old she would stay in the class her father taught. As a result Penny grew particularly close to him. He would take her to school with him each day, teach her through most of the morning and afternoon and then would return home with her in the early evening.

After school they would go for walks together in the woods and fields near their homes in Germany and Penny would never stop asking him questions about everything. 'She became so interested, so vital, so keen to know the reasons for everything,' he recalled with emotion in his voice. 'We had the most wonderful time together, a close and remarkable relationship between a father and daughter.'

Desmond recalled, 'I taught her to trust people; to understand that people were far less fortunate than we were; that people had weaknesses and sometimes could not help the way they behaved and the actions they took. Now of course I wonder whether, by teaching Penny to trust people, I was partially responsible for her being too trusting, to the extent she came to trust the young woman who was prepared to kill her in cold blood.'

As well as her schoolwork Penny fell in love with music and became proficient on both the recorder and the clarinet. She showed such talent that she was invited to play in various British regimental bands during their tours of duty with the British Army of the Rhine, a job she loved. She would also play in concerts held in schoolrooms and garrisons on Sunday evenings, and Nick and her parents would often attend. 'She loved us being there,' Norma recalled. 'She loved having our support when she was on stage. I think it gave her confidence.'

Penny also discovered she had a clear singing voice, and teachers encouraged her to join the school choirs. When fifteen, Penny would be chosen to sing most of the solo parts in Christmas carols. Her pièce de résistance, which the local German people adored, was 'Silent Night', which she sang in near-perfect German. Later she would be invited to become the lead soprano in the King's School staff choir, which had acquired a formidable reputation.

Not surprisingly, she also took to the stage, often playing lead roles during the four years she attended Kings School in Gutersloh, North Rhine Westphalia. Understandably, her parents became tremendously proud of their daughter's achievements.

Penny was also academically gifted, passing her eleven plus examination with flying colours. Her IQ at that stage was an impressive 132. At King's School she became one of their star pupils, taking ten 'O' levels and passing them all. Her school report of July 1979, when attending King's, reveals the extent of her popularity and her commitment to studying. Her group tutor wrote, 'Penelope appears to have settled extremely well and made friends. A quiet and serious young lady who works well. A very pleasing report. Her help in the library has been appreciated. Conduct is excellent. Punctuality, good.' Her head of house wrote, 'A most impressive young lady. Penelope is cheerful, has a well-developed personality and I trust will be a confirmed asset to the house.'

All her marks for monthly assessments showed Penny gaining only 'A's and 'B's. Teachers' comments were also full of praise: her integrated studies teacher wrote, 'Penelope's standard of work and contributions in class have been of the highest quality. She is an able and enthusiastic pupil.' In most other subjects teachers were also full of praise, describing thirteen-year-old Penny's work as 'conscientious' and 'of a high standard', her attitude as 'keen and enthusiastic'.

Penny would grow up to become an attractive teenager and a quite stunning young woman. Tall, slim, with long fair hair, a good figure, a beautiful face and an engaging, warm smile, she would command attention wherever she went. Her natural good looks, however, would not always make life easy, for her looks and personality would sometimes cause envy among some of her peers.

As Norma explained, 'Penny never had a nasty thought in her head. We had always encouraged her to be generous to people, to like them and to be honest and genuine with everyone. And she was. And perhaps because of that she found it difficult to believe that everyone wasn't the same. She became too trusting.'

Penny also had the most remarkable eyes; her left eye was speckled, her right blue and green, an effect that people found fascinating and would often comment upon. It also gave her an additional, almost unique attraction.

She earned a family nickname, 'Concorde'. Penny believed her nose to be too large and, when a teenager, would become embarrassed, fearing she looked ugly. She would not believe her parents, who tried to allay her fears, assuring her that her nose was not out of proportion and did not spoil her looks. Nevertheless, she kept the nickname and learned to live with it.

The tall Penny, with a model's slim figure, would be just sixteen when she first met Duncan McAllister. Chatting to one of McAllister's fellow officers at the a bar of the officers' mess in Lippstadt one evening, a young man she had never met walked up to them and they were introduced. Penny would say later that she was stunned by his behaviour for, after only a couple of minutes, Duncan stepped back, looked her up and down in a rather condescending, brusque, sexist fashion, nodded, and said, 'Yes, not bad.'

Then he turned on his heel and walked away.

No one had reacted that way towards Penny before. Usually the young officers who were introduced to her showed politeness, interest, and most stayed to chat, attracted to the young woman who had style and presence and appeared older than her sixteen years. But here was a young officer who behaved arrogantly. She stared after him in disbelief as he walked off. She thought him ill-mannered and aloof and she did not like it. Yet in that brief encounter Penny had noticed something. He was different.

Duncan McAllister

★ ★ ★

When Duncan McAllister set out to write his aide-memoire of the whole, shocking tragedy he pulled no punches. He entitled his first chapter 'The Sod'. He was referring to himself.

Duncan Edward Alexander McAllister was born on 8 June 1961, ruining his mother's day, for she had wanted to sit at home quietly and watch the royal wedding of the Duke of Kent and Katherine Worsley at York Minster. Soon after the wedding celebrations began, however, Judy McAllister went into labour and baby Duncan arrived later the same day.

His father David, then twenty-five, was a

captain in the Royal Army Service Corps stationed at Yeovil, Somerset, and had only recently been given permission to move into married quarters. At that time the army decreed that no officers were allowed married quarters until the age of twenty-five.

The son of a wood machinist at Hull docks, Duncan's grandfather lost his job during the great depression and his father remembers the deprivations of the 1930s, living a hand-to-mouth existence. The war years that followed, however, were fun for David McAllister, who amassed a substantial shrapnel collection and won a reputation as a young tearaway.

David McAllister became quite a sportsman and when just sixteen, Manchester United scouts wanted him to sign apprenticeship papers. But his father refused, insisting that the young David complete his education instead.

Duncan's mother, Judy, was only three when her father went off to war with the RAF, serving as ground crew in India. She would not see him again until 1945, when she had turned eight years old.

Rather than do two years' National Service, David decided to sign on for three years and joined the Education Corps as a sergeant, with the same pay as a regular NCQ. Stationed at Halifax with the Duke of Wellington's Regiment, David met Judy at a Young Conservative dance and they married in 1956.

Writing of his formative years, Duncan McAllister said, 'As a young boy I would always look for trouble. I wasn't thuggish or violent, I just had a knack of finding things to disrupt and managed to get into loads of trouble.

During the next five years the family moved from Hull to Bushey to Farnham as David McAllister was posted around the country after gaining a commission and joining the Royal Army Service Corps.

At the age of seven Duncan still remembers an event that would dictate his sexual preference for the rest of his life. He wrote, 'Auntie Angela, one of my mother's former schoolfriends, came to stay and she would constantly cuddle me, showing great affection. Blonde, voluptuous and warm, Auntie Angela would forever be picking me up and holding me close to her ample bosom. During those weeks I became someone who would forever be attracted to large-breasted women.'

Duncan spent the next three years in Hong Kong with his parents and two sisters, Maxine and Isobel, his father having been given command of 56 Squadron Royal Corps of Transport. But the posting would be a disaster for Duncan's education; by the age of ten he could neither read nor write! Fearful that his son would become a an uneducated young rogue, David McAllister decided he would have to send Duncan to boarding school in Britain. That first night at Slitheroe House, the junior part of Rishworth School near Halifax, Duncan recalls, 'As my mother drove away that day I felt my whole world had come to an end. How could my parents leave me with total strangers? That night, a bewildered and miserable young boarder cried himself to sleep.

Duncan McAllister's first brush with the opposite sex was not of his own choosing. Indeed, it was more a matter of survival. Kathy Taylor was not yet a teenager, but her brother, nicknamed 'Niger', learned that she had decided young Duncan McAllister would, become her boyfriend. Duncan recalls, 'I wasn't given much option. I was informed by Niger that I either dated his sister or he would punch me every day until I agreed. The relationship lasted all of four weeks until Kathy focused her attention on a new victim and I was thankfully released from this unwelcome commitment.'

At the age of thirteen, young Duncan had finally learned to read and write and also managed to catch up with most of his contemporaries. Now he really enjoyed boarding school, especially the sport, playing rugby and cricket and swimming and running for the school. He also met Julie Bowskill, a thirteen-year-old with long strawberry-blonde hair. They remained teenage sweethearts until Duncan left Rishworth at the age of sixteen. During those last three years Duncan had been working hard and left with eight 'O' level passes, three 'B's, five 'C's and two fails. His parents thought he had done very well, but Duncan was disappointed and dejected, feeling he had let them down.

The decision had been taken for him to attend Welbeck College, where young men study for science qualifications for army technical corps, with an automatic entry to Sandhurst assured at the end of the two-year 'A' level course. Duncan thoroughly enjoyed Welbeck and gained the required 'A' levels.

During school holidays Duncan had met Debbie, the daughter of a staff-sergeant at an air mounting centre in South Cerney, Wiltshire, where his father was stationed. Bubbly, slender, fair-haired and pretty, Debbie would become the first real love of his life. They wrote to each other while he studied at Welbeck and spent holidays together. She lived three miles away from Duncan's home in Ashton Keynes. Her mother died when Debbie was fifteen and she began spending more time at Duncan's home. When Duncan was seventeen and Debbie a year younger they had sex together for the first time.

Within months, Debbie moved into Duncan's parents' home and the teenage sweethearts were given a bedroom to share. They were young, happy and in love. Duncan would spend the week at Sandhurst, training to become an officer and indulging his passion for sport, and then he would race home for weekends of bliss in the arms of his teenage sweetheart. Life was near-perfect.

Having gained a commission, Duncan went for intensive signals training at Blandford, Dorset, from March to September 1981. Then, at the age of twenty, he was posted to Soest in Germany. Miserable at being parted from Debbie, the young McAllister had a crisis of confidence. On the phone from Germany he asked

Debbie to marry him and they became officially engaged.

Alone back home, where she continued to live with the McAllister family, Debbie would spend her evenings and a weekends with a group of young people, many of whom studied at the nearby Cirencester Agricultural College. The inevitable happened: she fell in love with someone else.

She flew to Bavaria for a week's skiing with Duncan, but the holiday was a disaster. 'I knew something was wrong,' Duncan recalled, 'but she kept denying it. I went home on leave and found a letter in our bedroom from someone called Richard. It was a love letter.

'I was distraught, devastated. My fiancée, the girl whom I adored, had been having an affair with someone else while living in my parents' home.'

Confronted with the love letter, Debbie confessed and she and Duncan split in January 1982. Debbie, however, would go on to marry Richard and have two children.

Six months later Lieutenant Duncan McAllister walked into the officers' mess at Lippstadt in Germany and saw a beautiful young woman painting a mural on the wall for the Royal Signals summer ball that weekend. He drove back to his base at Soest twenty miles away wondering who she could be.

Exactly one week later Duncan would meet the girl in the same officers' mess. She was talking to his best friend, Lieutenant Colin McGrory. He recalled,

'Standing at the bar I saw this stunning girl. I recognized her as the girl I had seen the week before. She captivated me, yet I had never met her. I can't remember what she wore that night. I can only recall she was tall and slender with long, light-brown hair. When I came closer, wanting Colin to introduce me to the woman I presumed was his girlfriend, I also noticed her stunning smile and beautiful eyes.'

He went on: 'What possessed me to be so rude to her I just don't know, yet I did look her up and down and I did say "Yeah, not bad" before walking away.

'Why I acted like that I don't know. I presume it was jealousy. When I walked away I remember being instantly angry with myself for acting in such a bloody, rude manner to someone who seemed absolutely wonderful.

'Later that evening I asked her to dance, but even then I didn't apologize for my rudeness, which I should have done.'

Duncan asked Penny what she did, and when she replied she attended school he asked what subjects she taught. 'I was stunned when she told me she was studying for 'O' levels. I took her to be at a least twenty.'

That night Duncan asked Penny for a date, but when she said she could not go out the following night Duncan thought she had no interest in him. Duncan was unable to forget the lovely girl to whom he had been so rude, so four months later, he decided to call at Penny's house on the off-chance she might be at home. When he knocked at the door her mother Norma answered. She said, 'You're Duncan, aren't you? Come on in and have a coffee.' Norma told him that Penny had talked of the young Signals officer she had met at the mess, and suggested Duncan go to the hall where Penny was a rehearsing a play.

He recalls, 'I walked into the hall and saw Penny on stage. When she looked down the hall and saw me she leapt off the stage and ran towards me as though we had been friends for ages. I was overawed, flattered and very happy.'

Duncan invited Penny to a disco at Soest and can still remember her arriving dressed in a short A-line bottle-green mini skirt, a bottle-green sweat shirt with a three pieces of fake fur on the bodice, tights and red suede ankle boots. 'We had the most wonderful evening,' commented Duncan, 'and at 1 a.m. I took her home, only giving her a single kiss on the cheek. I was smitten.'

The next night, Duncan took Penny to a pub in Lippstadt that sold Guinness, and they talked non-stop for the entire evening. Walking through the town later that night Duncan stopped in the middle of the street and turned to Penny, saying, 'I cannot imagine you with anyone else. I really want you as my girlfriend. If you can't agree to that then I'll have to walk away.'

Penny replied, 'Yes, I agree. I would like to go out with you.' And they kissed.

Duncan McAllister had discovered within a matter of days that Penny would be someone of real importance in his life. 'I believe it was love at first sight,' he said. 'I was captivated by this wonderful girl.'

Two weeks later Duncan was posted to Norway for six weeks on a ski course. He wrote to her, saying 'I love you', and Penny replied also expressing her love. Throughout his stay in Norway Duncan would listen over and over to the rock band Foreigner's famous song, 'I've been Waiting for a Girl Like You'. Duncan had played the song to Penny before he had left for Norway, explaining to her that the words expressed how he felt towards her. He sent it to her. Until the day, years later, when Penny would be brutally murdered in the peace and quiet of an Irish forest, they would frequently play that song, instantly bringing back the tender moments when they first fell in love.

Duncan returned to Lippstadt three days before Christmas and on 23 December Penny accompanied him to his regiment's drinks party at Soest. 'Both of us knew in our hearts that we would make love that night,' Duncan recalled. 'We both knew we a were in love, we had told each other so often in our letters. There was nothing said between us. When we arrived I took her hand and we walked to my room together holding hands. I had never touched Penny before; we had barely kissed. We spent the next one and a half hours locked in each other's arms, making love. I knew I was absolutely in love with her and I knew then that I wanted to marry her.

'Penny of course was a virgin but she had told me that she so wanted us to go to bed. She knew I loved her. I loved her so very much, and I think she too had fallen in love with me.

'We then left for the drinks party and later I snaffled a bottle of champagne. We returned to my room, where we made love again. I was in seventh heaven. Outside, snow was falling and I phoned Penny's father, asking permission for her to stay the night in Soest. Understandably, he refused, but the return journey was hell. It took us two hours through the snow rather than the usual thirty minutes.'

Four days later, Duncan was posted to an army ski lodge in Zweisal, Austria, for eight weeks and Penny won permission from her parents to go and stay with Duncan for a week's holiday. 'Bliss is the only word to describe that week with Penny,' Duncan recalls. 'I would be running at 5 a.m., skiing each day at 8.30 and home by 4 p.m. Penny learned to ski and we would spend the nights together as though we were on honeymoon. After that, everyone understood we were an item.'

Throughout 1983 Penny and Duncan spent as much time together as they could. For much of the time he stayed with Penny at her parents' home. 'We weren't allowed to share a room,' Duncan commented, 'but her parents knew that every night we slept together in her bed.'

In September 1983 Duncan was posted back to England, to Tidworth, near Salisbury. The next two months were hell for both Penny and Duncan. That enforced separation convinced both Penny and Duncan that they wanted to be with each other so much that they would have to marry.

In November, Duncan could wait no longer. He phoned Penny at her home in Lippstadt and proposed. 'Fantastic, wonderful, darling,' she said. 'You don't know how much I love you. I never want us to be parted, ever,' she said.

'We won't be, I promise you,' Duncan reassured her.

Susan Christie

★ ★ ★

The young woman who would gain nationwide notoriety for her deadly obsession with a handsome army officer was born in August 1968, a year before the Troubles in Northern Ireland became so intense that the British Government sent in the troops to keep the peace.

Susan Christie's father had joined the British Army as a young man and spent most of his career serving in England and Germany. Born an Ulsterman, Robert 'Bob' Christie would later join the Ulster Defence Regiment as an NCO and become a senior warrant officer.

Bob Christie adored his daughter Susan. To many it seemed he believed his daughter could do no wrong: he doted on her, praising her and continually fussing over her. Others would comment later that they believed Bob Christie spoilt Susan during her formative years.

Undeniably, a strong bond developed between father and daughter, far stronger than the bond between Susan and her mother. Susan would become inseparable from her father; she became completely dependent on him.

In her latter teenage years, however, there would be a role reversal, with Susan becoming the dominant partner in the relationship. Then, although she would always look to her father for advice, she did what she wanted, disregarding his wishes. The girl who had sought his advice and approval for everything she did had outgrown the dependency.

Susan Christie would later brag to friends and acquaintances, 'I can twist my father around my little finger.' It was no idle boast.

From an early age Susan decided she too wanted to join the army, to follow in her father's footsteps. As a young girl she would take delight in helping her father don his dress uniform, and she would watch him on parade whenever possible.

Bob Christie took great pride in his daughter, encouraging her in everything she did. He also wanted to instil ambition in Susan, encouraging her not simply to join the army, become an NCO and enjoy army life, but to take all the right examinations so that she would have the qualifications to gain a commission, become an officer.

Her father's ambition for Susan would dictate the course of her life and instil in her a single-minded determination to better herself, to achieve goals her father had never attained for himself and, in so doing, make him proud of her.

When Susan was twelve, her life of roaming around England and Germany, living with her parents and younger brother in various army married quarters, came to an end when Bob Christie decided to settle down and return home to his beloved Ulster. He joined the Ulster Defence Regiment as an engineer and settled in Lisburn.

Susan had attended a number of different schools overseas, changing them whenever her father was given a different posting, like all army children. She had enjoyed her early school life, always fitting in, but never reaching any great heights in school or sport. All this would soon change.

Now, however, it was time to study for her forthcoming 'O' Level exams and Bob Christie realized that a stable background would be necessary for his daughter to achieve the necessary standard. She attended Forthill Girls' High School, Lisburn, in an area of the province frequently at the centre of Northern Ireland's Troubles.

Her teenage life was dominated by the presence of troops, armed troops in flak jackets and helmets, in armoured Land Rovers and armoured personnel carriers on the streets of her town, near her school and in the shopping precincts. As for every other young person in many parts of Northern Ireland, hardly a week would pass without a bombing, a violent killing or a wounding in the streets and areas around Lisburn.

After taking 'O' Levels, Susan went on to complete a secretarial course at Lisburn College of Further Education. She enjoyed the college, though she was, in many ways, still young for her age, for throughout her early teenage years Bob Christie had taken care not to let Susan spend too much time out, alone. He was, understandably, fearful for her safety. As a full-time soldier he saw at close quarters the full horrors of life in Northern Ireland.

As a result, Susan remained very much a 'Daddy's girl' not only at school and when attending the secretarial college but for some years later, even when she became a fully-fledged soldier at the age of twenty-one.

A teacher at Forthill Girls' High a School would say later, 'Susan had that butter-wouldn't-melt-in-her-mouth look about her. She appeared the picture of innocence. I remember her as something of a loner, definitely not one of the in-crowd. Perhaps one could say Susan Christie was an insignificant member of the school, easily forgettable.

'And yet when I met her at a party, when she would have been seventeen, Susan had matured to a remarkable degree. No longer was she the shy violet, the little childlike teenager. She had become a far more confident young woman with a personality to match her confidence. I remember her marching up to me with a big smile on her face and introducing herself. I was very pleased that she had become more confident.'

In November 1986, at the age of eighteen, Susan Christie went some way towards achieving one of her life's ambitions by joining the UDR as a part-time private soldier, known as a 'Greenfinch'. She enjoyed the life and, encouraged by her father, would do well in all the courses.

In July 1989, a few weeks short of her twenty-first birthday, Susan Christie became a full-time member of the UDR. Trained and encouraged by her 'Daddy', the name by which she always referred to her father, Susan Christie began to shine. Without great difficulty she became 'best recruit', a most distinguished achievement, and she came first in most of the army courses she attended.

Another UDR Greenfinch who trained with Christie would say later, 'Susan was a perfectionist and she was determined to be the best at everything she undertook, whether it was tackling an assault course, map reading or ironing her uniform.

'Everyone who trained alongside Susan soon had the impression that she was a very determined young woman, and very, very ambitious. We all knew her burning ambition was one day to gain a commission, and most of us believed she would do so.

'When out on exercises or working and training together with a group, Susan would become bossy, and nearly always take command to such a degree that she could become domineering. As a result, she was not the most popular person in the cadre. She didn't seem to mind that. She spoke differently to everyone else, having more of an English accent than a Northern Irish one, due, she would tell everyone, to the years she spent in army quarters overseas, attending English schools. Some of us, however, suspected she put on the English accent to make herself different; her accent gave her confidence and made her feel superior.'

Most of the Greenfinch recruits would drink and smoke. Not Susan. Her father had brought her up to shun both the evils of smoking and drinking and she frowned on anyone who indulged in these vices. That, however, would change when she fell in love.

Annette Gascoigne first met Susan Christie in 1989 on their joining the UDR as full-time private soldiers. They met while attending a 'Methods of Instruction' course, prior to joining the NCOs' training course. Annette, from Norfolk in England, naturally spoke with an English accent and, as a result, they formed an immediate bond.

Annette, who married in 1987, would say later, 'Because of our English accents we were both treated as outsiders by most of the other recruits. They of course were mostly staunch Ulstermen and women and very proud of it. They felt that we weren't part of the team and, to a certain extent, we found ourselves ostracized. Neither of us had a circle of friends and, understandably, we became outsiders, and sometimes felt we were loners. Our accents brought us together. We were also both fiercely ambitious. Soon after we met we became friends, and, for a time, close friends.'

No-one would get to know Susan Christie to the degree Annette did during those years. They would talk together for hours at a time, confiding in one another. Annette, however, an intelligent, mature young woman with perception and understanding, saw through much of Susan Christie's behaviour.

Sue and Annette spent three weeks together with twenty other privates undergoing the NCO course at Ballykinler. They worked together, swotted together and virtually lived together. Both sailed through the course with flying colours, Susan Christie passing out top of the cadre and Annette second. This meant both would be prospective candidates for a commission at a later date.

Annette described Susan Christie at that time as 'bright, domineering, petulant, self-centred and aggressive, but with a bubbly, engaging personality that often made her the centre of attention, which she loved, craving acknowledgement and praise for everything she did. She always wanted to be outstanding at whatever she was doing. She was a truly competitive person, determined to win, ambitious to succeed, to prove herself better, superior, different to everyone else.'

Susan Christie, however, believed she had a problem; for she was not very happy with her body. Annette explained, 'Sue is only five feet tall with mousy brown hair which she would highlight. She believed her body was out of proportion, and she was convinced she had a big bottom and legs like tree trunks. She knew she was short and stout, rather dumpy, the female image of her father. She resented him for that.

'She also knew, however, that she had well-developed breasts, and wore a thirty-eight-inch bra with a "C" cup. She knew that certainly attracted the men, as well as much attention and many remarks. She would always dress to show off her breasts, wearing tight sweaters and tight shirts, tucking them into her jeans or skirt to emphasize their size and shape. Quite often she would attend discos wearing a low-cut shirt with no bra at all.

'She would often go further than that. She would arrive for work at the barracks wearing a tight T-shirt with no bra. She fully realized that turned on the guys and she revelled in it.'

Annette continued, 'Sometimes Sue could look very attractive, particularly when in a happy, gregarious mood. On the other hand she could also look forbidding and dowdy, petulant and unhappy, sulky and moody.

'It seemed she never tried to hide her feelings or her moods, giving the impression of a spoilt child, still believing at the age of twenty-one that she could get her own way by sulking and appearing sullen. But Sue also knew that she could attract men by her bubbly personality, which many men found appealing. Sue could be a wonderful asset at a party but only when the centre of attention. If someone came into the room, or joined the group, who Sue felt was more beautiful, attractive or engaging, she would break into an instant sulk.

'She didn't like other girls stealing the limelight. If men paid more attention to another girl in the group, Sue would become instantly huffy. One could almost sense her animosity to the intruder and the effect on Sue's behaviour towards the poor girl would nearly always be rude, sometimes openly belligerent.'

Susan Christie would always seek the attention of young men, but she would remain a virgin until she fell in love with Captain Duncan McAllister, the husband of a young woman whom Sue immediately saw as a rival. During her teenage years, Susan had hardly any boyfriends and virtually no sexual experiences whatsoever. She found it difficult to relate to potential suitors, finding most of those who invited her on dates lacking in one area or another.

Annette recalls one boyfriend Susan did date soon after she joined the UDR. Susan told Annette, 'He was a very good-looking bloke whom I found attractive and we began dating. He was, however, very religious. I wanted to kiss him, to pet him and, more than anything I wanted him to make love to me. I wanted him to take my virginity. I was nineteen and felt that I should no longer be a virgin.

'It was my hard luck that he did not believe in sex before marriage. I tried everything to persuade him to go to bed with me, but he simply refused. We kissed and petted, but nothing more. I was very fond of him and, in some ways, I do believe I loved him. But nothing could come of the romance so we simply drifted apart. Later, I think he decided to enter a religious order.'

Instead of dating young men Sue loved to go out in the evening to discos, ten-pin bowling or to the cinema. She would, more often than not, go out with a group of people, mostly young soldiers whom she became matey with during the day.

As Annette revealed later, 'Sue appeared to have a very raunchy approach to sex, but in reality that was not the case. She became a terrible flirt, deliberately egging men on. I would watch her toying with some young chaps, either in the way she moved on the dance floor or the way she chatted to them, tantalizing them, moving her body suggestively, touching them and giving them the come-on.

'And yet it was all for show. She had no intention of dating them, going out with them or even kissing or petting with them. She seemed to need their attention as a boost to her confidence, to prove to herself that she was sexually attractive.'

Susan Christie would sit in a disco making open remarks about the men, as though leching after them.

'Get a load of him' or 'Look at that arse' or 'He's a bit of alright' were some of her favourite phrases. Sometimes she would go further, saying 'I wouldn't kick him out of bed', but she would never take the initiative. It was all talk.

Annette noticed the way Susan reacted whenever men were, around. 'She would instantly begin flirting if she had the slightest interest in them. She would thrust out her breasts deliberately, laughing, trying to gain their attention in whatever way she could. She would laugh out loud, smile, speak rather loudly and make sexual remarks, some of which they could not possibly fail to hear.

'It all seemed contrived to make her the centre of attraction, to draw attention to herself and to make herself desired by men, even when she didn't particularly fancy them. At first her behaviour seemed way over the top but after a while one became used to her attention-seeking and barely noticed it. But the men noticed it.'

Susan's great kick would be to find herself surrounded by a group of men, whom she loved to entertain and flirt with. She would always pepper her chat with double-entendres, always sexually motivated, suggestive and intimate. She had powerful, intelligent eyes that attracted the men but she would often end up laughing in their faces if they tried to kiss or fondle her.

On those occasions Susan would show how provocative she could be, dipping her finger in her drink and then sucking it seductively, leaving nothing to the imagination. She would do the same when eating an ice lolly, pushing it into her mouth slowly, sucking it provocatively, leaving no one in any doubt that she was simulating sucking a man's erect penis.

As Annette said, 'If she believed any man paid her any attention then she would always go to great lengths to tell me about the man, how attractive or handsome he was, what car he drove or what he did for a living. If officers paid her attention then she would be really pleased with herself. But to most men Susan Christie was the quintessential prick-tease, offering everything and giving nothing.'

Perhaps the one word that many believe sums up Susan Christie is 'flirt'. Many people would describe her flirting as 'outrageous', particularly some of the young men and women who joined the diving club. To some club members she would make openly suggestive remarks, or flagrantly tease them, to watch the effect. But there was never any follow-through.

And yet there was a sad side to Susan Christie's sexual craving. If any man did pay her attention, even the faintest, she wanted the world to know, as though she had won a beauty contest. And the more she would boast of such conquests, the less interested people became in her.

During the time she spent with the 11th Battalion of the Ulster Defence Regiment, Susan Christie won herself a most unenviable reputation.

One of the battalion's most popular sergeant-majors, Frank Drew, had been accused by Christie of sexual harassment. The case went before the company commander, who questioned Christie and Sergeant-Major Drew about her allegations. The G company commander did not believe her, but she insisted the sergeant-major had harassed her. The case therefore went before the commanding officer, who had to make an unenviable choice between believing a female private soldier's word or that of a trusted sergeant-major with a good record. It was known that Frank Drew was a rough diamond but, nevertheless, a good NCO.

In the end, the CO took Christie's side and Frank Drew was busted down to sergeant and moved from the 11th Battalion. There were very few people among those in the company who knew both Christie and Sergeant-Major Drew who believed that there had been any truth in her allegations. As a result, Susan Christie became so unpopular among her contemporaries in her company that it was found necessary to move her. She was posted to UDR Headquarters.

Later, Susan Christie made another accusation of sexual harassment, this time against an officer in the Headquarters Company. Once again delicate inquiries had to be made, an investigation authorized, and a report compiled to check if her allegations contained any substance. The investigation found the allegations were baseless.

The case was almost identical to that involving

Sergeant-Major Drew. There was no independent evidence against either man, no witnesses to either allegation of sexual harassment. Susan had no evidence whatsoever against the officer, and after being interviewed by senior officers she was persuaded, in her best interests, to drop the accusation. On this occasion she agreed.

An officer who had formerly served with the 11th Battalion of the UDR would say later, 'That Susan Christie is nothing but trouble; she's ruined a good sergeant-major's career with her false allegations. I am afraid I do know her but sincerely wish I didn't. She is a woman men would be well advised to steer clear of.'

Married, Together and in Love

★ ★ ★

The bride would be the calmest person on the day of her wedding, in August 1984. Though only eighteen years old, Penny remained cool and quietly confident that day while all around her bustle and last-minute alterations made everything appear to be in turmoil. With only one hour to go before she was due at the church, Penny, wearing nothing but a skimpy bikini, was sunbathing in brilliant sunshine in the garden of Duncan's parents' home in Ashton Keynes. She was chatting away to Duncan's grandfather while munching her way through a box a of Maltesers.

Two hundred guests attended the wedding of Penny Squire and Duncan McAllister at the Church of the Holy Cross in the beautiful Cotswold village. Later, there was a cocktail reception party at the South Cerney officers' mess and that night 120 of the guests stayed on to attend a disco and buffet supper. Drink flowed and Penny and Duncan were dancing and drinking until 2 a.m.

That night Penny wore the blue and green hand-painted silk dress Duncan had bought as a special present for their wedding night. It was to be the same dress in which she would be buried in the same church just six years later.

Penny and Duncan flew to Tunisia for their two-week honeymoon. It would prove to be only the beginning of their life of travel together. 'Life is for living,' Duncan would tell Penny as they would jet off somewhere exotic for a week or two of diving, sailing or skiing. Duncan explained their philosophy: 'We didn't want to spend our early years together sitting around at home, gardening or watching television. One day we planned to have a family, but we both agreed that the early years together should be as enjoyable as possible. And both Penny and I wanted to spend as much time together as possible. Penny would always tell me that her life was our life, together, as an item, a team, and that's the way we led our lives, throughout our six years of marriage. We were inseparable and we both loved it that way.'

Though living only on a junior army officer's pay, Penny and Duncan did appear to lead almost a jet-set existence. They were a most handsome couple; Penny with her sensational good looks and Duncan, particularly in his uniform, an impressive figure, athletic, fit and capable.

Penny was determined to attend university and Duncan agreed that she should complete her education. This was the primary reason he decided to attend the Royal Military College of Sciences at Shrivenham, Wiltshire, where he remained for three years, taking a degree in applied science. He explained, 'That meant Penny could attend Bristol University and we could live together in married quarters at Shrivenham. It was the ideal solution.'

It was not to be. Penny failed to gain the necessary 'A' level passes to enable her to take a place at Bristol in September 1984. She passed both geography and English with 'A's but passed history only at the second attempt, on retaking the exam the following year. This meant she could not start her university course until a year after Duncan began his three-year course at the army college.

Perhaps it was not surprising that Penny failed one exam, for she had not only changed schools in the middle of her 'A' level studies but, in the run-up to the exams, she had been busy planning her wedding.

It was, nevertheless, a bitter blow for Norma and Desmond, who wanted their talented and intelligent daughter to go to university, to fulfil her potential and have the experience of further education. Both Norma and Desmond had talked long and hard to Penny when Duncan had asked Desmond if he would give his permission for them to become engaged, since Penny was only seventeen. Their wish that she should complete her education was the reason they hesitated before consenting.

Penny had always been keen to attend university, gain a degree and find a worthwhile, challenging job. Both Norma and Desmond had always encouraged her to believe that attending university was the natural culmination of years of study, and she had never wavered. But Norma had a problem enforcing this, for she too, like her mother before her, had become engaged at seventeen and married at eighteen. It therefore proved difficult to persuade Penny to gain a degree before contemplating marriage. Penny, however, had been adamant and believed she and Duncan had found the solution: Penny would study at Bristol while Duncan took his science degree at Shrivenham.

She never did attend university. Norma would say a later, 'It was a waste of a good brain and a natural talent that she never went to university. But it was her choice, her decision and I know she never regretted it. She would say that Duncan's life was her life and she wanted their marriage to be like that.'

While Duncan continued his studies each day at Shrivenham, Penny would spend her first year of married life simply enjoying being a young bride in love. Each day she would walk her Gordon Setter, Jock. She would then prepare lunch for Duncan, who would return for an hour each day from the college less than half a mile away.

They lived in married quarters, a 1930s three-bedroomed semi-detached house with a huge garden, backing on to the woods surrounding the college golf course.

Penny wanted to involve herself as much as a possible in Duncan's life and particularly in his work. Because it seemed unlikely that she would attend university, she decided to learn what she could of Duncan's applied science course. When Duncan returned home each evening, he would sit down with his textbooks and together Penny and Duncan would go through the lectures so that she could keep up with the course.

Duncan recalled later, 'If there was any essay I had to write about social sciences or current affairs then I would take the relevant books home and give them to Penny. The following day Penny would write the essay and hand it to me that evening. It was marvellous. Generally, I was awarded an "A" for those essays. Penny was very bright.'

Nearly every weekend during the winter Duncan would be playing rugby and Penny would go with him to both home and away matches. They would enjoy the fun after the game, having a drink and a sing-song, and at the invariable parties she would, more often than not, be the centre of attention. Summer weekends would be lazy, loving days and they would go for long walks with Jock, occasionally stopping for pub lunches.

It was during their years at Shrivenham that their passion for diving began. Duncan recalled, 'We wanted to find a sport in which we could both actively participate. We attended an open night at the college diving club and decided we would give the sport a try. We both loved it. Twice a week we would attend evening lectures and during the summer months we would travel to a dive site with the other club members, usually somewhere on the south coast. It was great, because we both got the same kick out of diving. We had found something we could enjoy together.'

In the summer of 1985, one year after their wedding, Penny and Duncan took off for America, to Plymouth, Massachusetts, for a wonderful fifteen-week holiday. Duncan volunteered to join other divers excavating and raising the wreck of the *General Arnold*, which sank in heavy weather in December 1778 at the end of the American War of Independence.

He commented later, 'That was a glorious holiday. The problem had been funding the trip and the holiday. In the end we sold our 2CV Citroen car for £2,500 and that gave us enough money for the air fares and some money over so we could enjoy ourselves while in the States. Penny had a great time.

'The decision we made then is a perfect example of how we led our life together. I always wanted Penny to accompany me wherever I went and sometimes we didn't have the cash. So we would find ways of raising some to go off on our expeditions.

'On occasions, I would be sent away by the army leading some expedition, such as diving or skiing, and I always wanted Penny to be with me. Because Penny wasn't part of the army, however, I would have to pay her air fares, which were sometimes quite considerable. To raise the money we would pool our resources and if necessary sell something so that we had the money to be together and enjoy those occasions. Sometimes of course I would have to work hard but, to us, they seemed more like holidays because we were together. We never regretted those times; they were special. They kept our marriage strong.'

During the 1986 Easter holidays they enjoyed a ten-day diving holiday in Cyprus. And to celebrate their second wedding anniversary in the summer of 1986, they went on another fifteen-week expedition, enjoying a second honeymoon in the Cayman Islands before flying on to Plymouth to continue diving on the *General Arnold*.

In the autumn of 1986, Penny took a job,

managing one of the Principles fashion shops. A year later she quit so that she could accompany Duncan on a four-week expedition to Muscat in the Persian Gulf over the Christmas and New Year period. Duncan recalls, 'The management told Penny that she would not be permitted to take a month off work to accompany me to the Gulf and she was told she had to make a decision, to forget the four-week holiday and keep the job or accompany me to Muscat and lose her job. She had no hesitation; she quit and came with me.'

In June 1987 Duncan learned he had gained his science degree and that he would be posted to 21 Signals Regiment (Air Support). It was ironic that he was posted to Gutersloh, where Penny had spent her teenage years, living with her parents and attending school there. Duncan was appointed as Signals Officer to Air Support, working with RAF Harrier jets and support helicopters.

This job did not last long. Two months later, Duncan was invited to lead an RAF diving expedition to Estartit on the Spanish Costa Brava. As usual, Penny went along too and returned with a wonderful suntan.

After six months of winter in Germany, living in married quarters, Duncan was again offered a new opportunity to travel, leading another diving expedition, this time to Belize in South America. Accompanied by twelve army divers, Duncan, with his beloved Penny, spent a magical month diving in wonderfully warm waters.

By this time Penny too had become a keen and competent diver but she only enjoyed diving in warm waters where there was good visibility. She hated diving in cold waters where visibility was poor, if not zero, and the freezing water quickly numbed her arms and legs. Penny's apprehension and dislike of diving in cold, dark waters would later provide the opportunity for another young woman, captivated by Duncan, to become close to Penny's husband. The unseen consequences would be tragedy and horror.

Penny's wonderful holidays and expeditions with Duncan were not all spent diving. In November 1988, Duncan was invited to run the Signals Regiment ski hut in Bavaria for seven weeks. Duncan had thirteen assistants, including ski instructors, cooks, drivers, mechanics and barmen, helping to train the sixty skiers. Penny and Duncan were given the luxury of an apartment above the lodge in the middle of a lovely picturesque Alpine village.

Building on her earlier skiing experience, Penny became an expert skier and the two of them had an idyllic few weeks together enjoying the wonderful conditions. Life was near-perfect and they were still madly in love.

Duncan recalled those early years of marriage. 'We enjoyed being together whatever we were doing. We became inseparable. Everything we did together was an adventure. And that's what makes the appalling tragedy seem so much worse. I didn't need to stray. I had the world's perfect wife. She had everything: fantastic looks, a sensual and loving personality, and a sense of humour. I also had her total love and devotion. No man could have asked for more.'

And yet it would not last.

Both Duncan and Penny were thrilled when Duncan received his next posting, to 3 Infantry Brigade Headquarters and Signal Squadron in Northern Ireland. 'I'd always wanted to go to Northern Ireland because I wanted to work within a theatre of operation. Now was my opportunity. And Penny was only too happy to leave Germany.'

Understandably, many army wives preferred to stay in England rather than risk accompanying their husbands to Northern Ireland, where the Irish Republican Army were then continuing their bloody campaign of violence, much of it directed towards army and police personnel. Servicemen's wives knew only too well that the IRA's main targets in Northern Ireland were service personnel of whatever rank.

'You don't have to come with me,' Duncan told her. 'You can stay with your parents if you like.' But Penny would hear none of it.

Before going to Northern Ireland, Duncan had to attend a fourteen-week training course at Warminster, a junior staff course involving tactics and staff procedures. During the week, Duncan, along with 100 other officers, lived a bachelor life in the mess. But at the end of the week he would dash back to Wanborough, and to Penny.

One lunchtime Duncan received an urgent message to phone his parents and heard the surprise news that Penny had been rushed to hospital with suspected appendicitis. The operation had gone ahead immediately and she was back in the ward, recovering.

Duncan recalled, 'I spent the next couple of weeks commuting. It was a ninety-minute journey to be with Penny every night. In all truth it was a wonderful excuse to be with her. I had missed her so much during the weeks. It also made me realize that Penny was more important than anything else in my life, including the army.

While Penny convalesced at home Duncan had an unenviable decision to make concerning Penny's Gordon Setter, Jock, the dog she adored. Jock had been unable to settle while in quarantine kennels and the vet believed he would never regain his old composure. Penny could not make the decision and left it to Duncan.

He said, 'That night I went home and suggested we take a walk along the dirt track near our home. I told Penny: "I've had Jock put down."

'Penny just kissed my cheek and said, "I know."'

They did not have much time to mourn Jock

because within days the news of Duncan's posting came through. They had been allocated married quarters in Armagh. Penny was thrilled, but before moving to Ireland she dearly wanted another dog. In fact they found two Gordon Setter pups, one of which they named Barton after their vet, and the other Monty, simply because Duncan liked the name.

Their married quarters would be in an area named 'The Clump', a good-sized four-bedroomed house with a large kitchen and an open-plan lounge/dining room with french windows leading to a patio and a lawn from where they could view Armagh city.

Duncan recalled that first night together in Ireland. 'Penny came and sat on my lap, asking playfully, "Do you love me?" and I nodded.

'She then asked, "How much?" and I replied, "Enough."

' "Enough for what?" she asked, a big smile across her face. "Enough to cover any eventuality," I replied.'

Duncan has been unable to forget that little, inconsequential scrap of conversation since Penny's death, for when his love for Penny was put to the test he failed her totally.

During that autumn and the winter of 1989/90, Duncan McAllister worked hard, putting in long hours and concentrating on his task as a signals officer with operational responsibilities. He relaxed in the officers' mess, where Penny became popular because of her warmth, affection and understanding. The British Army had no diving club in Armagh, so in February 1990, Duncan and Penny decided to form one. Penny was happy to help organize the club, the lectures and expeditions, though she had no desire whatsoever actually to take part in freezing dives in the waters around Northern Ireland.

Following a two-week diving trip to Cyprus to train six novice divers to 'sports standard' it was decided to recruit more members. Two young women, both privates in the Ulster Defence Regiment, decided they might learn to dive. One was Annette Gascoigne, the quiet, attractive wife of Corporal 'Bamber' Gascoigne. The other was her friend, Private Susan Christie, a small, chunky young woman, a bubbly, extrovert twenty-one-year-old soldier who loved the limelight.

Addressing them that evening in the club lecture room was Captain Duncan McAllister, the club's chief diving instructor, whom Christie had never met. Throughout the evening she hardly took her eyes off the thirty-year-old army regular as he explained the principles of diving. And later, when they all had drinks, Christie quickly learned that the beautiful, tall, slender woman with the smiling eyes and fair hair was Penny, the captain's wife. Susan Christie ignored her.

Lovers

★ ★ ★

Duncan McAllister hardly noticed Susan Christie during those first few meetings of the diving club, but he slowly became aware that she would want to sit next to him, would pay attention to everything he said, and would want to stand next to him at the bar and seek his attention.

He also noted her remarkable figure, which she would show off by wearing tight shirts, revealing her well-developed bosom.

'It began as a joke,' Duncan said. 'The lads would comment that Susan didn't need a buoyancy jacket for diving because she already had her own built-in buoyancy. She loved the joke and responded happily, smiling and feigning embarrassment. The more the jokes went on the tighter became her sweaters and skirts. I believe she loved the attention.'

Ironically, Duncan recalled that the twelve months before he became embroiled with Susan Christie had been the happiest of his life. 'It seems extraordinary,' he said, 'but it is true. I was wonderfully happy with Penny; our life together was idyllic. We never had an argument and wanted to be with each other all the time. We were in love. And I was thoroughly enjoying the responsibility of my job in the regiment.'

And yet in May and June of 1990 Duncan realized that he was becoming attracted, sexually attracted, to Susan Christie. He noticed that she constantly craved his attention, spent lectures sitting and watching him, never taking her eyes off him and always laughing and joking when the lectures ended and everyone sat around enjoying a drink. And he had begun flirting with her, too.

On 4 July 1990, Duncan organized a dive on the wreck of the Chirripo, which was lying off the Irish coast in thirty metres of water, and he arranged it so that the only two people left in the surface boat were Susan and himself.

He wrote about that moment in his aide-memoire, 'The time had come to confront Susan about the situation — her constant craving for my company had become noticeable ... she sat in the boat with her back towards me ... the silence became overwhelming ... I tried to say something but I couldn't ... the atmosphere was electric, an energy building between us ... my mouth was dry and my mind was beginning to race.'

Finally, with only minutes to spare before the divers surfaced, Duncan said, 'Sue, I'm going to say something which may be way out of order and, if it is, I apologize now. But I feel we need to clear the air.'

Susan did not reply, nor did she turn to face Duncan. So he continued, 'For some time now I've had the impression that you like me and I admit I like you too. However, others have noticed as well, including Penny, and I think we need to talk. I'm sure people think there's something going on. It wouldn't be so bad if there was, but there isn't. I think we might have to curb the way we react to each other. But if I've got this all wrong I'm sorry.'

Still not looking at Duncan, Susan replied, 'You haven't got it wrong and you don't need to apologize. I would never have mentioned it or said anything, you know.'

As the divers surfaced and began swimming to the boat, Duncan said, 'I'll arrange for us to travel together to the dive on Saturday. We can talk then. OK?'

For the first time throughout the conversation their eyes met. Susan said quietly, 'Yes.'

Duncan recalled, 'As we sped back to harbour Susan sat next to me, pressing her legs against mine and every now and then increasing the pressure, as though wanting to catch my attention. And I didn't want to move my leg. I knew then that Susan was telling me that my suspicions of our mutual sexual attraction were correct.'

On Saturday 7 July Penny decided she would prefer to go shopping rather than spend yet another weekend diving; this gave Duncan and Susan their opportunity to talk. As they drove together to the dive site, Duncan recalls he decided to raise the matter immediately and, after a few minutes' chat, he asked Susan, 'When you say you'd like to see me outside the club you do know that we are talking about an affair, don't you?'

Susan replied, 'I'd like to get to know you away from the club, yes.'

Because Susan had not mentioned the word 'affair', Duncan continued, pressing home the point. He needed to know that Susan understood what was a being suggested, that they would have an affair.

'You do know I am talking about an affair, don't you?'

'Yes,' Susan replied simply.

Duncan maintains that it was on that journey that he explained to Susan for more than an hour all the disadvantages of having an affair with a married man, including the difficulties and loneliness, the desperation, the secrecy and the lack of attention.

Duncan recalled, 'I told her that we should be honest, that we both wanted each other's bodies, nothing more, nothing less; that we didn't love each other but that we were discussing an affair out of lust, and a desire to go to bed together.'

Susan smiled, caught Duncan's eye and looked away.

Duncan claims that later he told her, 'I'm not going to lie to you. The affair will end when I leave Ireland or sooner, depending on what happens. I will never leave Penny. I love her and I'm very happy with her. I don't have a good reason for doing this and I'm not going to give you any excuses. I like you and I want to sleep with you.'

He claims he warned Susan, 'I don't want a long-term commitment and I'm not looking at this as a permanent relationship. And I must warn you that if I ever think Penny knows about us I'll end it immediately.'

Duncan suggested that Susan mull over all he had said and think about all the consequences. She replied, 'I agree. I didn't realize there would be so many bad points.'

They arranged that Susan would phone Duncan at work and give her reply. But only after Duncan warned her, 'Don't breath a word of this to anyone.'

Two days later Susan met Annette Gascoigne for lunch and discussed the weekend's diving.

Annette recalls probing for information, suggesting Susan paid a lot of attention to Duncan McAllister throughout the weekend.

Susan replied, 'I just really enjoy his company. You know that. Anyway, he likes me too.'

Then Annette stung Susan by saying bluntly, 'You haven't got a hope. Look at you compared with Penny. What could Duncan see in you?'

Hurt by Annette's rebuke, Susan told her, 'Well, he's suggested we have an affair.'

Annette replied, 'You're joking. What are you going to do? You're not going to take him up on it, are you?'

Susan answered, 'No, I've got no intention of becoming involved. He's made his views very clear and he won't leave Penny.'

Probing further, Annette quizzed Susan. 'What did he say?'

Susan then told Annette the gist of their conversation and Annette advised her to stay well clear of Duncan and forget any thought of an affair.

Susan commented, 'Oh, don't worry so much, I'm not that stupid, I don't want some dead-end relationship.'

Two days later, on Wednesday 12 July, Duncan was sitting in his office when Susan called. 'I really would like to see you outside the club,' she said. They arranged a meeting for forty-eight hours later. The date was Friday 13 July. They agreed to meet in the car park at the far side of a beautiful lake one mile from camp on the Hamiltonbawns Road.

Duncan recalled what happened. 'Susan was already there when I arrived. She got out of her car and walked towards me. I felt nervous and a shiver ran down my spine as I looked at her. Dressed in jeans with a light cream blouse tucked tightly into her waist Susan looked very sexy. The see-through material stretched across her breasts. At that moment I was filled with sexual excitement.'

He went on, 'At that moment I knew that Susan was there of her own volition, knowing the purpose of the meeting. In short, she was offering me sex on a plate if I wanted it; and I did. Susan looked very attractive that day and I was enticed by her coy, nervous smile and her sparkling eyes.'

Susan said, 'I've brought a picnic blanket if we need it.' She fetched the blanket and the two walked to a spot above the lake which afforded a view of the car park yet was sheltered from the main road. For a while they sat and chatted in the sun, not even touching each other. Then Duncan asked, 'I don't know if I can kiss you, touch you or what? I can feel the sexual tension between us. Are you sure about this?'

She replied, 'I wouldn't be here, otherwise.'

Duncan recalled, 'Susan returned my stare and smiled, not moving a muscle. I needed no further encouragement, and leant forward to kiss her gently on the lips. I paused and then sank into a long embrace with her, my hand exploring her neck, her shoulders and stomach, brushing her breast as I caressed her.

'She responded and didn't try to stop me touching her. Susan lay on her back, her bosom thrust towards the sky, and I sensed the expectancy inside me. As I nibbled her neck and shoulders I slowly unbuttoned her blouse, then let my mouth reach for her breast. I took her nipple into my mouth, sucking gently through the lace fabric until the nipple became erect. Susan moaned as I continued kissing her breast.

'I removed her flimsy bra material and began kissing her exposed nipple. I ran my fingers up and down her side and across her stomach in a soft, soothing motion. After a few minutes I lowered my hand to the outside of her thigh and she tensed. To reassure her, I moved my hand back to her breast and she relaxed.'

Duncan reassured her, 'Don't worry, I won't do anything that you don't want me to. I felt you go tense.'

Susan replied, 'I'm just nervous at being in the open, that's all.'

Then Susan asked whether she could touch Duncan. 'Be my guest,' he replied, and she began fiddling with his zip, tentatively playing with it as a they kissed and cuddled. Slowly, she began to unzip his trousers and when Duncan made no move she slipped her hand gently into his boxer shorts, easing his penis into the open air. Then she lay her head on his chest and continued to fondle him gently.

For ten minutes they remained locked together, but they both realized time was pressing. Duncan a looked at his watch. It was nearly two o'clock and both had to return to duty.

Duncan said, 'I'm glad we've broken the ice. I did enjoy it. Any regrets?'

'No, none,' she said.

'Do you want to meet again?'

'What do you think?' she asked, smiling up at him.

They agreed to meet the following week. As they drove back to the barracks, in separate cars, Duncan recalls, 'I was on a high, like an excited schoolboy. I'd tasted forbidden fruit and wanted more. There was no sensation of guilt, just pure sexual arousal. I was looking forward to our next meeting.'

The Affair

★　★　★

When Penny came to her husband's office to travel home with him that evening the enormity of what he had done hit Duncan like a shock wave.

He would say later, 'I avoided looking into her eyes for the first time in our life together. Yet even as I felt the awful guilt I knew my weakness would still get the better of me in the future. Susan had offered her body to me and I couldn't say no. It had nothing to do with my feelings for Penny; they were still the same. I felt my marriage was still wonderful, alive and glowing. My lust for Susan was based on pure animal desire and I was at fault. I had no excuses.'

That night Duncan found himself being short, if not sharp, with Penny, and she realized he was annoyed at something. But she had no cause to guess at the real reason. Duncan knew he had become angry, primarily with himself, and, as a result, had become ratty and evasive. To Penny he pretended his army work had been causing problems. He vowed to himself that he would not act like that again.

Diving that weekend proved difficult for Susan, Duncan and Penny. Susan began to sulk as she realized Duncan was not paying her the attention she craved; and Duncan, fearful of showing any affection towards her, responded cautiously towards the young woman whom he had been kissing and caressing only a few days before. Penny too wondered why Susan Christie, to whom she had a shown nothing but kindness, had become so offhand towards her.

As Duncan and a new recruit surfaced from the dive Susan Christie suddenly keeled over, clutching her stomach, and collapsed on the deck. Everyone looked stunned, not knowing how to react, for she had not even complained of feeling ill that day. Back on shore Annette and one of the other divers helped Susan to a car as they waited for the ambulance to arrive.

Susan asked Annette, 'Please will you fetch Duncan and ask him to accompany me to hospital? I feel afraid, going on my own.'

Duncan went to see Susan and told her that in the circumstances he felt he could not go to hospital with her, but reassuring her that Annette would accompany her. Duncan recalled, 'I felt like a real shit at the time, but I had no adequate reason to go with her.'

Susan Christie was kept in hospital, for observation as the doctors could not diagnose what, if anything, was the matter. The following day Annette spoke to Duncan, telling him that Susan wanted to see him, alone, in hospital.

Duncan told Penny he would be visiting Susan and explained that she had requested he go alone. 'A little melodramatic isn't it?' Penny asked after Duncan had explained the situation. 'I'll see you later then,' she said. 'Be good.'

Susan sat up in bed happy and smiling broadly when Duncan walked into the ward. She looked the picture of health and happiness.

'Well, how are you then?' he asked, giving her a peck on the cheek.

'Fine, thanks. I'm much better,' Sue replied. 'The pain has nearly gone. Now it's more of a grumble a than a real pain.'

Duncan sat on the edge of the bed holding her hand as the two looked deeply into each other's eyes, saying hardly a word, but pressing each other's hands affectionately, revealing the strength of their desire for each other.

'The doctors have diagnosed a suspected ovarian cyst,' Sue explained, 'mainly because they could find nothing else wrong with me.' She went on, 'Actually the doctors weren't sure what had happened to me so they think a cyst was the most likely cause. I think I had a cyst once before.'

Susan was released from hospital the next day, told to convalesce at home over the weekend and to take a week off work.

On Wednesday 25 July, Susan and Duncan once again met at the lakeside, the stomach pain forgotten, the hospital stay not mentioned.

Duncan recalled, 'It was a lovely, warm summer's day with the sun high above us as we lay on the blanket together and started to kiss and caress. Her response was willing and eager. In no time her blouse and bra had been discarded and we were entwined in a passionate embrace.

Duncan asked her, 'Are you sure about this, because the other day I sensed you were nervous.'

'I've never been with anyone like this before.'

'What about your former boyfriend David, whom you told me about? You must have been close to him?'

'Yes, we were. But we only ever petted.'

'So you've never been to bed with someone?'

'No I haven't,' she said. 'I'm a virgin. I wanted to sleep with David but he wouldn't. He refused. He didn't believe in sex before marriage.'

'What?' said Duncan. He was surprised and nervous at becoming involved with a young woman with no sexual experience whatsoever. 'I think we had better talk.'

Sue slipped back into her blouse. For more than an hour they talked through Susan's teenage dreams and her wishes. She told Duncan how she had always wanted her first lover to wine and dine her, then seduce her in a four-poster bed in a lovely country hotel, with candles lighting the room.

'But,' she said, 'now I want you to make love to me. I want it to be you.'

Susan began undressing again. Duncan held back. 'Are you sure?' he asked.

Susan retorted, 'Yes, I'm sure. And I want you to be the first one. I've thought about it and I want it to be you. I want to make love with you.'

She pulled Duncan towards her and began kissing him. 'I want you to teach me,' she said as she removed her jeans and pants and lay naked on the blanket.

Duncan recalls, 'My hands wandered everywhere and Sue gave me access to her whole body. I wanted her to enjoy the experience and searched out the most sensitive areas, using my mouth, and fingers to stimulate her. After a period of concentrated arousal Sue climaxed several times.

'I cradled her in my arms and held her close. Then Susan suddenly moved on top of me and straddled me with her legs, her breasts swinging just above my mouth. I reached up to cup them in my hands.'

'You're still dressed,' she said.

He recalls, 'Susan undid my trousers and delved

into my boxer shorts to release my straining erection. Without a word from me she moved down my body and I felt her hot breath on my penis. It was obvious Sue had never done that to a man before.

'It was an erotic yet comical scene and the two of us laughed and joked as she tried different techniques of arousing me, asking me which of the various ways I preferred.

'At that moment I wanted to make love to her, to be inside her, and I wanted to be the first man ever to make love to her. She told me she had only started taking the pill a week before and begged me to be careful.

'She lay on the blanket and just stared at me, not uttering a sound, as I lowered myself down and entered her very slowly and deliberately. It wasn't a frenzied event. I took my time, wanting Susan to feel all the physical and emotional aspects of her first sex act.

'Sue reached a climax and shortly after, I withdrew as I had promised. She screamed with delight as I ejaculated in front of her.'

Susan then drove off to see her friend Annette, who was in hospital recovering from a minor operation, while Duncan returned to work rather later than intended.

'Hi, Sue, you seem awfully happy. You look radiant, if not glowing. What have you been up to?' Annette queried jokingly.

'Oh nothing, I've just had a good day.'

'There's more to it than that, you look like the cat who's just had the cream. What have you been up to?'

But Susan refused to divulge her secret and gave Annette her present, a small prickly cactus. 'I thought you might appreciate a lot of little pricks,' Sue joked, roaring with laughter at her risqué gift.

Later, as they chatted, however, Susan Christie gleefully revealed her secret. 'I've just lost my virginity,' she confided.

'Who with?' Annette asked, rather surprised.

But Susan would not reveal the name of the man, saying only that he was an army officer, married, and a friend of her father's called David. Annette warned Susan to take care, for she feared she might get hurt having an affair with a married army officer.

Susan replied, 'Oh, don't worry, I know what I'm doing.'

On 1 August Sue, Annette and two other young women soldiers, all 'Greenfinches', were due to fly to Berlin on a two-week attachment. The day before Sue was due to fly out, however, she managed to find time for another afternoon with Duncan, walking around the lake in Hillsborough Park.

Duncan recalls, 'Once again it was a lovely summer's day, the forest crowded with people enjoying the warm weather. We both wanted each other desperately but it seemed too risky with so many people around. Finally, after much searching, we did find a secluded place and made love, quickly, intensely and passionately, hardly even removing any clothes.'

The Berlin trip proved a disaster. Annette recalled, 'Susan, another Greenfinch named Denise, and myself all shared a room. Berlin was hot and humid and tempers became frayed. Denise was a very pretty girl, dark and slim with a lively personality, and Susan Christie resented the fact she was not the star attraction among the soldiers.

'Denise could also be arrogant and she and Sue just did not get on. Eventually things became so bad we all sat down and a truce was declared during the two-week attachment.'

During a forty-eight-hour exercise the three girls, along with everyone else, were ordered to dig trenches and stay there the night, resting. Hours later, the junior NCOs came to inspect the trenches, did not consider them up to scratch, destroyed them and then ordered the young soldiers to dig new ones.

One of the recruits, however, had found an old woodman's hut and they all decided to seek shelter there for the night. Around midnight the NCOs returned, found the recruits sheltering in the hut, which was against orders, and smashed the windows as they screamed and shouted abuse at the recruits sleeping inside.

Annette recalled, 'The NCOs stormed into the hut, yelling and swearing at everyone, grabbing hold of the soldiers and forcibly dragging them outside.

Sue and myself hid under a table and when the

commotion had died down we walked outside.

'One of the NCOs still had a recruit in a headlock and Susan went berserk, shouting, swearing and screaming at the instructors, accusing them of bullying. I was amazed by Susan's reaction. She seemed uncontrollable, raging at the NCOs.

'After a while, her outburst seemed amusing to the instructors and they began laughing at her. And the more hysterical she became, the more they laughed. Suddenly, Sue clutched her side and fell to the ground as though in agony, saying, "My stomach, oh my stomach, I've been kicked in the stomach."

'I rushed forward to help her and the instructors stopped laughing. They suddenly realized there could be serious trouble if one of them had indeed kicked a junior woman soldier in the stomach.'

Annette, however, was mystified by Susan's injury. Back in the hut Susan had not screamed in pain or even mentioned she had been kicked. Annette had been with her the entire time and no soldier had come near them while the furore was going on. Mindful of Susan's recent suspected ovarian cyst, Annette insisted she be taken to the medical centre for examination. After Susan had been examined Annette heard the doctors saying they could find nothing wrong with her, nor could they find any bruising to sustain her allegation. Despite this, though, the doctors decided to keep her under observation till the next day.

The following day the soldiers decided they did not want to complain about the bullying and all agreed to say nothing to senior officers about their treatment the previous night. Annette went to tell Susan the group's decision.

'It's too late,' Sue told her. 'I've phoned Daddy and I broke down in tears. He wanted to know what was wrong and forced me to tell him.'

As a result, Annette and Susan were questioned by a number of senior officers and Special Investigation Branch officers were called in to investigate the alleged bullying. Annette and Susan were ostracized by the other recruits for the remainder of the time in Berlin. Nothing would come of the bullying accusations.

But Susan Christie would not forget the incident.

Back in Northern Ireland, Sue phoned Duncan at home, ostensibly to ask about the next dive. Speaking quietly, she told him how much she had missed him. She also wanted to tell him of the Berlin bullying saga and how she had been kicked in the stomach.

Throughout the rest of August, and most of a September, Duncan and Sue continued their illicit affair, seeing each other privately twice a week, at diving lectures most Tuesday evenings and, of course, on weekend diving expeditions. During those two months the affair became more intense, their love-making more passionate. Whenever possible Susan would sit near to Duncan at lectures, at the bar afterwards or during diving expeditions. If at all possible she would sit next to him, or face him on the boat so she would always be near him or in his sight. Susan even went so far as to ask Duncan for one-on-one lessons on all diving matters so that she could progress faster. But he declined, saying he didn't have the time.

Susan Christie was falling in love, unable to control her passion for the man she knew she could never have to herself. Penny, however, was not blind to what was going on. She too attended the diving lectures, she too accompanied Duncan on their diving expeditions, even if she didn't want to dive in the cold waters of Northern Ireland. She noted not only the attention Susan Christie was giving Duncan, but the attention, the smiles, the glances that they gave each other. And Penny also noted that Duncan had not of late been so keen on their lovemaking, not so passionate, not so attentive as he had been throughout their marriage. She did not, of course, know that Duncan was having an affair with Susan Christie, but she had deep suspicions.

It was around this time that Penny found she was pregnant. She was surprised. All her married life she had been taking the contraceptive pill and had never given a second thought to the possibility of falling pregnant. She had no reason to know how many weeks pregnant she was. She decided to say nothing to Duncan until she had seen the doctor.

Her first instinct had been to run to Duncan and tell him the news, even though they had not yet decided to start a family. Yet something held her back. She was worried about Susan Christie. She did not know, but she suspected that Duncan was having an, affair with her. Penny did not want to force Duncan into a corner. She wanted him to end his relationship with Susan of his own accord, not just because she had fallen pregnant. Penny wanted Duncan to stay with her because he loved her, and for no other reason. She resolved to wait and see, and in the meanwhile say nothing to him.

Penny did not want to confide in Duncan, nor anyone else she knew in Northern Ireland. Nor did she want to tell her mother until the pregnancy was further advanced. Neither did Penny want Norma to know she suspected Duncan of having an affair. Within a few days, however, Penny lost the baby. She did not know what to do or whom to turn to. Penny was determined to keep the pregnancy a secret, particularly from Duncan. It is not known where Penny went for medical help that day.

Penny told all this to only one person, her great friend and confidante, Major Clare Harrill, a career officer in her thirties, whom Penny had met a few weeks after arriving in Ireland. Clare, however, had been posted to Germany. Desperate to confide her secret in someone she could trust, someone to whom she could turn for advice, Penny flew to see her one weekend in early September.

Clare said later, 'Penny flew to Germany so she could discuss the whole matter. She needed to talk to someone. She told me everything that had been going on. She told how she suspected Duncan was having an affair with Susan Christie. And she told me about the miscarriage.

'Penny told me that she felt she couldn't tell Duncan about what had happened. And she hadn't told him because of his affair with Susan. The last thing Penny wanted was for Duncan to return to her simply because he felt sorry for her over the miscarriage. Penny was deeply upset but she showed immense courage and a deep love for Duncan. She was a most remarkable woman.'

Penny remained confident that Duncan's affair would be only a fling. She hoped and prayed he would soon get it out of his system. Penny found it difficult to believe that Duncan fancied Susan, since she could see that Sue had no film star looks, little sexual appeal and appeared so often to be sulky and moody. All that mattered nothing to Penny. She just wanted Duncan to return to her, but worryingly, she noticed that Duncan appeared to be becoming even closer to Susan.

Duncan himself confessed later, 'I was growing more fond of Susan. Our meetings were full of fun and excitement and I found myself drawn increasingly to her. We were becoming closer than I believed we ever would and I realized the affair had developed into something more than a lustful, physical relationship.'

The sexual trysts with Susan Christie would

occur every time they met at lunch breaks during the week. Sometimes they would make love in the open air, but more often than not in the back of a car. Susan thoroughly enjoyed the affair, the illicit sex, and threw herself with abandon into their passionate bouts of love-making.

In the company of others, however, Susan found it difficult, almost impossible, to cope with the relationship. She would become angry when Duncan did not pay her sufficient attention, though she understood he could not be seen to be favouring her. Understandably, Susan craved open affection from the man she loved, for when alone together their passion for one another had become intense.

For his part Duncan knew that he must retain his cool, detached authority as chief diving instructor. He also knew he would face disciplinary action at least and would probably be ordered to resign from the army, if senior officers ever discovered he was having an affair with a private soldier. He knew full well that the army code still demanded that no sexual affairs take place between officers and other ranks, for the simple reason, so the army judged, that it could be prejudicial to good order and discipline. Sometimes, Duncan would worry that his affair must one day be discovered by the authorities and he knew full well that this would mean his army career would be blighted, if not finished altogether. Sometimes he would vow to end the relationship for any number of reasons — for Penny, their marriage, his career, their future — but his feelings for Susan Christie had become increasingly powerful, urgent, satisfying, and so he would push his fears to the back of his mind. And continue the illicit affair.

For nine months Captain Duncan McAllister took the most enormous risks with Susan Christie. And yet as he would sit at his army desk and think of making love to Sue the excitement and the sexual thrills he found in the affair so fuelled his libido that he could not bring himself to walk away and end it. Susan's understandable feelings of rejection and anger towards Duncan would frequently surface, manifesting themselves in many ways during the months of their relationship. Unable to control her emotions, Susan would become sullen and miserable. On other occasions she would flirt madly and openly with other members of the diving club, knowing she was deliberately goading Duncan, who could only sit and watch her behaviour.

More worrying for Duncan, however, was Susan's attitude to Penny. She was furiously jealous of Duncan's wife, not just because she shared her lover with Penny, but because Penny was so popular, so beautiful, so tall and slim. In most company, Penny was by far and away the most attractive woman. Susan simply couldn't bear it.

Susan would be rude, sharp and dismissive towards Penny, openly ignoring her and even refusing to talk to her whenever Penny said something to her, even when it was just 'Hi' or 'Hello'.

Penny refused to feel upset or irritated by Susan and would always go out of her way to be kind and open towards her, even when she felt hostility from the girl who so obviously had designs on her husband, and who Penny believed in her heart was having an affair with him.

Duncan recalled, 'I appeared to be dealing with two different people. When I challenged Susan about her behaviour in the diving club she would become instantly apologetic and use her charm to appease me. She would become thoughtful and understanding.

'Susan would also make sure that I saw how she was reacting though she would never challenge me and make me the object of her anger and jealousy. It would always be directed at a third party.'

When confronted by Susan's jealousy, Duncan would debate whether he should end the affair, but he could not bring himself to do so. He confessed later, 'I couldn't walk away. I can only say it was my deep sexual desire for Susan that would constantly overrule my rational thoughts.' He also claimed that he began to feel a sense of loyalty to Susan 'because he had taken her virginity'.

Occasionally, Susan's wild flirting with some of the young, single soldiers in the diving club ended in tears, with Susan accusing them of trying to kiss her or force themselves on her. Sometimes she would drink too much, flirt wildly and lead on some of the soldiers. If one or other then tried to kiss her she would react violently and run to Duncan for protection.

Duncan would also find himself becoming angry at Susan whenever he saw her blatantly playing with people's emotions. She would sometimes flirt too much with one soldier, sometimes with two, frequently throwing glances at Duncan to see his reactions. He knew her flirting was a deliberate attempt to make him jealous, and yet he knew he was her only lover. It annoyed him to see her deliberately leading on some of the young soldiers.

Sometimes she would accuse the soldiers of a making passes or groping her but, for the most part, Duncan saw how she was behaving and told her in a no uncertain terms that she was mainly to blame for the awkward situations in which she found herself. Susan Christie did not like that.

On occasions, their lust for one another and disregard of their own security, in such a potentially dangerous environment as Northern Ireland, nearly ended in disaster. Both knew the risks they ran. Both knew that if their secret rendezvous had been discovered by the IRA, or any IRA sympathizers, they would face abduction, torture and almost certain death.

Duncan McAllister told of one near escape. 'This occurred on our first and only meeting at night. I had been attending a brigade night dinner, dressed in dinner jacket and black tie. We had arranged to meet at midnight. We drove to the lake and were making love in the back of the car. We were desperate for each other and our passion that night was intense.

'I had remained almost fully dressed, still in my bow-tie, and Susan had simply taken off her knickers. We were in the act of making love when we heard the sound of cars, their tyres screeching as they approached. Then we saw their headlamps blazing and the vehicles skidded to a halt next to our car. I was deeply scared, convinced this was the IRA. My heart was beating furiously as I believed we were about to be executed. Susan and I lay still in the back of the car, not daring to move a muscle.

'Stupidly, I had forgotten to lock the car doors and I tried, as quietly as possible, to reach forward and lock them. I couldn't reach the handles so we lay as still as possible, praying we would not be spotted. Then I heard the noise of laughter and sighed deeply. They were joy riders on a wild, midnight drive.

'It took some minutes for us to calm down. My heart continued thumping, for I had convinced myself that IRA gunmen were in those cars. That killed our nocturnal activities for that night and for evermore. We agreed we would never meet again in such circumstances. I had been stupid and foolhardy.'

Both Susan Christie and Annette thoroughly enjoyed the thrill of diving and were becoming proficient after six or more months. As chief instructor, Duncan would take it in turns to dive with the recruits, one by one, teaching them the correct techniques and procedures to ensure their safety and enjoyment.

Susan Christie would always try to dive with Duncan as her partner and very often she succeeded. He realized, however, that he must not show favouritism and would dive with the others as well, but when he told Susan he was about to dive with Annette, Susan told him that Annette didn't like diving with him and preferred to dive with one of the other instructors.

Annette was surprised, and a little upset, that Duncan, the chief instructor, who had introduced her to the sport, never asked her to partner him when diving and always found herself paired with another instructor. She became more surprised when discussing the subject with Susan, for she told Annette that Duncan was unwilling to partner her because he did not like her very much.

Annette recalled, 'Susan told me that information in confidence and I had no reason to disbelieve her. After all, I understood that Sue and I were good friends. As a result, I never asked Duncan to dive with me because I had no intention of embarrassing him. But it did hurt.'

However, Susan Christie did confess to Annette, after only a few weeks of dating Duncan, that she was in fact having an affair with him.

Annette recalled, 'Sue first told me that Duncan only wanted an affair with her, not that they were having one. Then she confessed later that she and Duncan were sleeping together. I knew the risks they were taking, particularly Duncan. I knew he was risking his career and his marriage. I also could not understand why on earth he would be having an affair with someone like Susan Christie when he had such a wonderful wife in Penny. But it was none of my business. I simply hoped that they both realized what they were doing.'

Susan began acting in odd ways, not only towards Penny, but also towards other women in the diving club. It seemed Susan was determined to ensure that she would be the only woman who would become close to her lover. She would be rude to them for no apparent reason, criticize them in front of Duncan and she would go out of her way to make them feel awkward and out of place at diving club gatherings. Sexual jealousy now motivated every aspect of Susan Christie's life.

Ticking Timebomb

★ ★ ★

In September 1990 Duncan McAllister had to conduct open water safety tests, needed by some of the more experienced divers for their next qualification. This meant that the club would be short of experienced divers that day. It also meant that Penny and Susan Christie, the two women who wanted Duncan, body and soul, would be joined together by a single lifeline as they dove in the dark waters off Northern Ireland.

First, Duncan had to ask Penny if she would agree to dive at all. 'Pen, Pen,' he asked, 'would you mind diving this weekend, because we have a real problem. I know I've never asked you to dive in these waters before but do you think you could bear it, just for once?'

Penny, who Duncan knew full well hated the idea of diving in cold, dark waters, asked him why it would be necessary.

Duncan replied, 'Because if you don't agree it means that a number of club members won't be able to dive this weekend because there aren't enough experienced divers to partner them.'

With a smile, Penny said, 'All right then, but only for you.'

Duncan loved that side of Penny's nature. She would always agree to help out, even if it meant doing something she didn't really want to do. Duncan, not for the first time, realized just how lucky he was to have Penny as his wife.

'Thanks darling,' Duncan said, giving her a kiss on the cheek. 'I knew you would come to the rescue.'

Duncan worked out the various pairings and told Penny that her partner for the dive that day would be Susan Christie.

'OK then,' said Penny.

Then Duncan went over to Susan Christie with the good news that she would be able to dive that weekend. 'Sue, great news. Penny has agreed to dive today, which means you will have a partner after all.'

'What do you mean, Penny will be my

partner?' snapped Susan.

'Well,' Duncan explained, taken aback, 'it's the only way I can work the rota so that everyone gets a dive, otherwise it can't work.'

But Susan Christie would hear none of it. 'I'm sorry, Duncan,' she said between clenched teeth, 'but there is no way I am going diving with Penny. I don't have any confidence in Penny, you know that. I've a never even seen her dive,' she exclaimed angrily.

'Please,' said Duncan. 'She has agreed for the sake of the club. You can't back out now that I've arranged everything.'

'I'm sorry,' Susan replied adamantly, 'but I have no intention of diving with Penny. I flatly refuse to go with her. If that is the only option then I won't dive at all.'

Susan stormed off and an embarrassed Duncan informed his wife that Susan had decided she did not want to dive that day. But he did not tell her of Susan's explosion and flat refusal.

Susan's outburst showed Duncan how unpredictable and demanding Susan Christie could be, so very different from Penny. Duncan began to feel that Susan would become increasingly difficult to handle. Yet, despite his misgivings, the affair continued and Duncan and Sue would still meet, and make love, whenever possible.

The following seven months revealed Susan Christie to be a young woman desperately in love, yearning for attention, and sometimes acting like a spoiled child. More importantly, she was unable to come to terms with the realization that one day her lover would be posted away from Ireland, leaving her behind.

During the coming months Susan Christie revealed another side to her nature, that of a cold and calculating young woman hell bent on having her own way, whatever the cost. Annette Gascoigne sometimes witnessed this hard, cold side of Susan Christie, a side which would surface whenever they discussed Penny.

Annette said later, 'The more Sue became involved with Duncan, the more she came to hate Penny. And Sue made no bones of the fact that she hated Penny. She was totally open in her hatred and opposition, revealing to me and others how implacably jealous she had become of her.

'She would sit and talk to me about Penny from time to time. Susan would invariably describe her as "that stuck-up bitch"; at other times as "that dolled-up cow".'

She would constantly criticize everything about Penny, picking holes in whatever clothes she wore, her make-up, even her physical appearance. Sue knew that Penny had always been embarrassed about her nose, thinking it too big, and Sue would refer to 'Penny's great big conker'.

'And yet, with my hand on my heart,' Annette remembered, 'I can say that I never once heard

Penny say anything against Sue, never criticized her.'

Annette told how she would shake her head in disbelief, hearing Susan's constant criticism, when Penny was head and shoulders above Sue in looks, personality, appearance and sexuality.

Annette commented, 'Throughout the entire time Penny spent in Northern Ireland I cannot remember anyone, except Susan Christie, saying a bad word about her. She would always be happy, smiling, understanding and a friend to anyone in time of need. She was truly remarkable woman.

'And remarks about her patience and personality by everyone who knew her were said not only after her death, but during her lifetime. Without doubt, Penny was an exceptional person.'

Annette also saw how the affair had its effect on Duncan's relationship with Penny. She recalled, 'Sometimes I noticed Duncan would be rude, off-hand towards Penny. I knew what was going on and would feel genuinely sorry for her. She was the innocent party and yet it seemed she would sometimes be the butt of Duncan's abruptness.

'Sometimes in public Duncan would embarrass Penny. For example, I remember him telling Penny one day, in full view of everyone and in quite a loud voice, "I do wish you wouldn't put your hair up like that; we've talked about that before. You ought to put it down." And Penny would do so.

'It just wasn't the way that I believed a husband should speak to his wife in public. But sometimes Duncan would speak abruptly to people, even Penny, without meaning to be rude or offensive. That was him. But it was embarrassing for everyone around at the time, not only Penny. I would look at Penny and see the hurt she felt on such occasions, especially when Duncan would make such remarks in front of Susan Christie, the woman Penny believed he was having an affair with.'

And that was not all Annette noticed. 'I remember watching Duncan and Sue carrying on together, flirting, sometimes openly in front of the other divers. This usually went on when Penny wasn't there. When Penny was present I would see her watching the two of them, checking their eye contact, their glances, their smiles.

'Sue revelled in those occasions, of course. She was a natural flirt and would encourage Duncan to flirt with her. Duncan may have believed it was innocent fun but both Penny and Sue knew there was nothing innocent about the way they were behaving towards one another. It was no wonder that Penny believed very early on in their affair that something was going on.

'There seemed nothing more Penny could do. They appeared to have a good marriage; they got on so well together. She seemed to absolutely worship Duncan and would do anything for him, anything to please him. To many, Penny McAllister would be the perfect wife, not only because of her wonderful model looks but her personality, cheerfulness, friendliness and attitude towards everyone. She would always help out; whatever needed to be done she would happily help with, even dirty or mucky cleaning jobs, and always do so happily.

'After diving trips, for example, when Penny had helped steer the boat, carry the bottles, clean the gear, act as diving marshal and generally be everyone's dogsbody, she would be the person who would volunteer later to prepare and cook a meal for everyone. She was selfless. I marvelled at her and sometimes felt so very sorry for her.'

On occasions, when Penny had not participated in a diving expedition, Susan and Duncan would sit together in the back of Annette's car driving to and from the diving site. At the end of a day, Susan would lay her head on Duncan's lap and fall asleep.

Alone together, Duncan and Sue's passion for each other would encourage them to take the most extraordinary risks, which they knew could put their very lives in danger. But their lust for one another drove them on. Only a matter of a few weeks after their first fright, they experienced another heart-thumping scare when they went one afternoon in search of a new place to make love, a disused quarry not far from Lisburn barracks.

Duncan recalled, 'Susan had discovered a

conservation area which had been a quarry. It seemed quiet, and deserted. We climbed to the top of a steep bank and made our way around the quarry to a secluded, hidden spot behind some bushes. We lay down. Sue removed her shirt and we began kissing and petting. Sue was wearing a tight red lace bodice beneath her shirt and I buried my head between her breasts as she put her arms around me and pulled me closer.

'We were in this passionate embrace when suddenly I heard a movement in the bushes behind us and my heart missed a beat. I hoped it might just be an animal but then I saw a shadowy figure, a man, watching us. My heart beat faster. Instinctively, I thought the man must be an IRA gunman who had discovered that we were both army personnel. Living and working in Northern Ireland of course makes everyone fearful of attack at any time, and we were so vulnerable.

'I pointed him out to Susan, my heart pounding, ready for the sound of gunfire. Nothing happened. We could see the man quite clearly as a shadow and wondered why he hadn't opened fire. We were sitting targets. I then realized, hoped, prayed that the figure was that of a peeping-tom. He began to move, to retreat away from us. He realized he had been spotted and was making good his escape.

'I stood up and advanced towards the bushes as the man disappeared into the distance.'

Still shaking from the shock, Duncan turned to Sue, who was busily dressing, and said, 'I never thought I would be glad to catch a peeping-tom. Thank goodness we hadn't gone any further.'

Sue had now seen the funny side of the situation and said, with a big smile, 'You should have seen your face.'

Duncan replied, 'I can tell you I was worried. Can't you just see the headlines: "Captain with half-naked private found shot".'

The peeping-tom had put an end to thoughts of making love that day, so Duncan and Sue lay on the blanket, chatting for a while, enjoying the afternoon sun. Only weeks later, however, the full realization of the risks they had been taking came home to them. They read in the newspapers and heard on television that two young lovers, one a member of the UDR, were shot dead by an IRA hit-squad while cuddling in their car on the banks of Lough Neagh.

In late September 1990, Susan Christie and some other recruits were to make their first dive on the Chirripo wreck. Fortunately, conditions were good with a calm sea, no current and a bright, sunny day. Visibility along the top of the wreck that day was better than usual, with shafts of light piercing the green murky water. The divers could see the brightly-coloured conga eels, sea urchins, fan worms and delicate flora, making the dive interesting and satisfying.

Though only thirty metres down, Duncan insisted on a precautionary safety stop on the way back to the surface to make sure the divers were safely inside the diving compression tables. He did not want any of his divers suffering from a 'bend', the decompression sickness that affects divers if they surface too quickly or overstay the time limits for that diving depth.

That particular dive had been a high spot for the club and everyone returned to shore happy, joking and laughing. It had been a most successful dive. Back on shore Susan and some of the others were larking about, happily throwing each other off the jetty into the water.

When they all stopped for fish and chips on the way back home, however, Susan turned to Annette and asked her to look at her face. 'It feels really sore,' she said. 'Is it all right?'

Annette noticed it was a little red and suggested the cause could have been the oily waters of the harbour. She knew Susan had highly sensitive skin.

Susan joked, 'You never know, it might be a bend,' and laughed.

Overhearing the remark, Duncan said, 'You don't want to say things like that, you had better touch wood.'

Despite the great day's dive, however, Susan felt Duncan had not paid her enough attention and began to sulk. As she left that evening to drive home Duncan went over to her. 'I'm sure the rash on your skin is only from the water but take care. If you develop any other symptoms consistent with decompression sickness contact me or one of the others immediately. Promise?'

Susan nodded. 'I will,' she said. 'But you could have been nicer to me. I really wanted to talk to you today.'

'I know and I'm sorry,' Duncan replied, 'but you know I can't, with everyone around. I'll speak to you tomorrow. Look, I've got to go, Penny's watching us.'

Susan Christie wound up the window of her car, looking unhappy and miserable as she drove away. The following morning Duncan received a phone call from club member Lance-Corporal Jock Grey informing him that Susan had been trying to contact him all night. She believed she was having a 'bend', experiencing joint pains in her knees and ankles.

Duncan was worried. He and Penny had been home all night and the phone had not rung. Ever since becoming an instructor not one of his pupils had ever suffered a bend because of his attention to detail. He was also confused because he was certain there was no way Susan could have suffered a bend. Duncan had dived with Susan; he and others had dived on the Chirripo that day, and surfaced together, yet no one had reported any ill effects or the slightest symptoms of a bend.

He immediately phoned Dr Galway, an expert in decompression sickness at Craigavon Hospital, near Lurgan, warning him to stand by in case it might be necessary for a diver to use the recompression chamber at the hospital. He gave Dr Galway the dive details so he could prepare the chamber for their arrival.

Duncan phoned Susan at home and discovered that her pains were becoming more severe. However, Susan refused to allow Duncan to visit her home to collect her for the trip to hospital. She explained, 'I don't want my father to see you pick me up. I don't want him to know about the bend; you know he's against me diving.'

Susan managed to drive her car from her home to Lisburn barracks and walk unaided from her car to where Duncan was waiting nearby. She didn't appear to be in pain. On arrival at the hospital she walked without support and with no visible pain.

In the hospital Duncan left Susan sitting comfortably while he went to find Dr Galway. Two minutes later he returned to find two nurses tending to Susan, who had collapsed in pain and was unable to walk without assistance.

Later, Susan explained to Dr Galway that she was suffering from a stiff left shoulder and numbness in her left arm below the elbow. Dr Galway took her to the recompression chamber and went through the dive profile in detail with McAllister. Dr Galway could not understand how she had suffered a bend. It simply did not make sense, for she had not overstayed her time limit at depth nor had she resurfaced too fast. Dr Galway knew that taking into account the two-minute safety stop on the way to the surface Susan was, technically, well inside the limits. Yet she was complaining of pains symptomatic of decompression sickness.

There was another point. Duncan McAllister had partnered Susan throughout the dive. If she had indeed suffered a bend then McAllister would have expected to experience some of the same symptoms. But he had not.

Based on the symptoms she described to Dr Galway, Susan Christie underwent a session of recompression; she was then taken back to a hospital ward for further examination, X-rays and observation. She told Dr Galway that the time in the chamber had cured the numbness in her ankles and knees but her shoulder was still stiff.

Duncan spent the entire day at the hospital with Susan. He recalls, 'On occasions she would become scared and uptight, fearing the effects of the bend. I would try to calm her.'

Later, Dr Galway suggested a second treatment to rid Susan of the pain in her shoulder, starting at 9 p.m. and continuing till midnight. Susan asked Dr Galway if Duncan could stay with her in the chamber and he agreed. When the second treatment was completed Susan still complained of stiffness in her shoulder, which Dr Galway found difficult to comprehend.

Susan then told Dr Galway, 'Perhaps I should tell you that two days ago I fell off a twelve-foot-high wall during an assault course exercise, injuring my left shoulder.'

Dr Galway looked amazed, glanced with suppressed astonishment at Duncan McAllister, unable to comprehend why Susan Christie had not mentioned the fall earlier. In that instance Dr Galway was not convinced Susan Christie had in fact suffered a bend, but had been feeling the effects of the earlier fall. He felt she may have wasted his time. If so, however, he had no idea why a young woman would feign decompression sickness, spend two sessions in a recompression chamber and the entire day in hospital, for no apparent good reason.

Susan Christie would have known all about the bends. At diving lectures the new members were told how to spot any symptoms which might indicate they were suffering a bend, such as aches in the joints, rashes on the skin, mottling of the skin and a feeling of pins and needles. She would also have known that one of the golden rules of diving is that if ever divers believe they may be suffering from decompression sickness they should never try to sleep it off but inform one of their colleagues immediately.

The decompression lecture is perhaps the most important lecture new divers receive. It lasts for three hours. And everyone is left in no doubt that a bend can be extremely serious. At the end of that lecture every member of the diving club had received the location and telephone number of the recompression chamber at Craigavon Hospital.

The reason is that if the effects of decompression are not treated immediately in a recompression chamber then the effect will always become progressively worse, leading to extreme pain. It would be extraordinary if Susan Christie, fearing she had suffered a bend, did not inform Duncan or one of her colleagues the night she felt unwell. Her bend would remain a mystery.

Sometime after midnight, Penny arrived at the hospital to drive Duncan home after his sixteen hours caring for Susan. Duncan told Penny of the surprise announcement Susan had made after undergoing treatment in the chamber, telling the doctor that she had suffered a fall from the high wall only a couple of days before. Penny was not in the best of humour. She wondered why Duncan had found it necessary to spend all day at the hospital with Susan Christie. She understood he felt responsible as the chief diving instructor, but she could not understand why he felt it necessary to stay with her, sitting by her bed for sixteen hours.

Duncan, however, felt Penny was not being fair. On this occasion he defended Susan, believing she may have suffered a minor bend. On the drive home Penny commented, 'You know Susan didn't have a bend, don't you? She just wanted your sole attention and, what's more, she received it. Can't you see, Duncan, that she is stringing you along?'

Duncan took Susan's side, saying, 'I don't believe that. Surely no one would put themselves in hospital with a bend in order to gain sympathy.'

But Penny remained adamant. She said, 'Have you stopped to consider how many times Susan has apparently been ill, or suffered an injury, in the last three months? And do you realize how many times she has ended up in hospital within the last two months?'

As Duncan sat thinking, Penny went on, in an exasperated tone of voice, 'Can't you see that Susan is trying to monopolize your attention, Duncan? I won't say anything else, but just think about it.'

Penny had herself been doing a lot of thinking that day, but she did not tell Duncan this. She had telephoned her mother in England, however, and they had spoken about Susan Christie.

Norma recalls, 'Penny phoned and told me of a girl who had a so-called bend and that Duncan was spending the day with her in the recompression unit at Craigavon Hospital. Penny told me she thought the girl, whom she did not name during our phone conversation, was in fact playacting, demanding Duncan's sole attention. Penny sounded annoyed. Penny told me the girl was forever trying to attract Duncan's attention, trying to put herself between Penny and Duncan, but she told me that she could cope. I can hear her words now, telling me, "Don't worry Mum, I can hack it."'

After putting down the phone, Norma spent the next few days thinking of the conversation with her beloved daughter and hoping that she could indeed 'hack it'.

Norma knew, from her many years surrounded by army officers and their wives during her time overseas, all about the cauldron of sex, lust and extramarital affairs that exists on many service bases. Norma also knew that the women were as much to blame as the men, having noted the lengths some women would go to in order to ensnare an officer they fancied. Penny's phone call had worried her. She knew that Penny would not have even raised the subject unless she felt threatened.

She would say after Penny's death, 'I just hoped that she would be able to cope. I knew she was a beautiful, many would say a stunning young woman, who had many admirers. I also knew that her good looks and happy nature made many army wives jealous of her. From very early on in their relationship I had known that Penny was very much in love with Duncan, and loved being part of his life. But I also knew she was a most trusting person. I just hoped that the girl she mentioned wasn't too scheming.'

Susan Christie's father, Staff-Sergeant Bob Christie, of the Ulster Defence Regiment, a small, rotund man, was furious that the daughter whom he adored should have suffered from the bends as a result of a diving lesson. He believed there must have been some negligence on the part of Captain McAllister. Understandably, Bob Christie held McAllister, the chief diving instructor, responsible for his daughter's illness, for it was McAllister's duty to ensure the safety of club members.

Ever since Susan had become involved with Duncan, her father had sensed that there was some attraction between the two. The last relationship Bob Christie wanted for his daughter was an affair with a married man, particularly a married officer; and even more so with a young officer of the regular army who would serve for a few years in Northern Ireland and then leave the province for another posting.

He had seen other relationships between young UDR privates and regular officers and knew that most had ended in disaster. He did not want his daughter's heart broken by some casual affair with a married man.

Bob Christie did not contact McAllister or Dr Galway to ask what had gone wrong with the dive, preferring to seek the advice of the Royal Engineers Diving Section in Antrim.

Susan told Duncan of her father's concern and the lengths he was going to to try and discover what had happened to his daughter and who should be held responsible for what he believed had been negligence. Duncan said to her, 'If your father is thinking like that perhaps I had better have a word with him. I was the officer responsible. I am the person to whom he should be addressing his concerns. I believe it is my duty to phone him and explain what happened; take him through the diving tables and explain that it would have been impossible for you to have suffered a bend.'

'No,' said Susan, 'I don't think that would be a good idea at all. He's very angry with what happened and I don't think it would be a good idea for you to talk to him, let alone meet him. He believes you're responsible. You're not his favourite person.'

Reluctantly, Duncan took Sue Christie's advice and never phoned her father. Duncan would say later, 'I had intended pointing out to him that as Sue and I were diving together that day we either would both have suffered from the bends or neither of us. It makes no difference whether you are a man or a woman, experienced or inexperienced. If a diver surfaces too quickly from a certain depth that diver will suffer a bend.

'I also intended telling him that the dive had been correctly carried out, according to military diving regulations. However, whenever any divers in the club went to thirty metres plus, I always insisted that they did a compulsory safety stop before surfacing. In that way I ensured there was no possibility of anyone suffering a bend.

'There was another point. I wanted to ask Susan's father whether he thought that I would deliberately put myself at risk, because he knew I had partnered Susan on that dive.'

The trauma of Sue Christie's bend, however, would not be forgotten so quickly. Dr Galway informed Duncan McAllister, as the chief diving instructor, that Christie would not be permitted to dive for at least four weeks, as a precautionary measure. Sue had not realized the four-week ban was a mandatory prohibition for divers recuperating from a bend.

The news shocked her.

'Why can't I dive?' she demanded. 'I'm feeling fine now. There's nothing wrong with me,' she told Duncan when he broke the news to her.

In that instant, Sue had realized that not only would this mean she could not see her lover at weekends, but that she might not be permitted to take part in the club expedition to Ascension Island.

'Does this mean I can't go to Ascension?' she asked, a note of alarm in her voice.

'It all depends,' replied Duncan. 'If Ascension falls in that four-week ban then there is no point in you going to Ascension because it's a diving expedition; only divers would be permitted to go.'

Sue protested again and Duncan said he would have another word with Dr Galway to check. The twelve-day Ascension Island expedition was due to take place near the beginning of October. It would be touch and go whether Sue Christie would be passed fit to dive by then.

Dr Galway agreed to give Susan a medical check a couple of days before the team were due to fly out. If she had experienced no recurrence of decompression sickness, and if she felt in tip-top condition, then she might be able to go, but only on the condition she undertook shallow dives, with strict time limitations.

Duncan commented later, 'That calmed Sue to a certain extent. She had been looking forward to Ascension and I did feel genuinely sorry for her. She seemed very upset, almost distraught that she might not be able to come along. I tried to raise her spirits by telling her that I thought she would probably be passed fit to dive.

'I somehow felt protective towards Sue at that time. I found myself being drawn closer to her. My involvement with her had become more than just straightforward lust and sex. It now encompassed a strong emotional bond between us. I realized then that I had become attached to Sue and very fond of her, far more so than I had ever originally intended or considered likely when the affair began.

'And I was certain that Sue had fallen in love with me. But I did not realize to what extent she had become involved.'

Over a pub lunch one day in late September 1990, Susan had been pressing Duncan as to why he never told her, openly and straightforwardly, that he loved her. 'You never say "I love you", she pressed him. 'When I say I love you, then you just reply "Good" or "That's lovely", but you never tell me that you love me. Why won't you, Duncan?'

'My answers mean that I love you,' he lied to her.

'Then why don't you just tell me, in the same way as I am always telling you that I love you,' she replied.

Duncan had no good answer because in his heart he knew the truth. He would say later, 'I knew that if I told her I loved her then that would be a major commitment on my part and I was frightened of making that commitment. I was in love with Penny. I couldn't tell Sue I loved her because to me that would be a betrayal of Penny. Sexually, I was already cheating on Penny. I could not bring myself to betray her love as well. And I felt that if I told Sue I loved her that would be betraying the love between Penny and me. I would just feel terribly, terribly guilty.'

Walking down Hillsborough High Street after that lunch, Sue turned to Duncan, held his arm and said gently, 'I love you.'

Duncan did not reply immediately. Then he stopped her and turned her towards him so they were standing still in the middle of the street facing one another. 'Sue,' he said, 'I want to explain to you. I love you, I do love you but please don't think that means I don't still love Penny.' Then, looking into her eyes, he stressed the last four words, saying, 'But I do love you.'

Sue's face lit up; she was ecstatic. She looked into her lover's eyes and smiled broadly, so very, very happy that the man she adored had finally said he loved her. She threw her arms around his neck and kissed him on the lips, oblivious to the shoppers and passers-by. Sue had never been so happy in her life.

As they walked down the street, however, Duncan explained his love for her, saying, 'I love you, but not how you may think. Do you believe that you can love two people at the same time? Do you believe you can love two people in different ways?'

Susan nodded to both questions. 'Yes,' she said, 'I agree.'

He went on, 'Well, that's how it is when I say I love you. I do love you but not in the same way that I love Penny. So please don't confuse the two loves because they're different. Penny's my wife and you're an extremely close friend. I just don't want you to think this will change anything. Do you understand what I'm saying?'

Susan looked up at Duncan, squeezed his arm and said with a smile, 'Yes I do.'

A few days later Penny flew to Germany for a weekend with Clare Harris, and Duncan invited Sue to stay the weekend at his married-quarters home overlooking Armagh. Fearing that neighbours might see Sue arrive at the house, they arranged that she would stay away until darkness fell.

Duncan recalled, 'Just after nine o'clock the doorbell sounded and I rushed to let Sue in, fearful she might be seen standing on the doorstep. We stood there looking at each other, the moment highly charged as we both realized that this would be another major step in our affair.

'We were desperate to make love, to get into a double bed together and spend as much time as we wanted making love to each other. We were like two cats on a hot tin roof, the air somehow alive with sexual tension. Sue wore a tight blouse, revealing her wonderful breasts, and a knee-high skirt and high heels.'

Duncan said, 'You look fantastic, and so sensual', and they kissed passionately as they stood in the hall, unable to take their hands off one another, so keen were they both to strip naked and make love as they never had before, in a bed.

Duncan recalled the moment. 'I held her close, her body straining, forcing herself against me. I ran my hands over her backside and the tops of her legs and felt the suspenders through her skirt. Suspenders have always heightened my sexual arousal and Sue knew that full well because I had often told her. Now my mouth went dry at the excitement to come.'

Sue disentangled herself, walked through into the lounge and lay back on the sofa. 'The suspenders are for later,' she said and smiled wickedly at Duncan. He desperately wanted to race her off and make love there and then, so sexually charged did he feel. Instead, he said, 'I've some wine cooling in the fridge. Would you like a glass?' In less than half an hour they sat and drank the bottle of chilled rosé, while their hands searched each other's bodies, kissing and hugging one another. They opened another bottle but took only a sip. They could wait no longer. Duncan took Sue's hand, pulled her from the sofa and led her upstairs to the double bed in the spare room.

There, by the side of the double bed, Duncan had placed a chilled bottle of champagne with two fluted glasses. Sue let out a squeal of delight when she saw the champagne and turned to him, so happy to be alone at last, in a bedroom with the man she loved.

Duncan said, 'Well, you said you wanted this to be a special day. I know it's not the first time we've made love, but it is the first time in a bed and we can make love again in the morning.'

Sue and Duncan made love through the night, wallowing in the luxury a whole night alone had given them. In between bouts of love-making, and sipping champagne, they talked and chatted as though it was the first a opportunity to get to know each other, completely.

They talked about Ascension and Sue's father's attitude to diving. 'Daddy doesn't want me to go diving any more,' she said. 'He would be far happier if I never went diving again.'

'Is he happy about you coming to Ascension?'

'No, Daddy doesn't want me to go.'

'Does that mean you might not be coming?'

'No way. He won't stop me. I know how to get round him. I can twist him around my little finger.'

Duncan would comment later, 'I could tell by the way that she made the remark that Sue was not exaggerating. She was quite boastful of her ability to get her own way with her father whenever she wanted to. It was as though she had a hold over him.'

During Saturday and Sunday Duncan went diving with the club as usual, but the nights he spent with Sue, at his married quarters. Sue and Duncan spent Saturday night and most of Sunday night making love. Sue did not leave until the early hours of Monday morning after they had spent some more hours together in bed. For the first time in their relationship, they also found time to talk, to get to know each other.

Later, Duncan confessed, 'I thoroughly enjoyed that weekend with Sue. I would be lying if I said otherwise. We had a marvellous time. I knew I was becoming fond of Sue, perhaps too fond of her, even though I found her exasperating at times. I knew Sue had fallen in love with me, but towards the end of the weekend I realized the situation between us had changed, become more serious. It was no longer simply a sexual relationship, based on lust for one another. We were becoming very close, too close, and that worried me. The intensity of the affair scared me.'

Two Loves

★ ★ ★

The idyllic weekend Susan Christie spent with Duncan would, however, end in tears, for Duncan decided their love affair had begun to take over their lives and that they had become too involved with each other. He decided that he had to say something to Sue, to warn her that he had no intention of ever leaving Penny no matter what.

On the Sunday evening Duncan broached the subject. He began gently. 'I think we need to discuss our affair, Sue, and see where we go from here.'

She sat down on the sofa beside him, wondering what her lover would say.

He coughed, cleared his throat and began the speech he had rehearsed a dozen times. 'I think it might be best to go back to a platonic relationship, like we had before.'

Susan looked at him, stunned. They had been enjoying a wonderful, weekend, their first together. Everything had gone perfectly, their love for each other had never been greater, their love-making never more passionate, and now, suddenly, Duncan was getting cold feet.

'But why?' she protested. 'I thought we were both happy with the way everything's going.'

Duncan began to explain. 'Bringing you here has made me realize things might get out of hand,' he said, turning towards her. 'You know I'm really fond of you but I know in my heart that I would never leave Penny. I don't want you to get too involved and then get hurt.'

He stopped for a second and then continued, 'And there is another point: we're taking too many risks.'

The tears began to well in Susan's eyes as she realized that all her hopes of a long love affair with Duncan were evaporating by the second. Between tears, she said, 'I don't want that. I want to keep seeing you. I know it will end when you leave Ireland, but I want it to continue until that time'. After a pause, she went on, 'I can handle our affair ... You can't expect me to go back and just be friends ... It wouldn't be fair ... I'd have to leave the club and everything.' At that Sue broke down, tears flooding down her cheeks as she finished speaking.

Duncan would say later, 'I felt a complete heel. I didn't want to hurt her and yet here I was hurting her. I tried to explain everything to her as she sat next to me, sobbing.'

He told her, 'Listen, Sue, can't you understand that's why we must stop, before you become too attached? It's better for you if we stop now.'

But Sue remained adamant, imploring Duncan to let the affair continue until he left the province. As the evening wore on Duncan's resolve began to wane. He had not the heart to end the affair. He also became worried.

Later, he confessed, 'I feared that Susan might create a scene if I forced the issue. Perhaps she would tell Penny; perhaps tell the army authorities of our affair, which could well end with me being asked to resign my commission, forced out of the army. I couldn't risk any of those possibilities so I decided to continue the affair.'

Before she went home in the early hours of Monday morning Susan had all but regained her composure and they had kissed each other a fond farewell. The affair would continue.

The following morning Duncan answered his phone in his office to hear Susan's happy voice on the end of the line thanking him for a 'lovely weekend'. There was no mention of the tearful discussion.

'I also want to ask you a favour,' Sue said.

'What's that?'

'I want us to conduct an experiment when we are in Ascension, if you would agree?'

'What's that?'

'I'd like to make love twenty metres underwater.'

Jokingly, Duncan replied, 'I'm sure I could get one of the lads to volunteer.'

Ignoring his attempt at humour, Sue added, 'I want to do that because it's something you have never done with Penny. You haven't, have you?'

Duncan replied, 'No, it's not something I've ever considered before. It sounds a very interesting proposition. We'll have to see.'

Forty-eight hours later, Penny, Sue and Duncan would all attend a diving lecture in the unit bar at Armagh barracks. Throughout the entire evening Susan Christie totally ignored Penny. At every opportunity Susan would snub Penny, pretending not to hear when Penny spoke to her and even deliberately turning her back when Penny asked her a question. Sometimes Susan looked blankly at Penny, refusing to acknowledge her presence.

Duncan was absolutely furious. He remembers thinking at the time, 'If you're trying to show Penny and everyone else that there is something going on between us, then you're doing a bloody fine job.'

The following morning, Duncan phoned

Susan from his office. 'What the fuck were you playing at last night?' he demanded. Before Sue could answer he went on, 'Don't you ever treat Penny like that again. I was infuriated.'

Duncan had never spoken to Sue in that tone of voice. She was shocked, but protested her innocence. 'I don't know what you mean; I didn't do anything wrong.'

But Duncan's fury had not subsided. 'Don't give me that. You know damn well what you were doing. You took every opportunity to put Penny down. Don't make any bloody excuses, because they won't wash.' And he went on, 'Penny's done nothing wrong. We're the ones at fault, so don't ever take it out on her again. I won't have it.'

He drew a deep breath and spoke slowly so that Susan Christie would understand precisely what he was saying: 'Let me make one point absolutely clear. If this ever happens again, I'll drop you like a stone.'

The tirade over, Susan replied timidly, 'I'm sorry, I didn't mean to upset you.'

Duncan became calmer as his anger subsided. He said, more quietly, 'You upset Penny, not me. I just a got angry. I'm sorry to be so hard, but you've got to learn that other people have feelings too. Anyway, enough said, let's forget it. I'll speak to you later.'

A few hours later Susan phoned back and said, 'Duncan, I'm sorry, I really am very sorry. I've thought about what you said and I was in the wrong; I'll try and be nicer to Penny in future, promise I will.'

Two days later on 21 September, Duncan had put on the kettle for a cup of tea when Penny walked into the kitchen. 'I had a very unexpected phone call today,' she said.

'Who from?'

'Susan.'

Duncan froze. Trying to hide his fear, he asked, 'What did she want?'

'She's invited me out for lunch tomorrow. She said it was to say sorry for the other night.'

'Oh, right. Well at least she realizes she was off with you.'

'We'll see,' replied Penny.

The first call Duncan made the following morning would be to Susan. 'Why didn't you tell me yesterday that you had invited Penny to lunch?'

'I didn't think it was important.'

'We're having an affair,' Duncan exploded, 'and you didn't think I'd be interested that you were inviting my wife to lunch. Give me a break.'

Sounding composed and confident, Sue said, 'I'm only trying to be nice, as you asked me to be. I don't see any harm in it. I'd like to get to know Penny better. I know I've been unfair to her.'

Duncan did not know how to respond, so he said, 'I asked you to be more civil and make an effort, not to invite her to lunch.'

'Sorry,' Susan replied.

'Well, next time please give me some warning if you intend to do something like that.'

Changing tack, Duncan went on, 'You must promise me that you won't give her the impression we are having an affair or that we're involved. And if Penny suggests we are having an affair I want you to tell me, OK?'

The following evening Penny said virtually nothing about her lunch date, simply telling Duncan, 'It was pleasant; we just chatted.'

But she did not say what they had chatted about. Throughout the weekend, Duncan could hardly contain himself waiting until the Monday morning to phone Susan and ask what had gone on.

'What did Penny say?' Duncan enquired immediately Sue answered the phone.

'She said she thought that I paid you too much attention and expected to take too much of your time. She also said that I had caused her a lot of anxiety because of it.'

Duncan wanted to hear every word of their conversation. 'And what did you say to that?'

'I told her that I liked you, but didn't fancy you in any way; that I was very attentive at lectures because I wanted to learn as much about diving as possible.' Sue went on, 'I told her that I would temper my actions towards you in future and assured her that I simply liked you as a friend.'

Duncan sighed with relief.

During the following two weeks Sue and Duncan would meet and make love in the back of the car whenever possible. As the prospect of twelve days on Ascension grew closer Sue tried to persuade Duncan to leave Penny behind. She would say, 'Why can't you find some excuse so that Penny can't go? She's not military. You could say the Ministry of Defence have refused to let her fly.'

Duncan, however, would not hear of the plan. 'I won't do that to Penny. I've had to agree to take this expedition as leave, so it's her holiday as much as mine; throughout our life I've taken her on all my expeditions and I'm not going to be so selfish and refuse to take her on this one.'

Duncan asked Sue if she wanted to go to Ascension.

'Yes,' she replied, 'I still want to go.' Duncan was not certain whether Sue would be able to cope with the circumstances, the three of them together every day, every mealtime, every evening.

'Are you certain you will be able to handle it? You know that we will have to be totally platonic towards one, another.'

Susan nodded. 'I know we're just going to dive. I can handle it. I don't want to miss the experience of diving in beautiful clear waters. Anyway, what about our experiment?' And she laughed mischievously.

He smiled. 'We'll have to see about that.'

Ascension

★ ★ ★

Penny McAllister seemed destined to spend two weeks alone at home in Northern Ireland while Duncan, accompanied by his mistress, Susan Christie, and ten other divers, went off on a wonderful expedition to the crystal-clear waters of the Ascension Islands.

When the team assembled at Brize Norton in Oxfordshire on 4 October 1990, for the nine-hour flight to Ascension, an RAF flight sergeant told Duncan that Penny was not entitled to an indulgence flight as the wife of an officer serving in Northern Ireland. This came as a shock to Duncan. He knew there might be a problem and had therefore obtained all the requisite signatures. Or so he believed. He produced the relevant documents signed by the authorities within the Ministry of Defence and the officer commanding the RAF base in Ascension. 'I'm sorry, but they don't have the authority,' the sergeant declared after examining them.

Duncan went to see the officer in command at Brize Norton and he supported his sergeant's decision. Northern Ireland, being a home base, meant that Penny could not be entitled to an indulgence flight. They agreed that Penny could fly on an RAF flight, but only if Duncan a handed over a cheque for £1,500 for a full return fare. Even then she would not be able to fly out for another ten days, by which time the expedition would be at an end.

There seemed no way around the problem. Penny burst into tears when Duncan told her the bad news. 'Oh no, no, no,' she cried as Duncan tried to calm her. He had never seen Penny so distraught. Duncan recalls, 'I took Penny out of the building for a walk in the fresh air. I had never seen her so upset, tears streaming down her face. I felt awful.'

Penny composed herself after a few minutes, realizing the problem was insurmountable. She said, 'When all this is over could we go away together, just the two of us, for a lovely holiday, alone?'

'Of course, I promise,' Duncan replied, giving her a kiss of encouragement.

As Duncan walked back into the terminal building Susan Christie ran up to him, a big smile on her a face. 'Isn't Penny coming with us?' she asked.

'No, it doesn't look like it,' he replied. Susan could hardly contain her joy.

Duncan decided to give the Ministry of Defence one last try. After several phone calls to officials in London and Northern Ireland, a compromise was reached permitting Penny to fly as a compassionate case. It would cost Duncan £450 return.

He walked back to find Penny and gave her the ticket. 'This is for you,' he said, smiling. Penny leapt to her feet, threw hear arms around his neck, and kissed him, saying, 'Thank you, thank you, darling.' Everyone greeted Penny's good news with delight, save for Susan Christie. Immediately she became sulky and miserable, giving Duncan dirty looks and totally ignoring Penny. Later, during a conversation, Susan gave vent to her anger, frustration and disappointment that Penny would be on Ascension as well. 'You obviously prefer to be with Penny rather than with me,' she said in a challenging voice.

'Don't be so difficult,' Duncan said, trying to persuade her to be more tolerant of the situation. 'We talked about this before and we both realized that these two weeks would be difficult.'

Susan would not be convinced. 'I just don't like seeing you with her all the time. And, what's more, you haven't paid me any attention.'

'When I can, then I will, but I'm not going to make it too obvious in front of everyone. You know I deliberately never kiss or hug Penny when you are around. You know that.'

Susan shrugged.

During the nine-hour flight Duncan spent time walking around the aircraft, chatting to everyone, but he spent more time talking to Susan Christie than anyone else.

Their arrival on a lovely, balmy, warm summer's day did not, unfortunately, change Susan Christie's rather downbeat mood. She would not eat the evening meal, saying she was not hungry.

Duncan said later, 'The real reason seemed to be that Penny had cooked the meal, which meant that Susan had to pretend to everyone that it wasn't edible. She tasted the food, made a fuss, and left it.'

Later that night, however, Susan perked up when she became the centre of attention during an arrival party organised by the Ascension Island Diving Club. Some members remembered Penny and Duncan from their previous visit to the island some months earlier, but it was Susan who gained the applause and attention when she sportingly allowed the men to see how many empty beer cans they could pile, one on another, on her forehead as she lay on the floor.

The following day diving began in the crystal-blue tropical waters. Twice Duncan dived with Susan and, as a result, she became far happier and extrovert. Never before had Susan, nor most of the others, dived without the hindrance of wet-suits and weights. Everyone felt so much freer and the brilliantly coloured tropical fish made the dives a magical experience.

That evening Duncan and Susan went off, with some of the other lads, to collect goods from the local NAAFI shop, Penny volunteered to stay behind and prepare the evening meal for everyone.

On their own looking around the, shop, Duncan asked with a smile, 'Happier now?'

'Yes, but it would be much nicer if you told me that you loved me.'

'I don't think that would be too clever with everyone around.'

'It's just that I don't know whether you are happy with me,' Susan protested. 'I don't know if I've upset, you, or if you still love me and I just find it difficult to cope.'

'Listen, you know I can't say those sort of things in front of everyone.'

Susan looked downcast.

'I know,' said Duncan, 'we will have a code. When we want to say we're happy, happy with each other, we will make reference to the sunshine, to reassure one another.'

'Like I could say it's a sunshiny day,' Susan bubbled happily.

'Exactly.'

Susan smiled happily, reassured.

The following day, however, problems arose. Susan only wanted to dive with Duncan, but he had other responsibilities. There were five other recruits with much less experience than Susan and Duncan, as chief instructor, would need to dive with them. Susan would complain when paired with one or other of the experienced divers and refused once again ever to dive with Penny. Her petulant behaviour returned. And she let everyone know about her mood by her scowling sullenness.

Duncan managed to have a quiet word with his troublesome mistress. She needed reassurance. 'You never tell me you love me,' she complained, 'even when no one is around. And you've said nothing about our experiment.'

'When the opportunity arises we will organize your experiment,' Duncan promised, 'but you must understand that you have to dive with others and I have to dive with other people as well.'

'OK, just as long as it's not with Penny.'

That evening Susan and Duncan returned together to the huts where they all lived. Duncan deliberately took a long way home, stopping at Pyramid Point, a romantic spot with a magnificent view of the setting sun. They kissed and cuddled as they watched the blazing red sun dip below the horizon.

'Where have you been?' Penny asked when Duncan walked into the kitchens, where she was slaving away preparing the evening meal for everyone.

'I've been off doing some errands and Susan wanted to come along too.' Duncan didn't try to hide the fact that Susan had gone with him.

Once again at dinner that night Susan refused to eat the food Penny had prepared, putting on a sulky mood, and many at the communal table passed comments about her lack of appetite. Duncan feared Susan might become ill if she did not eat and later went to her bedroom to discuss the matter.

'Hi Sue, how are you feeling?' he asked as he entered the room and found his mistress lying on the bed reading a book.

'I'm fine,' she replied. 'I think it's just the heat. I find I'm just not hungry.'

'I really think you should make an effort or you'll make yourself ill. If you don't eat something you could become a danger to your diving partner and I wouldn't let that happen. I would have to stop you diving, for your own safety as well as your partner's.'

Later Duncan recalled, 'Susan looked disgruntled at what I had said and went back to reading her book, not saying a word to me or even looking at me. After a while I got up and left without another word.'

The following day the chosen dive site, the China wreck, was considered one of the most glorious dives around the islands and everyone, including Susan, was keen to get into the water. Sue had been given permission by Dr Galway to dive during the trip to Ascension, but he had given her strict limits. He had also given those limits to Duncan as her instructor.

Sue begged to be allowed to dive the China wreck but, as it lay in thirty metres of water, Duncan refused to permit her to take part. Dr Galway had given her a depth limit of only twenty-one metres.

'Please, please, Duncan let me go,' she begged. 'I'm fine now, I really am.'

Duncan, however, refused her repeated requests. Instead they would dive as a pair to twenty-one metres only, while the rest of the divers went to thirty.

That afternoon, after moving to another dive site, Susan approached Duncan, a wicked smile on her face. She asked, 'When can we conduct my experiment?'

'How about later today?'

'Great. I'll go and take off my swimming costume.' Susan wore a swimsuit with shorts and a T-shirt over the top when diving in Ascension, so even if she took off her swimsuit she would still be covered.

Duncan too had been looking forward to the experiment. He had never tried having sex under water and was intrigued to see whether it would be physically possible, wearing all the gear, the life-jacket, the air tank with its webbing, straps as well as the mask, mouthpiece and tubes.

Duncan arranged for all the divers to have completed their time in the water before Sue and he entered the clear blue sea.

He recalled, 'We entered the water and swam well away from the jetty, following a rocky ridge. When I thought it safe I motioned to Sue to sink down to the seabed. I attached the surface marker buoy to an extra weight I had taken with me to stop it floating away. Then I turned to Sue.

'She sank on to the sand and lay on her back. I then expelled the air from my life-jacket and floated gently down on top of her. At first it proved difficult actually to have sex together because of all the equipment we were wearing, but eventually I gained access and we were locked together for a couple of minutes.

'I must confess that neither of us actually achieved orgasm, but the experiment had established that it was physically possible to have sex on the seabed.'

The embarrassing part of the experiment would occur when Sue tried to climb out of the water after surfacing.

Duncan explained, 'Because she wore no

swimsuit underneath, and the weight of the water pulled down her shorts, those on the surface nearly saw a naked Susan Christie. Desperately, she held on to her shorts as the other divers pulled her out of the water. They had no idea Sue was naked beneath her shorts and T-shirt, yet they seemed to enjoy the view as it became obvious Sue was not wearing a bra top under her T-shirt.'

That night at dinner a happy, bubbly Sue, the centre of attraction, chatted to everyone. Someone then asked her, 'How did you enjoy the China wreck?'

She glanced at Duncan and said, 'I saw a lot more Moray eels than I bargained for.

Only Sue and Duncan knew what that phrase meant. Later, passing each other in the, corridor, Duncan teased her for talking about eels.

With a mischievous grin, Sue said, 'You know there's only one moray I'm interested in.'

Duncan patted his crotch and replied, 'Oh, you mean Mickey,' and they both laughed.

Sue said confidentially, 'Will I be able to play with Mickey again before we leave Ascension?'

'We'll see,' he replied.

Conducting the underwater experiment seemed to change Susan Christie's enjoyment of the expedition and she became more friendly and outgoing to everyone, including Penny. But her happiness would not last. She sank into a sulky, depressive mood when Duncan agreed to honour a promise he had made to Penny, that they would dive on the China wreck together one moonlit night. Sue told Duncan she also wanted to dive with him that night and reacted sullenly when Duncan told her that he would be diving with Penny as his partner.

During the first week of the expedition, Susan Christie would not lend a helping hand as everyone else did. She would deliberately hold back, never volunteer to clean gear, fill cylinders or assist in the administration. Some of the other divers noticed this. During the following couple of days Susan Christie continued her moody behaviour and everyone noticed her bid to gain sympathy by not eating, complaining and generally drawing attention to herself.

Alone with Sue in the equipment room one night Duncan let fly. 'For fuck's sake, Sue, stop feeling so bloody sorry for yourself and help out for a change. You've done nothing but moan since we arrived and I've had enough. I know you find it difficult with Penny and me together but I find the situation difficult as well. I just don't make it so bloody obvious.'

He added bitingly, 'Officers don't show their emotions, Sue, they just get on with it. So for Christ's sake sort out your act. If you want to be an officer then start acting like a fucking officer.'

Sue looked at Duncan in a state of shock, but he had not finished. 'And while we're at it, you say that you want to command men, yet you cannot even stand on your own two feet. If you're in the field and things aren't going well for Susan Christie you can't just sulk and expect someone else to sort it out for you. You can't go running to Daddy. You're the one who must get a grip, to lead people, so just bottle up your emotions and get on with it.'

'I'm ...' Susan began, but Duncan interrupted her, still angry. 'You haven't lifted a finger to help since we arrived. You haven't offered to fill cylinders, clean the gear, help with the cooking or do anything. For God's sake just start pulling your weight, will you?'

Sue whimpered, 'I've tried to help, but every time I do someone else has done it before me.' Her face became contorted as though she was going to burst into tears at any moment.

Duncan ignored her excuses. 'Don't give me that rubbish. You could have always insisted it was your turn. This is an expedition, a team effort. I suggest very strongly that you try and help out and stop your childish tantrums.'

As he walked to his room that night Duncan thought of Penny's attitude when on diving expeditions. She would always collect the food, do the cooking, carry the diving gear, fill the cylinders, muck in with everyone and, more often than not, do more work than anyone else. And usually with a smile and a kind word for everyone.

During one dive in the second week, Susan

Christie broke the depth limit which had been imposed on her by Dr Galway by diving down to twenty-five metres. After she surfaced Susan denied she had broken her depth limit but her electronic depth gauge revealed the truth. It seemed extraordinary that Susan Christie would have risked diving to twenty-five metres only weeks after suffering a bend.

The following Sunday, when no-one dived, most lay around sunbathing. When Duncan returned to the huts he found Penny and Sue deep in conversation. They had been talking together for some time.

Duncan recalled, 'That was strange because Sue a had always told me how she hated being in Penny's company, was unable to remain in the same room with Penny, and found it almost impossible to bring herself to speak to her, hardly ever saying hello. Now they seemed content in each other's company, happy to talk together. I was perplexed.'

Towards the end of the expedition Duncan again found Penny and Susan deep in conversation at the bar one evening. Duncan approached and asked Penny if she would be staying or whether she wanted to come with him. To Duncan's surprise Penny declined, saying she wanted to stay and talk to Sue. Both young women seemed happy and relaxed together but their conversation seemed most private.

Later, Duncan asked Penny what she was

talking about, but she simply shrugged her shoulders. Susan told Duncan they were simply sorting out their relationship but that no mention whatsoever was made of an affair.

Following Duncan's harsh criticism Susan's behaviour changed dramatically. She became happier and more bubbly, chatting away to everyone and helping out in any way she could. She asked Duncan for one final dive together before the expedition ended and Duncan readily agreed. Their dive was great fun, and they pretended to kiss each other through their masks, touched each other affectionately, and sexually teased each other as they swam together in the warm, clear waters.

That weekend everyone enjoyed a barbecue in the balmy climate. Afterwards, some decided to continue the evening at the Volcano Club while others sat around chatting and drinking. As Duncan went into the kitchen Susan followed him, in a state of some anxiety, babbling about Jock Grey trying to interfere with her.

Hurriedly Duncan closed the a kitchen door and asked her what had happened.

'Jock's just come on, come on to me,' she stammered, breathless, distressed and in tears.

'What do you mean?' Duncan asked.

Between sobs, Susan replied, 'He tried to kiss me ... he tried to pin me against the toilet wall ... he blocked the door ... he wouldn't let me out.'

Duncan tried to calm her down to find out

what had actually happened.

'I didn't let him touch me,' she went on, trying to control her tears; 'I struggled to get out and kept telling him to stop.'

'So he didn't actually touch you.'

'No,' Susan admitted, 'but he did try to kiss me.'

Duncan recalled, 'Susan was always flirting with Jock and had done so for months. It seemed that he was simply asking for a kiss or trying to start a relationship.'

Duncan told Susan, 'You know Jock fancies you and you do lead him on at times. You can't blame him if he gets the wrong end of the stick. Talk to him and let him know where he stands.'

A few minutes later Jock came into the kitchen, asking where Susan had gone. He stayed and helped with the clearing up. At breakfast the following morning Susan actually sat next to Jock and there seemed no animosity between them, no sign that there had been any problem the previous evening. Driving to the airfield the following day with Susan, Duncan asked about the day she had spent sunbathing and chatting with Penny on the beach and, more importantly, what they had discussed. Sue assured him the question of an affair never arose.

On the way, Duncan looked at Susan and winked. He told her he had decided to make a detour to the base. Susan was surprised to find them bumping along a deserted track overlooking the airbase. Duncan stopped the van and turned to kiss his mistress. Sue responded with passion and eagerness. Minutes later they climbed into the back of the van, ripped off their clothes and made love, passionately and eagerly.

For the rest of that day Sue appeared happier than ever and did not complain in the least when Duncan told her he would be making the night dive with Penny. But Susan's newfound relaxed happiness did not last. The next morning she made her presence felt once again.

As Duncan walked out of the mess hall after breakfast he saw Susan twenty yards away leaning her head against a wall. He called to her, 'Sue, are you OK?'

Immediately, Susan Christie collapsed to the ground as though in a faint. Duncan called to the lads in the hall to come and lend a hand and ran over to her.

Duncan recalled, 'I was absolutely certain that Susan was playacting and believed this to be another of her antics, to gain my undivided attention. This time I would not succumb, lifted her up, and handed her to Corporal Hanlon to take to the RAF hospital. He returned a little later saying the doctors who had examined her could find nothing wrong, but that she would be detained overnight for observation.

That evening Penny and another girl went to

see the patient and talk to the doctors who had examined her. On her return Penny told Duncan, 'You know she's attention-seeking again, don't you? It's not only you, it's now everyone. The doctors could find nothing wrong with her.'

The next day Duncan went to visit Sue who had been allowed to leave hospital and rest in an apartment nearby. Duncan told her of the final dive, planned for later that day, in which everyone would take part.

'Can I come? I'm feeling fine now,' Sue said.

'If you think you're diving after collapsing yesterday you are mistaken. I'm not going to take the responsibility. I won't let you dive.'

'But I'm all right now,' she protested.

'I don't give a damn, Sue; you're not diving and that's final.'

Reluctantly Sue accepted Duncan's ruling and perked up when she realized she would be flying home with Duncan while Penny would have to take a separate flight back to Brize Norton. Duncan, Sue and six divers found themselves on their own, the only passengers on board an RAF Tristar aircraft capable of carrying 200 people. Sue and Duncan spent most of the seven-hour flight sitting together chatting.

Sue apologized profusely for her behaviour throughout the expedition and asked Duncan to forgive her. She acknowledged that her behaviour had been dictated by her obsessive jealousy and her incessant demand for his constant attention.

Duncan recalled, 'I knew in my heart that I should never have permitted Sue to join the expedition and that had been my fault entirely. I should have known that Sue would have been unable to stand watching Penny and myself together as man and wife. It had driven her to act emotionally and irrationally. Taking her along had been a mistake.'

When the two flights landed at Brize Norton, Penny had to travel to collect some belongings at Duncan's parents' home in Ashton Keynes. She would fly back to Ireland the following day. His father, Major David McAllister, recalled, 'I noticed one of the expedition members seemed to be distinctly more pale than everyone else and asked Penny who she was'. Penny replied, "Don't talk to me about that woman, she's been nothing but trouble and she's making a real play for Duncan."'

Penny did not expand further and Major McAllister deemed it prudent to drop the subject. He commented later, 'I remembered the conversation because that was the first and last time I ever heard Penny say a bad word about anyone in her life. It rather shocked me.'

On the flight back to Belfast, Susan and Duncan decided to stay the night together at Duncan's married quarters. Duncan had decided, however, to take the opportunity to break the love affair with Sue, unable to take the pressure he felt was increasing the longer the affair continued. Accordingly, back home, he suggested to Susan that they should have a cooling-off period.

Susan Christie burst into tears and spent the next few hours crying and pleading with Duncan not to end their affair. The following morning she asked Duncan for time to come to terms with his demand. In reality, of course, Susan was simply playing for time. She had no intention of letting the man she adored break off their affair.

'Do You Really Want Me to Kill Our Baby?'

★ ★ ★

On her return to duty the next day Susan Christie learned she would be moved to the operations room at Lisburn working two shifts, one of twenty-four hours, the other of twelve hours a week, which meant the rest of her time would be free. Within minutes Susan phoned Duncan at his office.

'Wonderful news. I've been moved into ops, which means we won't be restricted to only meeting at lunchtimes. I'll have much more free time to see you.'

Duncan recalls, 'It seemed Susan had totally

forgotten the conversation of the previous night when she had cried herself to sleep. She had completely ignored my suggestion that we should have a cooling-off period.

'Now, it appeared, she had plans to increase the time we spent together.'

Due to pressure of work, however, Duncan could not meet Susan during the first two weeks of their return from Ascension, but they spoke frequently on the phone.

On Friday 2 November Sue phoned, a note of panic in her voice. She said, 'I must see you, we have to speak. I'm pregnant.'

Duncan was thunderstruck. He recalled, 'I didn't know what to say. I needed a few minutes to gather my thoughts. I told Sue that I couldn't talk on the phone but would see her at 1 p.m. at our normal meeting place.

'After I replaced the phone I thought, "This isn't happening to me; please let it be a false alarm; God let it all be a mistake."'

Susan Christie was waiting at their rendezvous, by the side of Marlicoo Lake, five miles from Armagh, when Duncan arrived. The day was cold and wet. Susan clambered into the front seat of the VW transit van Duncan had borrowed.

'Are you OK?' were Duncan's first words.

'I'm fine,' Sue replied. 'I just don't know what to do. I had to see you. You don't hate me, do you?'

'Don't be stupid. I'm obviously a bit shaken,

but I'm sure we'll sort it out. I just don't understand how it's happened, that's all.'

'I don't know either. It must have been when I was ill in Ascension. I kept being sick after every meal; I couldn't keep anything down.'

Duncan interrupted, saying, 'You never told me you were sick in Ascension.'

She replied, 'I didn't want you to know, I thought you'd stop me diving.'

Sue went on to explain that during the two-week expedition she took her contraceptive pill every evening before dinner, but that she would be sick afterwards.

'But you never forgot to take your pill on Ascension?'

'No, never,' she replied.

Then Sue asked Duncan, 'Do you want the baby?'

Duncan did not answer the question directly, suggesting they should first get confirmation that Susan was indeed pregnant. Sue agreed and did not press him on the point.

The following day when they met, however, Sue wanted to know Duncan's feelings towards the baby despite not having confirmed she was pregnant. Sue pressed Duncan: 'I need to know what you think. I don't know what's best. I do know that I don't want to kill my baby ... it's your baby too.' And she started to sob quietly as she talked about aborting the child.

For more than fifteen minutes they talked around the subject, with Sue pressing Duncan for a direct answer and Duncan hesitating, feeling it would be best to defer a decision until he was certain Sue was pregnant.

Duncan later claimed, 'That day I gave Sue three options, after telling her that I would never leave Penny. First, she could have an abortion; second, Sue could have the child but the identity of the father would remain secret; third, Sue could have the baby and I would accept full responsibility.'

Duncan claimed that during the conversation he pointed out the advantages and disadvantages of each option. He pulled no punches. He told Sue, 'If you have an abortion then you can stay in the army, continue your career, keep our affair secret and there would be no need to tell your parents. Aborting the baby would also mean I would not have to tell Penny, nor would I be kicked out of the army.'

He continued, 'If you have the baby but don't reveal my identity you would have to leave the army, you would have to reveal your pregnancy to your parents and withstand the pressure to reveal my identity; the child would grow up without a father and you would have to cope with life as a single mother. The advantage of that choice would be that you keep the baby, I would remain anonymous, my career would be safe and I would then financially support the child.'

Duncan then explained the final option to her: 'You could have the baby and I could accept full responsibility. The disadvantages would be that you would have to leave the army, I would have to leave the army, my marriage would almost certainly fall apart, your parents would know and you would still be a single mother. It would mean that I would have no job and no means to support you and the child. However, you would then have the baby and your parents and the child would know my identity.'

That day Duncan was sure Sue wanted to keep the baby, saying that she burst into tears whenever the word 'abortion' was mentioned.

In his aide-memoire, written after Susan Christie's trial, Duncan wrote, 'My approach to Susan may have been without emotion. However, I believe such important issues should be decided pragmatically with emotion playing a part, but not being the overriding factor ... We examined each option several times that day ... but I always insisted the final decision rested with her ... Susan could see that an abortion was the most sensible choice, but I didn't feel she would be able to go through with it.'

On Monday 5 November, Sue and Duncan met again at Marlicoo Lake and, for security reasons, they decided to take the van and drive towards Tandragee before stopping to discuss the pregnancy. On an empty stretch of road both Duncan and Sue recognized Penny, driving her slate-grey Peugeot 205 towards them. Both Duncan and Sue saw the car, checked Penny was driving and saw her two black Gordon Setters in the back as she drove past. Penny, however, didn't see her husband nor his mistress, though both were sitting in the front of the van.

Later, while still driving towards Tandragee, Sue suddenly blurted out, 'I've decided to have an abortion, it's best for everyone. I'd like to keep my baby, but I know that I can't. I don't want to lose my career and —'.

Susan started to sob, unable to control the tears. Between the sobs, she stammered, 'Oh God, Duncan, it's my baby ... I don't want to kill our baby. I know I have to, but I don't want to ... it's my baby.'

Duncan pulled in to the side of the road and put his arms around Sue as she continued to sob. He said gently, 'You don't have to make a decision now, give it time. Wait until you've seen the doctor and everything's confirmed. I know it's not easy for you and I know you don't want to kill your baby.'

Duncan would recall, 'I stroked her head as she leant on me. I felt very sorry for her. I knew having an abortion would not be easy for her, especially as she seemed to want the baby.'

Then Sue said, 'It's your baby too. You have a say in this. Do you really want me to kill our baby?'

Later, however, having talked about all the advantages and disadvantages, Sue made up her mind. 'I'm going to have an abortion. It's not what I really want, but considering my parents, the army and everything, I think it's for the best.'

This time there were no tears. She asked Duncan, 'Now, tell me honestly, what did you want me to do?'

'I think you're doing the right thing for everyone,' he replied. 'It was my first choice and I'm glad that's what you've decided. My second preference was for you to have the baby, but not reveal my name. Lastly, I wanted you to have the baby and for me to own up and take full responsibility.

'Those were my preferences, Sue. But you know I would have done what you wanted. You know that; I might not have been happy, but I would have done it.'

Susan Christie told Duncan in the middle of November that she had been to see a woman doctor who had confirmed she was pregnant but told her she would have to wait for some weeks before having an abortion. She asked Duncan whether he could arrange a weekend away together because the doctor had told her to return in three weeks. Susan asked this in the knowledge that Duncan was going to the mainland later that month.

In the meantime Penny was due to fly home to

England for the weekend of 17-18 November to attend the twenty-first birthday party of Mandy, her brother's new girlfriend. It would present an opportunity for Sue and Duncan to spend more time together.

Susan Christie arrived at Duncan's house on the Friday evening with a video and two bottles of rosé. They hadn't made love since Ascension and after only a few minutes watching the video film they raced off to bed; their passion for each other had not in any way been dulled by Sue's pregnancy.

Duncan recalled, 'We would make love and then relax and talk about the pregnancy and the abortion and dissect the reasons why the decision Sue had made was for the best. Then we would make love again.'

The diving season had ended for the winter break and so Sue and Duncan took the two Gordon Setters, Monty and Barton, for an invigorating walk in lovely bright sunshine along the headland off Groomsport. Sue never mentioned the abortion again for the rest of the weekend.

The following weekend Duncan took Sue to England as promised. He felt she needed a break to help her recover from the trauma of finding herself pregnant. He had been scheduled to attend a military diving conference on the Monday and decided to take Sue with him, so they could spend the weekend together.

Duncan recalled, 'The atmosphere between us

that weekend was intense and the sexual excitement had returned. It seemed as though we had only just met and were spending the first night together in a hotel. We arrived well after dark, tired and ready to sleep, but the sexual tension was so strong. We spent half an hour in the shower together, making love in the hot steam, unable to keep our hands off each other.

'We dressed for dinner, Sue wearing a tight white blouse, and a tight, short black skirt, suspenders, stockings and high-heeled shoes. She knew she looked stunning and she did. The talk at dinner was studded with sexual undertones and neither of us could wait to get to bed.

'We ordered liqueurs and immediately went to our room. We tore off our clothes; the passion between us was so intense. The sex that night was stunning and we spent hours making love, time and time again, until we fell into a deep sleep.'

The following morning Sue and Duncan spent hours in bed before taking a late breakfast. They then took a passenger ferry across the estuary to Portsmouth. They sauntered through the town in the late-November sun, two lovers enveloped in each other, oblivious to those around them. They visited Seaworld and had a drink or two, they window-shopped and decided to buy and exchange Christmas presents that weekend.

On the return ferry ride across the harbour, Sue nestled into Duncan's shoulder as he shielded her from the fresh breeze coming off the water. As they passed the Victory, they watched the street lights of Portsmouth fade into the distance. Together, Sue and Duncan had enjoyed a wonderful day, and after a dinner, tired and exhausted, they went early to bed, making love only once before falling asleep.

Duncan spent Monday and Tuesday in the conference while Sue lazed around, went for walks along the seafront and did some shopping. Tuesday night, their last together, they spent having a romantic dinner at the hotel with wine and brandies and ended the evening in each other's arms, making love.

Back in Northern Ireland Sue continued to phone, each and every day, but Duncan's work had to take priority and he would go home every night to Penny.

On Wednesday 5 December, Duncan answered the phone as usual, half-expecting the call to be from a Susan. 'Duncan,' she stammered between tears, 'I must see you ... I've had a miscarriage ... I've lost my baby.'

'Are you all right? Where are you? What can I do?'

'I'm fine,' she cried, 'but I've lost the baby.'

'Try to stop crying,' Duncan suggested, trying to soothe her. 'Take deep breaths, try to calm down, then tell me what happened.'

Sue revealed she was in hospital, having been

admitted, the previous night. She told him, 'Last night I was on shift and started to get really bad a stomach pains. I began to bleed heavily and knew something was wrong, so I asked to go home. Instead I came here to the hospital. They told me that I had suffered a miscarriage and lost the baby. I really didn't want to lose the baby, you know.'

Duncan said, 'I know you didn't, Sue, and I am a so sorry it's happened.'

Duncan was concerned that Susan had told her parents, and so he asked her whether they knew. She said they did not know and promised that she would not tell them until she and Duncan had had time to talk about the miscarriage. He promised to see her the following afternoon.

Duncan met and chatted to Sue often during the following week and, after their first afternoon together, Sue appeared to be over the tragedy, mentioning the miscarriage less often. Surprisingly, she also continued to work all her shifts, requiring no time to rest and recover from the miscarriage.

On Friday 14 December, Duncan received a surprise which nearly revealed to Penny that he had indeed been having an affair for months. In all innocence Sue sent him a Christmas card, to the barracks, little knowing that Penny religiously collected all their mail and opened all the letters addressed to them both, especially the Christmas cards. Fortunately for Duncan, however, Sue had sent the card in an official envelope, addressed,

'Private: For Captain D.E.A. McAllister'.

Penny handed him the envelope, and Duncan ripped it open. Inside, it read:

Dear Duncan: have a lovely Christmas.
Thank you for introducing me to:
Diving
Making Love
Mateus Rosé
Underwater Sex
Seafood Platter
Oral Sex
Mickey the Moray
etc etc.

He recalled, 'I nearly died and my heart missed a beat as Penny asked to see the card. I said "Just a minute, there's something I must do immediately." I ran out of the office and down to the message centre, knowing I had to destroy the card and quickly. I shredded it in the secure waste and then remembered there were some cards in the orderly room. So I picked up one and handed it to Penny when I returned. It had been a near-miraculous escape.'

Sue appeared to be making a rapid recovery from her miscarriage and had returned to her old, mischievous personality, hardly ever mentioning the loss of her baby. Duncan would still see her occasionally, but the cold winter weather made sex in the back of a car not so enjoyable as before. They would meet less often, though the phone conversations continued.

By the middle of December, just ten days after her miscarriage, Susan Christie returned to diving, giving lectures to new members and instructing new recruits in the swimming pool during a novice diver training weekend.

Yet another surprise was in store for Duncan before the Christmas holiday. One night Penny told him that Susan Christie had phoned her, again asking for a meeting, this time suggesting a lunch date. In his aide-memoire, Duncan wrote, 'It made no sense to me at all that a woman who had recently lost a child by a married man would wish to have lunch with his wife. I was unnerved. I knew that Susan didn't like Penny and I knew that Penny had no friendship with Sue.'

The morning after the lunch date, Duncan picked up the phone to a raging, screaming Susan. 'You fucking bastard, you never told me,' she hissed down the phone.

Duncan had no idea what on earth had upset Susan. She then added, as though speaking through a clenched teeth, 'You bastard; why didn't you tell me Penny has had a miscarriage?'

Duncan went into shock. He had no idea that Penny had ever suffered a miscarriage, had ever been pregnant. He was also furious with Susan. He said coldly, 'First, what the fuck has it got to do with you if Penny has had a miscarriage and, second, I didn't know she had ever had one. Even if I had known, I would not have told you because it's got nothing to do with you.'

Later, Duncan would say, 'I was upset and confused at the news. Why, why, why hadn't Penny told me she had been pregnant and suffered a miscarriage? I had lost a child and known nothing about it.

'At that moment I hated Susan Christie. She had had no thoughts of my feelings or any sympathy for Penny. All that concerned Susan was that she hadn't been told. I was furious, upset, and emotional. I simply could not comprehend why Penny had never told me.'

Sue suddenly realized that she had upset Duncan and made him angry. She also realized he had no idea that Penny had ever been pregnant. 'I'm sorry,' she stammered, 'I thought you would have known. I didn't mean to upset you. I'm sorry.'

Duncan put down the phone confused, miserable and full of guilt. He recalled, 'I suddenly saw that I had been the father of Penny's child and had never known anything about it. I wondered how she had coped and, more importantly, why she hadn't told me. I felt incredible guilt because I had been supportive to Sue when she suffered a miscarriage but had not even known when Penny had been pregnant, let alone coping without me when she suffered the miscarriage. I felt awful, physically sick.

'My first thought was to go to Penny and ask her all about it. But I couldn't. I felt trapped because I would have to reveal that Sue had told me and then Penny would have known we were having an affair.

I could not understand why Penny had not told me. I knew there would have been a reason, in Penny's mind a very good reason. I felt that I had no right to demand of her that she now reveal all to me.

'Perhaps more importantly, the whole episode made me realise what a shit I had been to Penny, having an affair under her nose for so long. I vowed to end my relationship with Sue as soon as possible so that I could stay where I belonged, at Penny's side.'

It was at this point that Susan Christie's long-held ambition to become an officer became a factor in the whole affair. In order to obtain the requisite educational standard, Sue needed to attend a special three-month-long pre-training school at Beaconsfield in England. In order to qualify for an officer's course she first had to obtain an 'O' level maths pass and Beaconsfield would provide her with an intensive course. If she did not pass her maths, then she could not progress further with selection tests to become an officer.

And Sue had learned that her Beaconsfield course would start at the beginning of April 1991.

Duncan, of course, also knew this and began more and more to encourage Sue to study so she would have a greater chance of success at Beaconsfield. He decided that when Sue left Northern Ireland at the end of March to attend Beaconsfield it would be the time to kill their affair.

In his mind, Duncan had thrashed out his plans for his future relationships with both Penny and Sue before going home that night. He determined to let the situation continue until Susan went to Beaconsfield at the end of March. He could not bring himself to end the affair so soon after her miscarriage.

As he walked in the door, he casually asked Penny how the lunch with Sue had gone. She replied, 'Fine. We had a good chat and I enjoyed the meal.' She said nothing whatsoever about a miscarriage, and Duncan began to wonder whether Sue had been telling the truth about it.

Duncan also noted that after his traumatic phone conversation with Sue, she never again mentioned either her own or Penny's miscarriage.

Sue and Duncan saw little of each other throughout Christmas and the New Year, but they kept in constant touch by phone. Because of his duties Duncan found it extremely difficult to escape at lunchtimes or during the afternoon for a secret rendezvous with his mistress.

In mid-January, Sue phoned as usual one morning, asking Duncan if he minded if she began going out with other friends, not dating other men, but simply getting out as she was becoming bored sitting at home alone in her room most nights. Understandably, Duncan welcomed the request and encouraged Sue to go out and enjoy herself.

Corporal Jock Grey of the Royal Ordnance Corps had joined the diving club at the same time as Sue and had always been attracted to her. From time to time he had tried to date Sue, sometimes attempting to steal a kiss during a party. Despite rebuffs, Jock still hoped that one day Sue might agree to a date.

In early January 1991 Sue phoned Jock and suggested they go out bowling together. He was only too keen to accompany her, happy in the knowledge that as far as she was concerned they were going out together as friends, but hoping that one day perhaps they would date seriously.

Together they went ice-skating, to the cinema, to bingo and the occasional disco. Sue would, more often than not, be in great form, laughing and joking, thoroughly enjoying the evening. Sometimes they went out in a party, but more often than not on their own. These outings continued for some weeks.

At the same time, though, Penny began receiving 'odd' phone calls at home. The phone would ring and Penny would answer. There was silence. No heavy breathing, nothing. After a few seconds the phone would go dead, as though someone had replaced the receiver. It never happened when Duncan answered the phone.

Understandably, Duncan thought Sue could be the person responsible and challenged her about it, but Sue totally denied all knowledge. Duncan could do no more.

Unhappy that their relationship had become nothing but a succession of phone calls, Sue then urged Duncan to visit her at home during lunchtimes when she was off-duty. He began visiting her once every couple of weeks.

Sue had a room of her own in her parents' small house outside Lisburn, a sanctuary where her parents never ventured. She had her own telephone, her own TV, video and hi-fi, and would hardly ever enter other parts of the house, preferring to stay alone in her own world. At night she would nearly always stay in her room, watching one of the films from her extensive video library.

Sue had decorated the room prettily, in a most feminine way, with white lace trimmings, pretty-coloured curtains and covers. The walls, however, were covered with photographs of herself, nearly always in uniform, including a number of photographs taken on army courses. They revealed how proud Sue had become of being a competent, professional soldier.

Duncan would visit the house in the afternoon, and he and Sue would spend a couple of hours making love in the warmth and comfort of

Sue's bedroom.

On one occasion Duncan and Sue were in bed together actually making love when Sue's father unexpectedly arrived back home. Duncan recalled, 'When Sue said her father had just walked into the house I froze. I knew he didn't approve of me and could imagine that if he discovered I was having an affair with his daughter he would report the matter to my commanding officer to make sure I was either booted out of the army or immediately posted overseas, away from Susan.

'I was convinced we would be discovered and that then our affair would be public knowledge. Penny would have to be told and I would probably be forced to quit the army.

'Sue, however, knew her father better. She told me that he wouldn't come in, or knock on her door or even shout "Hello" or "Goodbye". I persuaded Sue to get dressed and go downstairs to see her father, to ensure he wouldn't come knocking on her door. I hid under the covers, praying he would not find me.

'Thank God Sue was right. Later, she came bouncing back into the room to tell me her father, had left the house. I was so relieved.'

Towards the end of January, Major Andrew Johnstone informed Duncan that he was being considered for two possible promotions, both staff jobs, one in Northern Ireland, the other in Germany. Duncan discussed his future with Penny.

She knew Duncan had thoroughly enjoyed being involved in operational work in Northern Ireland, carrying out duties for which he had been trained. She also knew his work in Germany would be more mundane, less exciting.

Finally, Penny said, 'I know you love your work here in Northern Ireland and because of that, and your career, I'm happy to stay here.'

'That's that, then,' Duncan told her. 'We're going to Germany. I know you would much prefer a settled life in Germany and maybe it is time for us to start a family.'

Penny threw her arms around his neck and kissed him.

Shortly after arriving in Northern Ireland, Penny had been asked to take over as manageress of the PRI (President of the Regimental Institute) shop of the 3rd Infantry Brigade Headquarters and Signals Squadron in Drumadd barracks in Armagh. The small shop sold sports kits, outward-bound gear, regimental goblets, plaques, statues and crystal ware. Penny also served coffee and hot chocolate and biscuits, and during the two years she held the job she became an agony aunt to many of the soldiers and their wives having marital problems. Officially, the job was part-time, four hours a day, five days a week, for which she received the princely sum of £35! Penny, however, would spend far more than the statutory twenty hours a week in her shop.

Yet she never complained. She believed that as the unofficial agony aunt she probably did more work for the regiment than in caring for the shop. She also believed it was more important work.

After the MOD had decided that Duncan McAllister would be posted to a staff job in Germany in June 1991, Duncan braced himself to tell Sue what the army had decided. The news shocked Susan, because she had believed Duncan would be spending a further two years in Northern Ireland.

'Oh no, you can't be posted yet,' she said in a panic. 'You've two more years here. Your tour of duty doesn't end for two more years. You can't go yet. What's going to happen?'

Duncan explained that he had no control over his postings; that he had to obey orders, like everyone else in the army. Susan of course understood that very well, having lived with the army all her life, but she was still unhappy and angry with the news.

The diving club held its Christmas party in mid-January. It was attended by ten people. Duncan McAllister sat between Penny and Annette, the first time he had not sat next to Susan at any diving event. Consequently, Susan did not appear to be enjoying herself very much, ignoring both Penny and Duncan throughout most of the boisterous meal and becoming rather drunk.

Duncan had invited an old friend, David

Allen, over from England to stay with them for a weekend. He was missing his fiancée, who was working in Northern Ireland. They had been engaged only three weeks, so Penny invited them to stay at their house together. They both came to the Christmas party.

Susan, however, became roaring drunk, and as a consequence totally incapable of driving her car home. It was therefore decided that she should come back with Duncan, Penny, David and Jill and stay the night in one of the spare bedrooms.

During the night Duncan left Penny asleep and stole quietly into Susan's room. In his aide-memoire Duncan wrote, 'I thought Susan would be sick in the night from so much alcohol so I decided to check she was all right. She was awake when I walked in and I sat on the edge of her bed.'

She said, 'Your friend David tried to get into bed with me. He wanted to rape me.'

Taken aback by her accusation, Duncan exclaimed, 'What?'

'David tried to touch me and get in my bed. He wanted to rape me.'

Duncan had been lying awake that night before going to Sue's room but had heard no conversation, no movement from Susan's room or from David and Jill. He was therefore doubtful, but wondered why Susan should make such a serious accusation.

He decided to try and calm the situation.

'Come on Sue, calm down. Nothing has actually happened. I imagine you told him to get lost.'

'But he tried to get into my bed,' Sue persisted.

'He didn't actually get in to the bed or touch you, did he?'

'No, I wouldn't let him.'

'Well no harm's done. You know he's only just become engaged, so please don't say anything to Jill.'

Sue agreed and Duncan stayed a while with her, comforting and chatting to her. Susan's accusation perplexed Duncan. He simply could not understand David contemplating such an action, considering he had not seen his fiancée since they had become engaged only three weeks before, and, besides, he would have been totally stupid to have risked trying to rape or make love to Susan Christie with his fiancée next door.

Duncan decided to say nothing to David. Some months later, however, after Penny's murder, Duncan did raise the matter with his old friend, telling him of Susan's allegation on the night of the Christmas party.

'She said what?' David exclaimed loudly, unable to comprehend what Duncan was saying.

'I know David, I know,' said Duncan, trying to calm his friend's anger, 'but that's what she alleged.'

'The lying bitch. I can't believe she said that.

Christ, what a bloody woman she is! I never went anywhere near her room. God, how could she say that!'

Days after the Christmas party Duncan had more bad news for the unhappy Susan. He told her that he and Penny were going to Germany for a three-week skiing holiday from the middle of February.

'But we've only got a few more weeks together,' Sue exclaimed, amazed that Duncan would want to leave her and go on holiday with Penny when they only had such a short time left to them.

Duncan recalled, 'At the time I did feel sorry for Sue as I could see she was devastated by the news. I could understand her point of view but I knew I would be going on that holiday. Sue did, however, make me feel guilty about leaving her.'

'That means we won't see each other on Valentine's Day,' Sue said. 'And we'll only have three weeks together before I have to go Beaconsfield. Please, please can we have one last weekend together before I have to leave?'

Duncan promised that he would try to organize one when he returned.

'You know I don't see enough of you,' Sue said unhappily, 'and I love you so very, very much.'

The Final Fling

★ ★ ★

Before flying off to Garmisch-Parten-Kirchen on Valentine's Day 1991 Duncan McAllister did not forget the woman he was leaving behind. Having felt occasional pangs of guilt towards Penny for cheating on her for so long Duncan now felt similar pangs of guilt towards Susan. She had simply fallen in love with him and during their months together Duncan too had become attached to Susan.

So he telephoned a florist and ordered a bunch of flowers to be delivered to Susan's home for Valentine's Day. He signed the attached card, 'Love Mickey', which he knew Sue would appreciate and understand. Duncan McAllister also knew that by signing the card 'Mickey' he would be concealing his true identity.

Leaving Penny in their holiday hotel, Duncan slipped out the next day and telephoned Sue at home, to check whether she had received the flowers and to see how she was coping.

He recalls, 'I knew Sue was miserable about me going away on holiday with Penny and I wanted to make sure she was happy. She seemed really happy about receiving the flowers and the card and said she looked forward to my returning.'

During their three weeks skiing in the mountains, enjoying romantic meals in the evening and making love at night, Penny and Duncan not only breathed new life into their six-year marriage, but genuinely felt they were enjoying a second honeymoon. They behaved as though they had just met, so wrapped up in each other, so in love. It would be their last holiday together.

Duncan would write in his aide-memoire, 'We enjoyed the best holiday we'd ever had together and neither of us wanted it to end. The skiing proved wonderful and after Penny rediscovered her ski legs we would go out on safari every day, finding a new mountain to ski down every morning.

'The sun shone virtually every day, the skies were a clear blue and the snow conditions near-perfect. We ate out every night, found new friends, danced until the early hours and then stayed in bed in the morning, so very happy to be together. We also discovered this lovely little Italian restaurant close to our hotel, which we both found romantic.'

Over dinner one night towards the end of their holiday Penny talked to Duncan of their future together. 'When we move to Germany later this year,' she said, 'I would really like us to start a family. It is the perfect time. It would be wonderful.'

Duncan put his hand on Penny's and said, 'So do I; it's a great idea.'

When Penny and Duncan arrived back in Ireland in March there would be only three weeks before Sue had to leave for her three-month course at Beaconsfield. By the time she returned to Ireland, in June, Penny and Duncan would have left the province for the new posting in Germany.

Duncan therefore believed the affair had only three more weeks to last but Susan Christie had different ideas.

A week or so after flying back, Duncan was relaxing at home when the phone rang. Instinctively, Duncan knew it would be Sue. 'Hi, Sue, what can I do for you?' he asked.

'Well, Jock and I are going to see *Teenage Mutant Ninja Turtles* this evening and I wondered if you would like to come along as well.'

Never before had Sue phoned Duncan at home, asking him to go on a date.

Duncan was slightly taken aback, and the film held no interest for him either.

'Thanks for the invitation, Sue,' he said, 'but I really don't think so. Had it been another movie, maybe, but not *Ninja Turtles*.'

'Please, for me,' she begged.

'OK. I'll ask Penny if she would like to come.'

Penny had listened to the conversation and shook her head. The Ninja Turtles held no interest for her either.

'Sorry, Sue,' said Duncan, 'but Penny's not keen either. Perhaps another time.'

'Suit yourself,' she said and banged down the phone.

An hour later the doorbell rang. Standing outside, smiling broadly, was Sue.

'Hi, it's only me,' she said.

'What are you doing here?' Duncan asked.

'I thought I might persuade you to change your mind.'

'I really don't think so. I really don't fancy the film.'

'I know,' she said, 'but I thought you might like to come with me.'

'Penny isn't keen either. Why don't you go with Jock and enjoy the film?'

'Be like that, then,' she hissed, turning on her heel and walking off.

Duncan followed Sue to her car saying, 'It's not that I don't want to see you, it's the film I don't want to see. Anyway, we wouldn't exactly be on our own, would we?'

Sue would not be placated. Angrily, she said, 'I'm not going to bother again. I try so hard to be nice to you and to Penny and invite you out and it's thrown back in my face.'

Duncan tried to calm her, telling her how kind she had been, but she would not listen, driving off in a huff.

Watching from the door, Penny asked, 'What was that all about?'

Duncan replied, 'Nothing, really. She's just miffed that we didn't want to go out and wondered if we had changed our minds.'

On Tuesday 12 March 1991, Duncan and Penny attended the weekly diving lecture, preparing Susan, Annette and some of the others for their dive leader examination. That night Duncan told everyone that the first dive of the season would be on the Chirripo wreck four days later.

Annette Gascoigne recalled the evening. 'After Duncan had announced the Chirripo dive Sue went over to Penny and asked her if she would partner her for the dive. The three of us chatted together about the Chirripo.

'I knew Penny hated diving in the cold, dark Northern Ireland waters but Sue became most persistent, finally pleading with Penny to dive with her that Saturday. It was obvious throughout the conversation that Penny had no wish whatsoever to dive that coming weekend.

'Yet the more Penny said "No", the more Sue tried to persuade her to be her dive partner. I felt something very strange was happening and yet I couldn't put my finger on it. There was something odd about what was going on. I kept asking myself why on earth Sue was asking Penny to dive with her.

'I knew Sue detested Penny and had done so for months. Sue had told me on many occasions that she would never agree to dive with Penny. She never wanted anything to do with her and now, for no apparent good reason, Sue was pleading with her to be her dive partner.

'Finally, and most reluctantly, Penny agreed to dive with Sue that Saturday.'

Looking back on the conversation and remembering Sue's insistence, Annette Gascoigne now believes Susan Christie had made up her mind at that time to kill Penny McAllister. And she knew how Susan intended to kill her.

Some time after Susan Christie's trial, Annette would say, 'Sue knew perfectly well that it would be so easy for her to kill Penny as they dived together. They would be connected to each other "buddy line" and visibility down below would be very poor.

'Susan knew how one diver could kill a partner while diving. A diver would simply need to swim up behind the partner and close off the air supply, by turning the small tap on the top of the air-bottle. Seconds later, with the person unconscious through lack of oxygen, the partner could turn the tap back on again. The diver would be dead when he or she reached the surface.

'There would of course be questions asked in such circumstances; there could be the deepest suspicion, but it would be all but impossible to charge and convict someone with murder or manslaughter.

'In my heart I now believe Sue intended to kill Penny that weekend and I also believe that was how she intended to carry it out. The perfect murder.'

As Duncan and Penny drove home that evening Penny told her husband that she had agreed to dive with Sue that weekend. 'I don't really want to dive, but Sue kept nagging me so I agreed.'

'I'm not sure that's a good idea,' Duncan said. 'I know you don't like diving wrecks and it'll be dark and cold. You haven't dived in UK waters for more than two years.'

Penny replied, 'I've said I'll dive and I don't want to wimp out.'

'It's not wimping out,' Duncan said, 'it's just being sensible. My advice is not to dive, but it's your decision.'

On that drive home, however, Duncan was

worried. He knew the vehemence that Sue had shown towards Penny when she had been asked to partner her on a dive. Now she was pushing Penny to dive with her. Over and over again he asked himself one question, which he found impossible to answer: 'Why?'

Two days later Duncan and Sue met again at their favourite lunchtime rendezvous and Duncan raised the subject of the dive.

'I just thought it would be nice to dive with Penny before I go on my course,' Sue replied. 'I might never get the chance again.'

'But you've never wanted to dive with her before and would go mad if I even suggested it,' Duncan persisted.

'I've changed my mind. I get on better with her now.'

Minutes later Susan surprised Duncan by announcing that she was not certain whether she really wanted to take a commission. 'I like being a soldier,' she said, 'and don't want to be shunned by my friends when I come back to the battalion an officer.'

'But gaining a commission is what you've wanted for so long and worked so hard towards.'

'Have I?' she asked. 'Or am I doing it because it's what my daddy wants?

'He's always pushed me towards a commission but I'm not sure that I want it any more.'

Sue and Duncan spent the next thirty minutes

discussing the matter, Duncan doing his utmost to persuade his mistress that she should go for a commission and Sue unsure of the future she really wanted. Finally, halfheartedly, Sue said she would continue to strive to become an officer.

Saturday 10 March proved an overcast, grey day, with no sign of the sun, and the waters around White Head slipway near the Chirripo wreck were distinctly uninviting.

'I'm not sure I want to dive today,' Penny admitted as she shivered on the harbour wall.

'Well,' Duncan said, 'if you're not happy diving, then don't dive. You know my thoughts on the subject. My advice is that you shouldn't dive.'

'I don't really want to dive,' Penny confessed.

'Then you mustn't,' Duncan said. 'Annette can dive with Susan.'

Annette and Sue both wanted to dive but, to give them more confidence, they asked Duncan to dive with them. He happily agreed.

At first the dive went well as all three descended slowly to the deck of the wreck's hull, about sixteen metres below the surface. Annette's left fin strap had come undone and she could not fix it, so Duncan went to her aid and fixed it. When all three were safely on the deck of the wreck they each gave the thumbs-up 'OK' sign and, led by Duncan, began inching along the deck. Then the dive began to go wrong.

In his aide-memoire, Duncan recalled, 'As we

headed towards the stern of the ship the slope of the ship's decking took us from the expected sixteen metres down to nineteen metres and I could feel the current picking up strongly. I checked my gauge. We had reached the agreed depth limit and I decided it would be prudent to head back towards the surface.

'I signalled to turn back and watched as they moved to one side of me. Suddenly their torch beams seemed to be getting further away. I knew in that instance that they were off the wreck, probably caught up by the strong current. Their lights were disappearing fast, going up and away from me.

'Then they were gone. There was no sense in trying to find them or catch them in the dark. It was better for me to return to the shot line and surface to the boat. I began my ascent, and ten metres from the surface the line went slack, indicating that Penny had dropped the anchor line to pick up Sue and Annette.

'I hit the surface and saw two other divers ahead of me. In the distance I could see Penny helping Sue and Annette into the boat. When they were safely in, Penny brought the boat over to me and the others and we clambered in too.'

Later, Annette told what happened. 'After Duncan gave us the signal to follow him we went to the other side of the wreck and somehow we both let go of the wreck and began to move away rapidly. I tried to use my fins to get back to the wreck but the current was too strong.

'I was attached to Sue, who was dive leader that day, and we began to ascend very quickly. I became worried that we were ascending too fast. I thought Sue would stop to check our depth and to dump the expanding air in her life-jacket, but she never stopped. We surfaced faster than I had ever done before and I prayed we hadn't done ourselves any injury.

'As soon as we hit the surface Susan was fucking and blinding at me, saying it was all my fault. We gave the "OK" signal to Penny in the boat, then we began arguing again, Susan shouting that it was my fault, which I would not accept.

'Sue then said she felt as though she was drowning, so I kept telling her to put air into her stab-jacket. For some reason she couldn't do it, so I swam over to her and did it for her. We tried to swim to the boat but the current was too strong and we weren't going to make it. So we gave the distress signal. In fact we gave the distress signal more to tell Penny to come and pick us up rather than from feeling any danger that we were drowning.

'Penny struggled a little with the anchor rope but then brought the boat over to us. There was no delay. As soon as she arrived I told Penny to leave me and help Sue into the boat. Penny went immediately and helped Sue out of the water. Sue was in the boat and I was sitting on the side of the boat before she put it into gear. Neither of us was dragged through the water.'

Later, Penny told Duncan what she had seen as Sue and Annette surfaced. 'I could see them arguing and shouting at each other. They began arguing as to whose fault it had been, blaming each other for their rapid ascent. Neither made any attempt to reach the boat and continued shouting at each other.

'I told them they were behaving like a couple of fishwives and told them to get a grip, swim to the boat and get in. They both gave me the thumbs-up "OK" signal and finned towards the boat. Then Sue realized she wouldn't make it to the boat and gave the distress signal. So I immediately started the engine and went over to them.'

Once on board, Duncan checked that Annette and Sue were OK. He knew from the fact they had only been down to a depth of nineteen metres and been on the bottom only ten minutes that the chances of either suffering a bend were virtually nil. Both told him they were feeling 'fine'.

Duncan told Sue that as a dive leader she should take the bulk of the blame. He pointed out that she failed to check her depth and failed to dump the expanding air in her life-jacket, both basic mistakes. And he pointed out to both of them that when surveying a wreck no diver should let go of the wreck for fear of being swept away by the current.

As all the divers sped back to harbour,

however, the thrill of having carried out the dive in testing conditions was apparent, for all of them, including Sue and Annette, were laughing and joking.

A couple of days later Susan Christie phoned Duncan's home, wanting to speak to Penny, not to her lover.

After the call Penny said, 'That was Sue, cancelling our walk in the woods.'

'I didn't know you were going for a walk with her,' said Duncan. 'In any case her dog Sapper doesn't get on with ours. The last time they chased him so much he had to be put in the car.'

'I know,' said Penny, 'but last week she suggested we go out together, take the dogs for a walk and then have a bite to eat. We've provisionally fixed a date for next Monday.'

That weekend Penny went off to Dublin with other army wives, and Susan arrived at Duncan's married quarters sometime after dark, to spend a last romantic weekend with him.

As before, Sue and Duncan did not stay long downstairs but went to bed early, needing to satisfy the sexual tension between them, wanting to make love. That night they hardly slept, making love four times before they finally fell into a deep sleep, their passion exhausted.

The next day began beautifully, the sun shining brightly on the waves. Sue and Duncan planned to dive with four others around Gunns

Island that day, hoping to play with the seals that frequent the area. But once in the water the seals disappeared and the first two pairs of disappointed divers came back to the boat.

The wind then changed direction and the wind chill factor increased considerably. The others wanted to return home, for they were cold and hungry, and Duncan, diving with Sue as his partner, happily agreed.

Sue had other ideas. 'I really would like to dive. I might not be able to dive with you again, Duncan. I'm off on my course in a week or so. Please dive.'

Duncan agreed, but put a time limit on the dive, not wanting the others to suffer too long in the cold. While the others shivered in the boat above the waves Duncan and Sue had their final dive together.

That night would also be the last they would ever spend together. They cooked a meal and sat on the sofa watching a TV movie, but not for long.

After kissing and cuddling they left the TV and went up to bed, as hungry for each other's bodies as they had been every time they had slept together.

Once again they made love with abandon and passion, hardly able to satisfy their lust for one another until exhaustion overtook them.

Afterwards they cuddled and Sue began to ask questions. 'I'll miss you when I'm on my course,' she said. 'Will you miss me?'

'Of course I will,' Duncan replied, 'but don't you dare mope around. Get out and enjoy yourself. It's the start of a new phase in your life, so go out and meet people.'

'How can you say that?' she asked, sounding hurt. As Duncan held her close and stroked her naked body,

Sue suddenly said, 'If ever I get married I'd like you to be there.'

'I don't know if I could do that.'

'Why not?'

'I just don't think it would be right. I think we would both find it hard. It's always difficult when someone invites old flames to wedding. I would only come if you invited both Penny and me.'

'I don't know if I'd want to invite Penny, but if I did, would you come? I'd like to think you would.'

Susan mused for a while. Then she said, 'Well, I would like to think we would remain close. I'm going to miss you so much, you know.'

She went on, 'I'd like to come back at weekends to dive and see you and the others.'

'That's great, but you do realize that it would have to be on a platonic basis?'

Susan looked up sharply. 'But why?'

'Because I would be with Penny.'

Tears welled in her eyes and Duncan held her close and she began to cry. They talked of the great times they had shared, of their love-making, of their love for each other during the past nine months. Duncan stroked her hair and her body and the tears stopped.

'Make love to me,' she said.

Duncan kissed her gently and they began to make love again, this time more slowly, until passion took over once again and they clung to one another, still craving each other's bodies, not knowing whether they would ever make love together again.

As they kissed and cuddled afterwards, Sue asked, 'Do you love me?'

'Yes, I do, and always will,' Duncan said. 'I'd like to think we could always remain friends.'

The next morning Sue and Duncan woke late and then joined the other divers cleaning out the boat and checking the diving gear. Later that day, they took Monty and Barton to the lake where they had first made love and let them loose, the big Setters racing around, enjoying their freedom in the wild country.

As they walked hand in hand, Duncan said, 'Will this place have fond memories for you or do you regret what happened between us?'

'Fond memories, of course,' she replied. 'I don't regret a thing. I wanted to have the affair and I want us to remain friends.'

As they began walking back to the car Sue made one last request. 'Will you make love to me here and now, the place where it all began?'

'Here and now?'

Yes,' she replied, 'I'd really love to.'

Duncan took the dogs back to the car and returned to Sue. In his aide-memoire, Duncan would write, 'It was a lovely warm day although only March. Sue chose the exact location, out of sight of everyone and dry under foot. I took off my coat and laid it on the ground for Sue to lie on. She slipped off her jeans and pants and, once again, I knew why our sex life together had been so exciting, so passionate, so wild. Once again we wanted each other as though it was the first time.'

It would be the last time they ever made love.

After a gentle, slow, final walk around Maricoo Lake they returned to their cars, kissed and hugged and said goodbye. Sue was in high spirits as she waved farewell, a smile on her face.

Duncan would write in his aide-memoire, 'It surprised me that she left in such good spirits. For me, there was a rush of relief throughout my entire body. It was finally over. I was a free man again. No more deception, no more lies.

'I thought I had achieved the perfect solution. It was over. No one got hurt, no one had found out. Susan and I were friends and I was back with Penny. By the time Susan returned to Northern Ireland we would be in Germany. It felt so good.

'The burden of months of strain and pressure to hold the situation together had gone in an instant. I had been waiting for this moment ever since making the decision to end the affair in Ascension. Five months of soul-searching. Now I had done it. God, it felt good.'

Duncan was busy tidying the house when the phone rang. It was Sue. 'I've called to say thank you, thank you for a lovely last weekend. I just wanted you to know how much I appreciated it.'

'Well, thank you very much,' Duncan stammered, surprised by the call. 'I'm glad you enjoyed it.'

'I'll ring tomorrow. Bye.' And she was gone.

Murder in the Forest

★ ★ ★

Duncan would have another extraordinary telephone conversation with Susan Christie the following day — about how she became stuck down a hole in the remote part of a forest.

She phoned Duncan at his office, hoping for a date, and then proceeded to tell him of her bizarre accident. She said, 'I found a new place to walk the dogs yesterday. I took Sapper there after I left you at the lake. It's a lovely forest. Monty and Barton would love it.'

'You'll have to show me where some day.'

'And I got trapped down a hole.'

'You did what?' said Duncan, surprised.

'It's true, I was trapped down a hole. I became stuck and couldn't get out. It took me ages to climb out because I kept sliding back whenever I tried to clamber out. I could have been left there because I was in a really remote part of the forest and no one was around. If I'd shouted for help no one would have heard me.'

Duncan asked what she was doing in the hole in the first place. Sue replied, 'Sapper jumped into it and couldn't get out. I tried to grab his collar and pull him out but I couldn't, so I jumped into the hole and pushed him out. Then I became stuck.'

Sue was laughing and joking about her predicament. It would be later that Duncan discovered Sue had been referring to Drumkeeragh Forest.

When Penny arrived to collect Duncan from the office he asked how Sue had taken Penny's cancellation of their rearranged Monday walk together.

'She insisted on making it Wednesday,' Penny said somewhat grudgingly.

'And you agreed?'

'Well,' Penny said, 'we have cancelled twice. I don't really want to go as I have so much to prepare before Mum and Dad arrive. I just feel I ought to go.'

On the morning of Tuesday 26 March, Sue phoned Duncan, as she had many times before. She would usually begin her conversations with a 'Hello' or a 'Hi' or 'It's Sue'. On that morning, however, the first words Sue said to Duncan were, 'What do you think would have happened if you'd been single?'

Rather taken aback, Duncan replied, 'Well, I don't think you can think like that because it's a hypothetical question. I'm married, so the question doesn't actually arise.'

'But what if you had been single?' Sue persisted.

'Sue, there's no point in discussing it.'

'But I want to know.'

'Even if I had been single it doesn't mean we would have stayed together.'

'Why not?'

Duncan explained again to Susan Christie that it was impossible to speculate, because couples break up all the time despite the best of intentions.

Sue would not be put off. 'But, hypothetically, if you weren't married would we have stayed together?'

Once again Duncan refused to answer her question directly, saying there were many reasons why they might have broken up at some later stage.

'But why?' she asked.

'Because you're a private soldier and I'm an officer so we could never have been seen together in public. It would have had to remain secret. Can't you see that?'

'But what if I got my commission?'

'Again you are talking about something which may not happen, Sue. I don't mean to be cruel but you might fail to gain a commission. Anyway, even if you did, you're UDR and I'm in the British Army. I would still be going to Germany and you'll always serve in Ireland whether you gain a commission or not. The likelihood of my ever returning to Ireland on posting is virtually nil.'

After a moment's silence Sue said, 'I could always get a transfer from the UDR.'

'You know that's highly unlikely,' Duncan argued, 'and it still doesn't mean we would ever be posted to the same place.'

Then he said, 'Sue, don't hurt yourself thinking of something that is just never going to be. Think of the good times we have have together and look ahead to getting a commission.'

The conversation never reached a logical conclusion, but Duncan would recall it some days later.

During that Tuesday, 26 March, Susan Christie would be on a twenty-four-hour shift in the operations room at UDR Headquarters. During her duty she found time to call Annette, having chatted to her earlier.

Annette recalled, 'She seemed perfectly normal when we spoke. We talked about the forthcoming dive leader exams and chatted for nearly ten minutes. For some extraordinary reason

Sue asked me whether I liked Duncan and I told her that I did. She told me of her plans to go out the following night to see some friends and wondered whether I would like to go too. She laughed and joked as though in one of her more happy, relaxed moods. Thinking back, I can find nothing untoward whatsoever about Susan or the conversation that day. In fact, she seemed very together. She never told me she was tired or depressed and seemed rather cheerful.'

The following day Sue Christie would go walking in Drumkeeragh Forest with Penny and the dogs, Duncan's words still fresh in her mind.

The morning of Wednesday 27 March was bright and the day promised to be warm and sunny. Penny drove Duncan to work because she needed to collect some stock for the PRI shop from nearby Lisburn.

The last time Duncan saw his wife alive was when she popped her head around his office door and said, smilingly, 'I'm off now. I'm just going into town to collect some daffodils for Mum, then I'm off to Lisburn. I won't be too long as I have some cleaning to do at home.'

Duncan asked, 'Are you happy about collecting your parents?'

She replied, 'They don't land until six o'clock, so I'll have stacks of time.'

'OK, have fun, see you later.'

Penny flicked her hair back from her face and

gave Duncan a wave before dashing away to collect the daffodils for her mother, walk her dogs and spend an hour in Drumkeeragh Forest with the young woman she knew was her husband's mistress.

As Penny cleaned the house, her mother Norma phoned to say they would be on schedule and expected to see her around six o'clock.

'What are you doing today?' Norma asked.

'I'm meeting someone to walk the dogs, then for lunch and then back home to clean, clean, clean,' she said laughingly.

'I'll let you get on then; see you later, love you both.'

'Love you Mum, I'm so excited you're coming over. I'll be at the airport to pick you up.'

At about the same time Sue Christie was phoning Duncan at his office, trying to contact Penny. She said, 'I've tried to get hold of Penny at home but there's no reply. Do you know if she's left yet?'

Duncan told her he presumed she had left for McBrides shop and was then going on to their rendezvous.

'I can't remember what time we were meant to meet. Do you remember?'

'Sue, I only know that you were meeting each other to walk the dogs, but I don't know where or when.'

'We were meeting at Hillsborough, but I can't

remember if it's eleven or eleven-thirty.'

'Why don't you go for eleven, Sue, and if it's eleven-thirty just wait around. It's only half an hour.'

'I'll do that. Speak to you soon. Bye.' And she was gone.

That afternoon Duncan, along with other officers, had to undergo a fitness test, a three-mile assessment run. Too warm for a tracksuit, Duncan ran in a singlet and shorts and found the going tough. He returned to the office sweating, out of breath and somewhat shattered.

'Duncan, I need a word.' His commanding officer Major Johnstone had walked into Duncan's office while he was still towelling off. It sounded like trouble.

'I've got some very bad news for you.'

'Don't tell me, they've cancelled my posting to Germany.'

'No. I don't know how to say this in any other way.' He paused a moment and then said, 'Penny is dead.'

Duncan wrote in his aide-memoire, 'I stared at him, not believing what I had just heard. I wanted to ask how, but I couldn't speak. He must have read my mind. I knew it must have been terrorists ... a bomb ... a shooting ... what?

'I tried to speak, but no words would come out. Then Andrew said, "She's been attacked by a man in a wood."'

He would write later, 'To be told your wife is dead is a horrifying experience. But to then think she has been killed in a sex attack is your worst nightmare. All I kept thinking was that I could not be hearing what I was being told ... it can't be true ... it isn't true ...she can't be dead ... she's not dead ... it's a mistake ... you haven't checked properly ... she's still alive.'

Duncan's head was spinning and, as he tried to sit down, his legs went from underneath him and he all but collapsed on the floor. 'No, no, no, no,' he kept repeating the same word, as he sat in the chair, his head in his hands.

Then Andrew spoke again. 'Duncan, there's no mistake, she's dead. There was another girl with her. She was also attacked. She's in hospital with stab wounds.'

Duncan would write later, 'All sorts of things were racing through my mind. I just hoped she had died quickly, that she hadn't suffered. I prayed that she hadn't been raped and the thought that she had been knifed to death was too much. Every time Andrew had told me something new the scenario worsened. I started to sob and to try and speak at the same time. I remember Andrew bending down in front of me, on his haunches, holding my shoulders and trying to comfort me.'

Between tears, Duncan said, 'Christ, Andrew, I just hope she didn't suffer ... I can't take all this in ... I know it's true but I don't want to believe it.'

Suddenly, Duncan thought of the dogs. 'What about the dogs? Where are they?'

'I'll try to find out.'

'Where did it happen?'

'At a place called Drumkeeragh, I think.'

'Where's that?'

Duncan got to his feet and they went over to the large wall map and finally found the forest, near Ballynahinch.

'I want to go to the scene,' Duncan said. 'I want to go down there.'

'We don't think that's a good idea,' Andrew said. 'We've sent down an army representative to act on your behalf and keep us informed.'

A little later, the brigade commander came in and sat on the chair opposite Duncan. 'I just want to say how sorry we all are for you,' he said. 'We're all thinking of you and you have our full support. If you want anything just ask.'

The brigadier went on, 'We've sent someone down there and we're doing everything possible. The police are there investigating. We've put a helicopter up and we have two battalions on the ground. If he's still there we'll get him.'

Little did anyone realize at that time what had in fact happened on that fateful day.

Penny and Sue had met as arranged at eleven o'clock at Hillsborough. Susan Christie had not brought her dog Sapper because she said he was ill. The two women had then driven in their respective cars to Drumkeeragh Forest, a remote and secluded spot which sits in the valley below the Slieve Croobe mountain range. Sue led the way, as Penny had never been before. They had parked their cars and begun their walk, the dogs racing everywhere, enjoying the fresh scents and the wild open forest.

They had walked together one full circuit of the forest, enjoying the beautiful views over Belfast Lough, and the smell of the trees just coming into leaf.

And they could see in the distance the two massive Harland and Woolf cranes.

Penny had enjoyed the walk in the spring sun so much that when Sue suggested another circuit she happily agreed. Susan Christie would say later that Penny talked non-stop about her parents coming out to stay for the weekend and of the forthcoming move to Germany with Duncan, which she was looking forward to.

Susan Christie would claim that during the walk she had apologized to Penny because of her earlier behaviour towards her, making the excuse that she had been overworking. She would say that Penny seemed really happy that day and excited about seeing her parents.

At the point in the walk which would have been the farthest from the car park, Susan Christie complained that her shoelace had come undone and suggested Penny walk ahead with the dogs while she stopped to tie it.

As Penny walked ahead with the dogs Susan Christie took a butcher's knife from the right-hand pocket of her tracksuit trousers. She had bought the boning knife some days before and had asked for the blade to be honed, to make it razor-sharp.

During her five years with the army Susan Christie had never been trained in unarmed combat but she had seen a number of displays. She had watched as a would-be attacker stealthily crept up behind a victim, seized the person around the neck with his left forearm, grabbing the chin and forcing the head backwards, exposing the throat. She had seen the attacker bring the knife around the front of the victim, slashing the exposed throat in one violent action. Slowly, the attacker would then lay the victim on the ground, killed within seconds, without a sound being uttered.

As Penny walked on along the forest path Susan Christie carried out the brutal killing in exactly this way. She crept up behind Penny, the knife in her right hand. She grabbed hold of Penny's neck from behind, forcing the head back, exposing her throat.

Then, with one slash of the knife, she buried the five-inch blade in Penny's neck, dragging the knife back hard towards Penny's right ear, almost severing the head with the violence of the movement. Penny's jugular vein was severed. Immediately, blood began gushing in spurts from the gaping wound as Susan Christie laid Penny down on her back on the floor of the forest. Penny had not uttered a sound.

Despite the fact that it was a warm, sunny March day Susan Christie had worn gloves throughout their walk, something she hardly ever did. As Penny lay dying, Susan then tried to stem the spurting blood as it pumped out of Penny's inert body in a dark, red stream, covering her gloves with blood.

Despite the horror of what she had done, Susan Christie continued with the rest of her plan, carrying out all her evil intentions in a meticulous fashion. She pulled down the tracksuit trousers she wore that day and, with the same knife, stabbed herself in the left thigh, at the same time deliberately ripping her cotton knickers. Christie realized only too well that if she was to fool the police and escape justice she had to make the police believe that she too had been attacked, and she wanted them to see her torn clothes and the stab wounds to her body.

Christie looked around but saw no one. She knew she had carried out the attack in the most deserted part of the forest and she also knew that Penny had not been able to utter a sound, let alone scream, throughout the violent assault. Only then did Susan Christie begin to scream as she ran towards the car park, knowing there would be people there. On the way she threw the knife into the undergrowth. Police would later find the keen-edged knife 260 yards from Penny's body.

Mrs Eileen Rice had gone to Drumkeeragh Forest that morning with her husband and their two children for a picnic in the warm March weather. Mrs Rice noticed a young woman with two dogs walking haphazerdly towards the car park. At first, she thought the young woman was laughing but then realized she appeared distraught and in tears.

She would say later, 'She was staggering about as though not sure of her actions and I ran up to her and held her by the hands to steady her. She was distressed and crying. I had difficulty making out what she was saying.

'Then I realized she was trying to tell me that she needed help for a friend who had been attacked by a man in the forest. It was at that moment that I realized something serious had happened. I shouted to my husband, telling him what had happened, and asking him to go and phone for the police. He went off to call the police while I stayed with the girl and her dogs. She kept urging me: "Help Penny, go and help Penny, please, please."'

'But I had no idea to whom she was referring and where this other person might be. The girl kept crying and I sat her down and tried to calm her while we waited for the police. She seemed uncontrollable.'

Mrs Rice decided she should find somewhere for Susan Christie to lie down and, with the help of her husband, took Christie to a nearby house in Drumaquoile Road, Ballynahinch, where a Mrs Teresa Morgan lived.

Ten minutes later the police and an ambulance arrived at the house. A local GP, Patrick McGtath, was also called to the scene and he examined Christie. He would say later, 'I noticed her hands were covered in blood although I could find no injuries. She appeared to be distressed and was crying and sobbing uncontrollably. She seemed quite shocked.

'She complained of a pain in her neck, her shoulders and her left leg. I noticed the presence of a small wound on her left thigh and the surface of the thigh was smeared with blood. I also found a number of scratches and abrasions on her left side, some tenderness at the base of her skull and on one of her shoulders.'

Dr McGrath cleaned and dressed the wound on Christie's thigh and checked to see whether any of the other minor scratches needed attention. While the examination was in progress Christie recovered her composure and talked a little to Dr McGrath.

'Please God help me. Oh God, help me,' she moaned.

'Do you believe in God?' Dr McGrath asked.

'Yes.'

'I am sure God will help you, then.'

Christie asked, 'Why didn't he help Penny,

then?'

'I am sure Penny is with God now.'

'It is Duncan who God should be looking after now.'

Detective-Constable John Horan talked to Christie after she was placed in the ambulance. She gave him a detailed description of the attacker, the same description she would repeat many times over during the next forty-eight hours.

Christie was taken by ambulance to Downe Hospital, where she was examined by Dr Deidre Bell. Dr Bell would say later, 'Christie told me that her attacker had tried to pull her trousers down. She told me that she had prevented this by kneeing him in the groin. She complained of a pain in her neck but she did not know whether the man had grabbed her by the neck.'

It was while Susan was being examined at Downe Hospital that the news of Penny's murder was being broken to Duncan.

He suddenly realized that Penny's parents, Norma and Des, were due to arrive at Belfast airport at six o'clock. He decided that he should break the news to them of Penny's murder, telling Andrew, 'I don't want them told by a complete stranger. It's my responsibility, I should tell them. It's going to be hard enough for them as it is. It has to be me.'

Duncan also needed to tell his own parents of Penny's death. He wanted to tell someone who would understand his total devastation at Penny's murder. He asked to be left alone and dialled his parents' home in Ashton Keynes.

'Mum, it's me.'

'Hello darling,' she said, 'don't tell me you're at Brize Norton and want me to pick you up?'

'No. Mum, listen. I'll only be able to say this once so please listen, please.'

After a moment's pause Duncan said, 'Penny's dead.'

Duncan McAllister then broke down, the pent-up emotion he had suppressed for more than an hour suddenly erupting. He burst out crying, unable to control the tears and the sobbing which shook his body.

After a while, as his mother tried to console her anguished son over the phone, Duncan fought to collect himself. 'Mum, I must go now. I can't speak any more. I'll phone you when I'm feeling better. Bye.'

An army helicopter flew Duncan and Andrew to Aldergrove and a small room was secured near the baggage reclaim. Duncan knew he had to keep himself together until Norma and Des were in the room and he had broken the news of Penny's death.

'Hi Duncan,' Norma said. 'We thought Penny would meet us.' Duncan kissed Norma on the cheek and shook Des by the hand. 'She wasn't able to come so you've got me instead,' he tried to joke.

'I suppose you'll have to do,' Norma said, and

laughed.

Duncan explained that for security reasons they would have to go to a nearby room and their baggage would be collected and brought to them. Norma took Duncan's arm and began asking about Penny, the dogs, the house and how far they would have to travel to their quarters.

'Why don't you sit down?' Duncan said.

'No thanks,' Des replied, 'I'd prefer to stand. I've been sitting for the past hour or so.'

'Des, I think you should sit down.'

Both Norma and Des looked at Duncan, knowing instinctively that something was wrong.

'Listen. There's only way I can say this: Penny is dead.'

Neither Norma nor Des said a word. They just looked at Duncan in total disbelief.

'I'm so sorry,' Duncan said weakly.

Suddenly Norma's cries and screams of anguish rent the peace and quiet of the room. Des moved over to his wife and put his arms around her shoulders as she shook uncontrollably, tears smearing her face, contorted by her anguish and despair.

Duncan's aide-memoire would reveal: 'I found myself transfixed to the door, unable to move forward in a bid to console her. As I viewed the scene of these devastated parents a deep sense of guilt invaded my soul. I had deceived them and I'd deceived Penny. I had been unfaithful to the one woman I had loved for the last eight months of her life.'

During the hour-long journey to Armagh, Des and Norma sat in the back of the car, holding each other and openly crying while Duncan and Andrew sat in the front, not saying a single word, listening to the pain of Penny's mortified parents.

The full realization of Penny's death hit Duncan, Norma and Des as they opened the front door of the house and walked in, the rooms full of the daffodils Penny had bought only that day; the food on the cooker waiting for Penny to prepare, the house clean and tidy, the way Penny had left it to show her parents. All three looked at each other, their eyes bloodshot by the tears they had shed, knowing the person they all so loved and adored would never come back.

There was a knock at the door and the chief clerk stood there with Monty and Barton. Duncan recalled, 'The dogs were hyperactive, on edge, nervous. He brought them into the kitchen and as he entered the dogs went for each other. They had never fought before, but now they seemed like wild animals intent on destroying each other. I managed to grab Monty and dragged him into the back yard. He was shivering and he cowered against the wall. Neither dog had ever behaved like that. It seemed extraordinary.'

That night Norma, Des and Duncan tried to eat some of the food Penny had prepared but for most of the time they sat and cried. Sometimes they would get up and stand in a circle in the middle of the room holding each other and weeping tears of anguish, frustration and unfathomable sadness.

Norma asked what had happened to Penny, but there was little Duncan could tell her because he had not been given any details of her murder. Norma asked what had happened to the other woman.

Later, she would say, 'When Duncan told me that the other woman was Susan Christie, the woman who had suffered the bends, I became unnerved. I felt something was amiss, something was wrong. I could not decide why I felt Susan Christie was somehow involved. But the fact that she was there unnerved me.'

That night Duncan walked into the bedroom he had shared with Penny to see her clothes scattered around, her belongings everywhere. He wrote later, 'Her very presence seemed everywhere. I found the T-shirt she had been wearing earlier that day, turned it inside out and held it to my face, breathing in her fragrance. I sat there for hours that night begging her to come back and telling her how much I loved her, desperate that I hadn't had a chance to say farewell. Eventually I placed her T-shirt on my pillow and tried to rest for a couple of hours. I needed her smell around me, to hold on to it as long as possible because I felt that night if I lost her smell I would have lost her for ever.'

Norma and Des were not permitted by police to visit the scene of the murder; nor could they see their daughter's body because it had not yet been prepared at the chapel of rest. The following morning they flew back to England to be with their son Nick.

Later that day, Duncan had his first interview with the detectives investigating her murder. They wanted to know whether anyone bore Penny a grudge, wanted to know details of her friends, of the members of the diving club, of her marital relationship, and they also wanted to know about the relationship between Penny and Susan Christie.

That evening Duncan was informed that Susan Christie had been released from hospital and had been taken home. Fortunately, she had not been badly injured, but was apparently still suffering from the shock of the attack.

Duncan phoned her but her father answered. 'Mr Christie, I'm sorry to disturb you but I wonder if I could speak to Susan; it's Duncan McAllister speaking.'

'I'm so sorry about your wife,' he said.

'I know, thank you. But I'm so thankful for you that Susan survived.'

'The police have said that she shouldn't really speak to anyone or be disturbed but she said that if you rang she would like to speak to you. I'll just go and tell her to pick up the phone in her room.'

'Duncan, I'm so sorry,' Susan stammered, hardly able to speak or string two words together. She managed to say, between sobs, 'I tried to help

Penny ... I really did ... I couldn't stop the bleeding ... I'm so sorry ... I really tried ... I promise.'

'Ssshh, I know you did. I'm sure you did all you could. There was nothing you could do, you had to save yourself. Just thank God that you're alive.'

'I really tried to help her, you know, but he came back. I ran and ran. I just left her there. I'm so sorry. I just turned and ran. Forgive me, please. I tried so hard to save her.'

'There's nothing to forgive; you did all you could. You had to run, you had to save yourself. I'm just glad one of you got away.'

A few minutes later, after Susan had calmed down, Duncan told her he was going to the chapel of rest to see Penny.

'I'd like to come with you,' Susan said. 'I'd like to see Penny and say goodbye.'

'I don't think so, Sue, I'd like to go alone.'

'But I'd like to go with you to support you.'

'I don't think so, Sue. You've just been attacked by the man who murdered Penny. You saw it happen, it would be just too much for you. It's too soon.'

'But I want to see Penny,' Sue protested.

'Not tonight, maybe in a few days. Would it help if I came round to see you?'

'Yes, I'd like that.'

'I'd like to talk to you too. No one is telling me what happened, so I would like to talk to you about it, if you feel up to it.'

'Come tonight.'

'I will, after I've been to the chapel of rest.'

Duncan wrote in his aide-memoire, 'As I entered the chapel I saw the coffin at the far end in front of the altar. I edged forward until I could see Penny, lifeless and cold. Even in death, though, she seemed serene and still very beautiful.

'Penny lay there in the same hand-painted silk wedding dress she wore at her wedding in 1984. The brooch Des had given her that day once again adorned the dress and the pearls I had given her on our wedding night were round her neck. I placed in the coffin the letter I wrote her the day before our wedding, which she had read on the morning when she woke.

'As I looked at her I again dissolved into tears as I tried to tell her how I felt. I told her over and over again how much I loved her. But after a few moments I felt drained, utterly exhausted by the experience, and I had to leave.'

Penny McAllister's body was later flown to England, and she was buried at the same church in Ashton Keynes where she had been married six years previously.

By then, however, the world knew the true identity of Penny's killer.

Confessions

★ ★ ★

Susan Christie was curled up in a ball at the top of her bed hugging her favourite teddy bear when Duncan walked into her room that night.

The moment Susan saw him she began to cry. Between the sobs, Susan Christie stammered, 'I am so sorry, Duncan ... I tried, I really tried to save her but I ran away ... I was so scared ... Please, please forgive me ... I didn't want to leave her alone ... I tried to stop the bleeding, but I couldn't.'

Duncan went over to his lover and put his arms around her, tears filling his eyes as he held her close. A few moments later, Duncan drew back from her and said, 'Look at me. There was nothing more you could have done. Penny was most probably dead already. If you had stayed he would have killed you as well. You had to run, you had to get away. You did the right thing.'

But Susan would not be consoled, repeating time and again, 'I really tried, I'm so sorry.'

Duncan told her, 'I know you did, Sue; you did all you could. Don't blame yourself, there's nothing to forgive. For Penny you must be strong. Be glad that you got away, for now there's a chance of finding this bastard. Try and calm down if you can. You were very brave, you could have done nothing more to save her.'

Sue seemed to calm down a little. She held Duncan's arm and said, 'I'll be here to help you; I'll help you get through it; I'll always be here for you.'

After they had talked for a while, and the tears had subsided, Duncan asked Sue to tell him what had happened at the forest.

Susan Christie told him, 'When we met at Hillsborough I told Penny that Sapper was ill and that's why I hadn't brought him. But we still decided to go ahead with the walk for the sake of Monty and Barton. They needed a run.

'We did one circuit and decided to go round once more because it was such a lovely sunny day. My shoelace came undone and I stopped to tie it. Penny went ahead with the dogs. Then I heard one of the dogs, I think it was Monty, begin to bark.

The dogs were out of sight, way ahead. Penny ran after them when she heard barking and I followed.

'I rounded a corner of the path and saw Penny lying on the ground with a man standing over her. I thought Penny had fallen and that the man was trying to help her. I called out to Penny as I walked towards them. She didn't answer. As I got closer I saw the blood and realized she had been attacked.

'I was transfixed, I couldn't move. The man then turned and lunged at me, pushing me to the ground. I was fighting with him as he tried to rape me.'

Susan Christie became distraught as she continued her story. 'He began to pull down my tracksuit trousers, ripping at my clothes. He was trying to stab me in the leg. He was hurting me, I could feel the knife going into my leg. It really hurt.

'He also cut me across my stomach as he tried to cut off my knickers. I was screaming for help. I started shouting, "Daddy, Daddy, help me" in the hope the man would think my daddy was coming and we weren't alone.

'As I was screaming for help Barton came running round the corner towards us, startling the man, who must have believed someone was approaching. I then kneed him in the balls and he let go and ran away.

'I then moved over to help Penny.'

Susan broke down again at that point in her story, sobbing for a few minutes until she managed to regain her composure.

'I tried so hard to stop the bleeding,' she said, crying again. 'God, Duncan, I am so sorry. I shouldn't have left her there, alone. I was a coward. I just ran and ran. I should have tried to save her, I should have stayed. I tried to stem the blood coming from her neck, I really tried.'

Susan then told how she had looked up to see the man standing on a hillock, looking down at her. She said, 'He just stared at me. I shall never forget those eyes for as long as I live. He then started to walk towards me and I just got up and ran for my life.'

Susan told Duncan that she continued running until she saw some young boys and she asked them for help but they just ran away when she approached them. She went on, 'I walked for ages, not knowing where I was. I started to run again and eventually I found myself at the car park. It was there I found the family. Monty and Barton had followed me.

'I told the man about Penny and pleaded with him to go and help her but he refused. He told me to get into the car but when I asked whether Monty and Barton could come as well he refused and took me to a nearby house where he called the police.'

When she had completed her story Susan Christie seemed composed, relieved that she had told Duncan exactly what had happened.

Duncan told her, 'I'm sorry I had to put you

through this, but I needed to know from you what had really happened. There was nothing you could have done, Sue; I think you showed real bravery and I'm glad you got out alive. I'm just so sorry for you, I can't imagine what you're going through.'

Duncan asked Sue to describe the man. She told him, 'He was average height, about 5 feet 9 inches tall and slightly built with short, mousey brown hair. He had blue eyes and was dressed in jeans, white trainers and a green jacket.'

Later Duncan told Susan that he had been interviewed by the police but had not told them of their affair because he felt it had nothing to do with Penny's murder and was indeed none of their business. Susan revealed that she, too, had avoided telling the police about the affair when asked about her relationship with Duncan.

He told Susan, 'Why should we both lose our careers and suffer even more after such a tragedy? And there is another point. I don't want a scandal surrounding Penny's funeral. Her parents have suffered enough. There is no need to make them suffer more, knowing we had an affair. It would be too much for them.'

And Duncan went on, saying, 'For Penny, for her parents, for our two families and for ourselves I think it is better if we don't reveal our affair. If they find out through their enquiries, so be it, but hopefully that won't be until after the funeral, if ever. I hope you agree?'

Susan nodded and went on, 'It would devastate my parents if they knew and, in any case, I agree for Penny's memory.'

'Good. I know it's wrong,' Duncan confessed, 'but I think it's for the best, for everyone. What did you say when they asked you about our relationship?'

'I've told them that you're just a friend. I won't tell them.'

It would be after ten o'clock that Duncan kissed Sue on the cheek and gave her a hug before leaving.

The following morning the police arrived at Susan's house, asking her to accompany them back to Drumkeeragh Forest so that they could reconstruct the crime. Already they had suspicions that Susan Christie had not been telling them the whole truth.

Dr McGrath had informed them that he believed the abrasions on Christie's thigh and stomach could well have been self-inflicted. However, they had no clue as to why she should have done such a thing.

That day three officers, one a woman PC, spent hours quizzing Christie, asking her many different questions and cross-questioning her about the alleged attacker, the man she had seen standing over Penny's body, the man who had tried to rape her. Christie became confused and began giving different answers to some of the questions the officers kept asking. She began to weep and cry and the officers would have to stop their questioning until she had become composed. Then they would begin again, making her go over her story time and time again, checking everything she said.

As the day wore on Susan Christie became more anxious and worried. She sensed the police were no longer treating her as an innocent victim of a stabbing and an attempted rape, and certainly not like a frightened witness who had been at the scene of a horrific murder. It seemed they were now treating her like someone who knew a lot more about the killing than she was admitting.

Yet that day Susan Christie stuck to her story of the man who had attacked her and Penny.

Duncan was at home watching television when the news of Penny's murder made the lunchtime headlines. The TV reporter said the police were looking for a man seen near the woods at the time of the murder, wearing trainers, jeans and a green Barbour jacket. Police believed the man had been driving a white Ford Escort XR2. The news gave Duncan confidence that Susan had told him the truth and, so he believed, verification by the police that there was indeed a chief suspect. He had every confidence the police would eventually catch the bastard.

At six o'clock that night Susan phoned Duncan. 'The police were really horrible to me,' she complained. 'They kept trying to confuse me. I didn't really want to go through with the reconstruction, but they kept pushing me.'

Duncan tried to placate her, saying the police had to use techniques like that to find out every piece of information to help them catch the killer.

'No, Duncan,' she replied, 'it was much worse than that. One of them, whom I've never seen before, was really nasty, a real bastard. The two who were with me all day were all right but the other one kept trying to confuse me.'

One of Duncan's friends agreed to drive over to Susan's house and bring her back to Duncan's quarters so that they could talk at length of the day's events. After they sat down, Susan complained again to Duncan about the one 'nasty bastard' police officer, who, she claimed, had been totally unfair during the questioning. 'I was only trying to help,' she said, 'and he was trying to confuse me all the time.'

She went on, 'When we reached the spot where Penny was murdered they made me stop and then fired loads of questions at me. They weren't gentle at all; they kept putting me under pressure. I found it so hard to go back to the scene and I was crying but they still forced me to walk right back to the spot where it happened. They didn't understand what I was going through.'

Susan complained that the nasty detective kept asking her about distances, about how far away the man had been standing, how far she had been from

Penny, how far the man had run away. She added, 'I just couldn't remember. I kept telling them that I was being attacked but they didn't believe me. Why wouldn't they believe me, Duncan?'

Duncan shrugged off the police's attitude to Susan, telling her that, in the police's eyes, everyone was a suspect until they had caught their man. It was simply their way of working.

Duncan then asked Susan whether she had seen the TV news that evening and she replied that she had not. He told her about the man in the Barbour jacket seen driving away in the Ford Escort XR2.

'Thank God someone else has seen him,' Susan said, a giant sense of relief in her voice. Duncan put his arm round her and gave her a hug, saying, 'Don't fret over the police. It will soon be sorted out. They now have a good description of the man and his car.' In an effort to help Susan, Duncan proposed that the two of them go back over her story so she would not become confused later if and when the police wanted to ask her further questions. Duncan wrote in his aide-memoire, 'For the next two hours we went through her story much more slowly and more sensitively than she had done that day with the police. And her story did not alter one jot from what she had told me the previous night.'

That night Susan pleaded with Duncan to let her fly back to England with him for Penny's funeral. Duncan did not like the idea. He was worried that it might appear that he and Susan were indeed close and, he feared, someone might suspect there was more to their relationship than simply being friends, members of the same diving club.

Susan then turned to Duncan and told him, 'The police know about Sandra. They asked Mummy and Daddy about my friends and they told them about Sandra Gordon, so they're bound to talk to her. What shall we do? We don't want them to find out about us.'

'So you think Sandra will tell them?'

'If they talk to her, yes.'

Duncan became scared. He now realized for the first time that there was a real possibility, a probability, that the police investigating his wife's murder would discover he was having an affair with the girl who last saw Penny alive. He knew immediately that such a revelation would have a devastating effect on everything.

Throughout his affair with Susan he had known the risk he had been taking, that if the affair became public knowledge there was every chance he would be forced to resign from the army, his career at an end. Now everything seemed so much worse than that. Penny was dead; Norma and Des, and his own parents, his brother officers and all his friends would find out that he had been having an affair with Susan Christie, a private in the UDR. And he felt certain he would be forced to resign from the army.

He knew now that the police would find out. He wanted to stop Sandra Gordon telling the police about his affair with Susan prior to the funeral. He needed to know exactly what Sue had told Sandra.

'But all the police will know is that you have been having an affair. They won't know my name. You didn't tell her my name or rank, did you?'

Susan Christie said nothing, but simply looked at Duncan and shrugged her shoulders. Then she said, 'I just had to talk to someone about us.'

'That doesn't matter. The important thing is she knows my name.'

'Yes.'

Under his breath Duncan swore. 'Well,' he said finally, 'it's not a case of if they find out about our affair, it's when.'

'I don't want them to find out,' Sue said. 'I don't want my parents to find out.'

'First, do you agree that we should try and conceal it until at least after the funeral?'

'Yes, I think we should.'

'You're going to have to talk to Sandra then, before the police do.'

'What shall I say to her?'

'Simply tell her all the reasons we've stated and see if she will agree to conceal the information. If she does tell them, your commission and my career will be over, because they're bound to tell the army.'

Susan agreed to phone Sandra that night and insist on meeting her the following morning. Susan would then ring Duncan and inform him of the outcome. Fearing Duncan's phone might be tapped, Susan went to a public phone box to call Sandra.

They both agreed, however, that if Sandra felt she could not conceal the affair from the police then they would have to go immediately to the police and inform them.

That night Duncan could hardly sleep. He tossed and turned, debating whether he should go to the police and reveal all.

He would write, 'My father had always told me that when confronted by allegations from authority it was imperative to be totally honest, no matter what the outcome. If honesty meant losing my career, then so be it. Compared to the loss of Penny it would be insignificant. I was convinced Susan was innocent and that revealing the affair would not alter the result of the police investigation. In fact, it would save them a great deal of wasted time. There would also be a slim chance that the police might treat my confession in confidence and not inform the army.'

After walking Monty and Barton the following morning Duncan had made his decision. He went home and picked up the phone, 'Ballynahinch incident room. Can I help you?' said the voice at the other end of the line.

'It's Captain McAllister here. I believe I have some information that might be of some use to you.'

Over the phone Duncan arranged to see the officer who had first questioned him. They arranged to meet at Gough barracks, one hour later.

Duncan entered a small office to find the detective sitting at a desk. He took the seat opposite and said, 'I'm here to give you this information, not because I think it will alter the case, but because I don't want you wasting your time going down blind alleys.'

The officer said nothing.

Duncan took a deep breath and continued, 'I was having an affair with Susan Christie. I'm sorry I didn't tell you the other day, but I just couldn't bring myself to tell you. There didn't seem any point.'

Duncan began to repeat what he had first said to the officer but then he became nervous, far more nervous than he realized. He began to stammer, something which had never happened to him before. He couldn't control the stammer; he could hardly speak.

The officer said nothing but stared directly at Duncan, making his efforts to speak properly even more difficult. Duncan told the officer of their plan to try and stop Sandra Gordon revealing their affair.

Finally the officer spoke. 'Well, Susan's down

at Ballynahinch at the moment so she hasn't seen her friend.'

'Susan should be told that I've told you.'

'She will be. Now tell me, how long has this been going on?'

For the next hour Duncan told the officer all about their affair, providing dates whenever possible.

At the conclusion he said, 'As I have told you all this in confidence can you assure me that you will not tell the army?'

The officer replied bluntly, 'I'm sorry, I cannot give that assurance.

At that instant, Duncan thought, 'I knew it. The police would tell the army whether it had anything to do with the case or not. So much for trusting the police and giving any information to them in the strictest confidence.'

The officer agreed that Duncan could take a flight that day to England so he could attend Penny's funeral, on the condition that he would then return to Northern Ireland, in case they needed to ask him further questions. He agreed.

Within minutes of arriving home before catching the flight, the phone rang. It was Ballynahinch police.

'Just one question, sir. Have you ever been to Drumkeeragh Forest?'

'No, I haven't.'

'Were you aware that Susan Christie went to

Drumkeeragh last weekend?'

'No, I wasn't. I knew she had taken her dog for a walk in a wood but she never said where exactly. Would it be possible to speak to her?'

'Why?'

'Because I want to tell her that it's all right to tell you about the affair.'

'Well you can't at the moment. She's gone for blood tests.'

'Will she be back soon?'

'No.'

Duncan said, 'Look. I'd rather you were straight with me. Are you saying you don't actually want me to speak to her?'

'Yes.'

'Fine, I understand.'

As the aircraft took off from Aldergrove, passing over the Mountains of Mourne, Duncan realized for the first time that there was a real possibility that Susan Christie had been involved in Penny's murder. He felt an icy chill run though him as the repercussions raced through his mind.

★ ★ ★

Duncan's father met him at the airport and the two drove to Ashton Keynes together, the atmosphere strained and almost unreal. As they drove, Duncan, stammering with nervousness most of the time, told his father of his affair with Susan Christie, the girl who had been with Penny at the time of the murder.

Mr David McAllister remembered seeing Susan at Brize Norton and he recalled the scathing remarks Penny had made about her at the time. He commented, 'I've had a feeling something was not quite right ever since I heard Penny was out walking in the forest with another girl.'

He asked Duncan to tell him everything that had passed between him and Susan Christie in the two meetings since the murder. Duncan told him all he could remember, leaving nothing out. As they approached the village, Duncan's father said he had one very important question to ask. After taking a deep breath he said, 'Tell me one thing. Were you involved in any way, any way at all?'

Duncan would write later of that moment, 'The question hit me like a thunderbolt. How could he possibly believe that I would do anything to harm Penny? He knew how much I loved her. I couldn't believe that he was asking me.

Duncan replied, 'No, no, I wasn't.'

'I didn't think you were, but I felt I had to ask you.'

Duncan would later write of his thoughts, 'if my own father had asked the question, then the police had every reason to suspect that I might be implicated in Penny's death. I had spent two nights alone since the murder talking with the prime suspect. I could understand that would look suspicious. Suddenly I felt that the police probably suspected me of being involved in Penny's murder. For the first time since her death I tasted fear.'

The following day David McAllister told his son that he wanted to know about the whole affair, from start to finish. They drove around, in the privacy of his father's car, for hours. Step by step, Duncan recounted what had happened from the first time they met at the diving club in March 1990 to the last time he had spoken to Susan Christie, two days after the murder.

At around six o'clock the phone rang in the McAllister home. His father answered. 'It's for you, it's the police.'

'Captain McAllister?'

'Speaking.'

'I promised to ring you if I thought the story was going to be released to the press. They've just been told that Susan Christie has been charged with the murder of your wife.'

Now the world would know what had happened. For nine months he had been desperate to ensure his affair with Susan remained secret, as though his very life depended on it. In that instant Duncan McAllister realized that everyone, the army, Des and Norma, all his friends, all Penny's friends and relations, everyone who had attended their wedding, would know that he had been having an affair behind Penny's back. And it was only a matter of time before they would all learn that the person who killed Penny had been his mistress for the past nine months.

Two more thoughts struck him. First, he wondered how many would think he too had been implicated in Penny's murder; and second, he wondered how many would lay the blame for her death at his door. He felt physically sick. Yet Duncan McAllister knew what must be done. Now that Susan had been charged with Penny's murder he had to face the music. His first phone call had to be to Norma and Des.

'Des, it's Duncan. I've got some bad news.'

There was no response.

'I have to tell you that I was having an affair with Susan Christie. I've just been told that she has been charged with Penny's murder. It will be in the papers tomorrow. I wanted to be the one to tell you.'

There was a silent pause. After a moment Duncan continued, 'I'm so sorry, Des. I don't know why I did it. I really did love Penny. I'm so sorry.'

Still there was no reply. This time Duncan said nothing.

Then Des Squire said slowly, 'Thank you for letting us know. I can't talk now, we'll speak to you later.' And the phone went dead.

As Duncan walked through the wind and rain the next morning into the beautiful country church in Ashton Keynes for Penny's funeral service he felt both humble and guilty. He also felt a fraud. Everyone he met offered their condolences, saying how desperately sorry they were for his having lost such a wonderful, loving wife. But none of them knew the truth. He did not want to see anyone because virtually no-one at that stage knew of his guilt, that he had cheated on Penny with the young private soldier who had ended up killing her.

Duncan did not know where he should sit in the church, for he did not want to embarrass Norma and

Des or intrude on their grief. He went to sit in the pew immediately behind them but Norma turned and saw him and held out her hand. She motioned Duncan to come and sit with them. 'Don't sit alone. Come and sit between Des and me,' she whispered.

'Are you sure?'

'Yes, we want you to be with us.'

As Duncan sat down Norma held his hand and Des put his arm around his son-in-law's shoulder, comforting him. Duncan would never forget that remarkable act of public forgiveness.

At the funeral wake afterwards, held in the officers' mess at nearby South Cerney, Duncan saw Annette and 'Bamber' Gascoigne, Jock and Chris, all members of the diving club. They were chatting together. He went over to them to say sorry for what he had done. He felt he had deceived them all the same way he had deceived Penny.

Annette said nothing, but stared straight at Duncan as he struggled to put together some sentences, striking the right phrases to show how sorry he was. He half expected Annette, a strong, open character, and one of Susan's best friends in Ireland, physically to attack him, strike him, smack him across the face. Instead, she moved forward, put her hands on his arms and whispered, 'I'm so sorry about Penny, you bloody, bloody idiot.'

Forty-eight hours later Duncan was ushered into a shabby interview room at Ballynahinch police station. Two detectives sat at a formica-topped table.

Duncan sat on a steel chair. They left him for five minutes, then returned.

'I'm Duncan McAllister and I'm here to help you as much as I can regarding the death of my wife Penny.'

The first question would be blunt and to the point. One of the detectives said, 'You have admitted to having an affair with Susan Christie.'

'Yes, since July last year.'

'What we can't understand is why you felt it necessary to have a fling with such a devious little tart when you had Penny.'

'I know that.'

'So why then?'

'I was flattered by her attention and we did get on well. She was completely different to Penny and I suppose that had its attractions.'

'But you must have fancied her in some way?'

'She could be attractive at times, but not in a classical way like Penny. I'm a breast man and I suppose I was initially attracted to her because she is well endowed.'

'You mean she had big tits?'

'If you want to put it like that, yes.'

'Susan says you were the one who came on to her and that you instigated the affair.'

'No, it wasn't quite like that. I admit I broached the subject, but this was because her attention and actions towards me were becoming noticeable. It was only when we discussed it three days later that we talked about an affair. It was mutual.'

Duncan told them of the start of the affair, of the sex by the lake before she went to Berlin.

Then they changed tack. They asked about the dive on 16 March when Duncan, Susan and Annette dived as a trio.

'Susan has said that she wasn't in the boat before Penny put the boat in gear. Susan says Penny tried to kill her by dragging her through the water with the engines revving hard. She thinks Penny tried to kill her on that dive.'

'That's not true. Both Annette and Susan were in the boat when she put it into gear to come over to me. If you want to check, ask Annette.'

The detectives did not answer but again changed the line of questioning.

'Ascension, tell us about Ascension.'

For ten minutes Duncan told them all about the Ascension expedition and they would throw in questions. Then, dramatically, they asked about the time one of the club members had allegedly tried to get into Susan's bed while she was staying at Duncan's home.

Two hours later the questioning began to take its toll on Duncan and his stammer returned. The more he stammered the more the pressure was applied.

Then they raised the issue of Susan's pregnancy. 'We believe you only gave Susan two options. She could either have the abortion or you would tell her to fuck off and have nothing more to do with her. You didn't give a damn about anything but your "career".'

Duncan could not speak properly and through his stammer he explained the three options he had given Susan.

Finally, they interrupted him, saying, 'What did you want?'

'I thought an abortion was best for everyone.'

'So you told her that, forcing her into a corner. Isn't that what happened?'

'Nnnoo,' Duncan stammered, 'I only told her that after she had decided to have an abortion.'

After the police broke for their lunch hour the questioning resumed.

'Tell us about the weekend you spent with Christie in England.'

Duncan spent the next five minutes relating details of the long weekend he and Susan had spent in Gosport.

'Christie says you went away to discuss the pregnancy. She says that you kept demanding an abortion and she was in tears most of the time.'

'No. I took her to England to get away from everything. The arrangement was that we would not discuss the pregnancy.

'You see, Captain McAllister, we have a major problem. Susan kills your wife and you then spend the next two nights alone with her. You even concoct a plan to deceive us. Can't you see our problem?'

'Yes I can. But I did come to you and confess of my own accord.'

'But you may have done that to protect your own skin. We think Susan is protecting you. We think there's something she is holding back; she's not telling us everything.'

Duncan replied, 'I came to see you because I didn't want you wasting your time. I believed Susan, I didn't think she had anything to do with it. I told the detective I didn't think the affair had anything to do with the murder.'

'The detective says you didn't say that. You never said that. You were just trying to save your own skin.'

Duncan looked worried; his stammer returned. 'Bbbuut I did tell him that.'

'Are you saying he is lying?'

'No,' he stammered, 'I'm not. He must have been mistaken.'

'So the officer is mistaken now, is he?'

The detectives switched their questioning.

'Susan's father has told us you demanded to see her on Friday night. Is that right?'

'That's untrue. I offered to help her. I didn't even speak to her father on Friday night.'

'He said you did. Why would he lie?'

'I don't know. I spoke to her mother at lunchtime and Susan phoned me in the evening.'

'He says you rang up demanding to see Susan. We think you are hiding something, and so is Susan.'

Duncan became extremely nervous and worried. He realized the police were trying to implicate him in a murder conspiracy. He also realized what the consequences could be.

He stammered, his nerves out of control, 'I'm not going to answer any more questions until I have a lawyer present.'

Then they turned on him. 'You're not with your army chums now, where you can order what you want and walk away. Don't think you can have a lawyer because you've decided you want one, old chap.'

One of the officers said, 'This is a very serious matter. You don't seem to realize the trouble you're in. You tried to obstruct the course of justice. You lied to the police. We believe there is something going on. Why don't you get down off your high horse and think of someone else for a change, not whether Captain McAllister will lose his career? Why don't you think of Penny?'

'I've lost my career and I do think of Penny all the time.'

'Why, then, didn't you reveal the affair?'

Because you lot weren't telling me anything and I didn't believe it had anything to do with the murder.'

'You thought that if we knew of the affair we would then suspect the two of you.'

'No. I just didn't want you to find out about it.'

'If you were so concerned about Penny, why didn't you come down to the scene? Most husbands would have come straight away, but you just sat back in Armagh.'

'I was told by the army that you, the police, would not allow me to visit the scene. That's why they sent a representative.'

'And you believed that, sat back and did nothing?'

'Yes.'

Then the police began questioning Duncan McAllister about his marriage. 'Did you and Penny have an open marriage?'

'What do you mean by that?'

'Susan says that you told her that you and Penny had an open marriage, that you could both have relationships with others if you wanted.'

'If that's true,' Duncan snapped back, 'why was I so careful about not getting caught?'

'Because of your career.'

'That's not true. I didn't want Penny to know. We didn't have an open marriage in that sense.'

'Did Penny ever have an affair?'

'Not to my knowledge, no.'

'Would it upset you if she had?'

'It would be hypocritical, but yes it would.'

'Susan Christie says that it was common knowledge that Penny had affairs with officers and soldiers.'

'That's not true. I would have known. Can't she just leave Penny alone?'

The detectives returned to the dive of 16 March 1991, and asked whether Susan had ever complained about it.

'No, she didn't. I think she was a little shaken by the fast ascent but once it was over we all had a laugh about it.'

'Would it surprise you to learn that Susan believes she might have drowned that day and was scared of getting another bend?'

'No way. She couldn't have had a bend that day.'

'And the drowning?'

'Well, she never mentioned anything to me.'

Again they changed tack, asking, 'Would it surprise you to hear that Susan is saying that as they walked the dogs Penny goaded her about her alleged bend?'

'Penny wouldn't do that, she hated confrontation. I've never heard her goad anyone or say anything nasty, even to people she didn't like.'

'Christie maintains Penny started to torment her, saying she had become a laughing stock in the diving circle, saying she was a bad diver, saying that everyone joked about her.'

'Penny wouldn't do that.'

'Christie says that during the walk in the forest she felt as though she was underwater and drowning. That she couldn't breathe and that Penny would not help her.'

'I don't believe that. Penny would have helped.'

'Christie then says that everything went black and the next thing she can remember is seeing Penny on the ground.'

The two detectives looked at each other and then left the room, leaving McAllister to sit and think alone. When they returned they appeared different men. 'Right, that's it. We'll just write a statement based on the interview. You can go.'

Duncan was nonplussed. He could not believe what he had heard. Then one said, 'We know we put you under pressure but it's our job to do that. I'm sorry we had to be so rough. To show there's no hard feelings we'd like to take you for a beer.'

Duncan replied, 'I understand you have a job to do. There are no hard feelings.'

'By the way,' one said, 'one small point. The boots you bought for Susan, were they short, brown ones with a small heel and a ruffled effect at the top?'

'Yes, why?'

'Because the bitch was wearing them when we charged her. I make no bones about the fact that I don't really like you, but I don't have to. Having said that, I hate that murdering bitch more. She's been telling us a load of bullshit since day one. I think she knows damn well what she did. She's not sorry one little bit.'

Duncan asked whether Susan had admitted to the murder.

'She says she can't remember. She just keeps saying, "I can't remember" in that silly annoying English accent of hers. She's a cunning little bitch all right.'

'So you don't believe she's depressed or ill, then?'

'Is she fuck. We have a saying: "She's bad, not mad." I didn't think much else has to be said.'

Waiting for Justice

★ ★ ★

Susan Christie spent days with detectives, spinning them a web of intrigue concerning Duncan, Penny and herself. She would talk to them for hours, explaining away everything that had happened, from the moment she had first set eyes on Duncan McAllister more than a year before.

She told the detectives how everything that had happened had somehow been due to someone else's actions or behaviour, accepting no responsibility for anything that had occurred. To a great extent Susan Christie appeared to enjoy the attention she received from the police, from the moment she had been taken to the police station for questioning at 9 a. m. on

Saturday 30 March twelve hours after she had explained to Duncan, in floods of tears, how she had fought off the man who had attacked and attempted to rape her, and who had murdered Penny in cold blood.

She enjoyed the way the detectives, the senior officers and the police officers treated her. She appeared to revel in the fact they would come to see her, to have a look at the young army private who had become the chief suspect in the brutal killing of a British army captain's beautiful wife. Susan Christie would eat the food placed before her with relish, enjoy the endless cups of tea and coffee offered her, and on many occasions the detectives could hardly stop her talking. She needed no encouragement to tell her story.

She would laugh and joke with the detectives and wanted to become a friend to the woman police constable who was assigned to her, chatting to her non-stop. Susan Christie would be in a happy, ebullient mood most of the time, showing not a jot of remorse or sorrow for Penny McAllister.

Susan Christie told her story with confidence and attention to detail, happy to add any anecdotes the detectives asked for. Time and again, as Susan told and retold her story to the detectives, she would tell them, emotion in her voice, 'I will never, never forget that man's face.'

Her demeanour would change only when they cross-examined her about the details of Penny's actual murder, urging her to describe the incident, the attacker, the circumstances. Then she would go to pieces, break down, the tears flowing down her face, making any conversation impossible. The sobbing would continue until the detectives were forced to terminate the interview and leave Susan with a woman police officer so she could compose herself.

By mid-morning on that Saturday, however, three days after Penny's murder, police were convinced Susan Christie was the killer. They were not sure, however, that she had acted alone. Understandably, they were suspicious, deeply suspicious, that Duncan McAllister had also been involved. They had to consider the possibility that Susan and Duncan had acted in concert to be rid of Penny. It would not have been the first time that a lover and his mistress had plotted together to commit murder to be rid of an unwanted wife.

It was at this stage that the detectives told Christie that Captain Duncan McAllister had gone to see them and admitted having a nine-month-long affair with her. Susan was stunned by their statement. At first she denied it, but then realized that Duncan's admission would make police realize that she had a motive, a very strong motive, for killing Penny.

She told the detectives, 'All right, it's true. I'll tell you everything.'

Susan then went into every detail of her affair. She could not stop talking. She happily revealed everything to the police. She also told them that

Penny had had full knowledge of what had been going on. She went even further, telling the police that Penny had also taken lovers, both officers and soldiers, while she had been in Northern Ireland.

She explained to the police that Penny and Duncan had practised what they called 'an open marriage', meaning that they would take lovers whenever they wished but without the adultery compromising their marriage. She claimed Duncan had told her this and that this was why Penny was apparently not bothered about their affair. Later, police would check Christie's allegations concerning Penny. They found not an iota of evidence suggesting Penny had ever had an affair with anyone.

It was at this stage that Susan Christie changed her story. The attacker, the man whose face she said she would never forget, disappeared, never to resurface in her story of the attack. From that moment on, Susan Christie would say that at the time of the murder her mind had gone blank and she could remember nothing. Whatever ruse the detectives tried, whatever pressure they applied, Susan Christie refused to admit to murdering Penny, although she would not deny it either. She would simply repeat, over and over again, 'I just don't remember anything, anything at all.'

She would repeat, time and again, 'My mind's a blank; I can't remember what happened. All I remember is seeing Penny on the ground with the blood pouring from her neck. But it couldn't have been me because I would never do anything like that to Penny.'

She was never to change this story.

At the Maghaberry remand centre in Lisburn, where Susan Christie was detained awaiting trial, she enjoyed her celebrity status. She would always laugh and joke with the staff as well as the probation officers on duty.

At first Christie was reticent towards the other inmates, but not for long. Soon she had become one of them, wishing those going to trial 'good luck' and commiserating with those, like her, who were having to wait months for their trials.

Susan Christie could, however, rely on the full support of her father, who was permitted to see and talk in private with his daughter every week. She needed his presence, his comforting understanding, his encouragement. And he was only too happy once again to be wanted and needed by the daughter he loved.

Those who witnessed their meetings in Maghaberry reported that Bob Christie seemed to take his daughter's murder charge and arrest far, far worse than Susan herself. He seemed cut up, distraught about what had happened. He was also angry that the authorities should have treated his daughter, as he put it, 'like a common criminal' while she was on remand.

Bob Christie would complain to anyone prepared to listen at the UDR barracks where he worked. He would seek their sympathy, suggesting the whole episode was really a huge mistake and that the blame for what had happened should rest mainly and principally on the shoulders of Captain McAllister.

Bob Christie would complain of the conditions in which his daughter was being held, not permitted to wear make-up, only permitted to wear specific coloured clothes and never permitted to eat bananas which, he explained, happened to be one of his daughter's favourite fruits.

During the first few weeks, following the initial shock of his daughter's arrest and murder charge, Bob Christie discovered many people who were prepared to stop and discuss his daughter's predicament with him. For a while he became the centre of attention in the barracks. But later, most people could not understand Sergeant-Major Christie's attitude to Penny's appalling murder, for he seemed interested only in the comfort and well-being of his daughter. They never heard him speak of the callous, brutal murder of Penny McAllister for which, quite possibly, his daughter had been totally, completely and solely responsible.

Only a few weeks after her arrest Susan Christie wrote to four soldier friends, all men, in the operations room at 11th UDR Headquarters where she had worked for the past six months. The letter provides a remarkable insight into the mind of Susan Christie at that time, facing a murder charge for which, if she was found guilty, she could expect to be given life imprisonment. Even with luck and remission for good conduct, she would still be facing twelve to fifteen years inside.

'No doubt I am the centre of gossip,' she wrote, 'but the only good thing to come out of this is that it has shown me my real friends.'

It went on, 'As this letter should really have been about what a great potential officer I was becoming, I'll tell you what a great potential model prisoner I am becoming ...'

She wrote that one girl in her block, from Andersonstown, 'has all the social graces of a retarded pig' but she dismissed most of the other prisoners because they were 'only petty criminals'. She also wrote, 'It can be very easy to turn into a living vegetable in prison. The only thing I have left is my sense of humour and on the days that I'm filled with self-pity and I'm ready to break down I just think of my mum and dad.'

She also chided her former squaddies: 'Hey, don't you forget that you guys still owe me that meal. I still want it and I also want the male stripper, so start saving for it (Grin!!)'

She ended, 'Take care and watch your backs, Love, Sue.'

Those last words, 'watch your backs' that Susan Christie wrote at the end of her letter were no accident. She had never used that phrase in everyday chat or when saying 'goodbye' to anyone. Everyone who knew her, and has read that letter, believes that she wrote that last phrase deliberately, as a joke. The phrase, however, revealed Susan Christie's attitude to the murder of Penny McAllister, her total lack of sympathy, remorse or feeling for the person whose life she took in such a cold-blooded manner. As a joke it was nothing but obscene.

Throughout the two-page, A4-size letter, Susan Christie did not write a single word of remorse or sorrow.

To Duncan McAllister, Penny's parents and in-laws, her brother Nick, her relations and her many friends in the army and in civvy street, Penny's death was distressing, tragic, heart-breaking. It took the people who had known Penny many, many months to come to terms with her gruesome murder.

In the weeks and months following the murder, Duncan McAllister had to hear some awesome truths. Penny's close friend, Clare Harrill, would tell Duncan some months after the murder of the miscarriage Penny had suffered when she realized the awful truth that Duncan was having an affair with Susan Christie. Duncan asked her one evening, 'I have to ask you one important question. Susan Christie told me that Penny had said that she had suffered a miscarriage. I didn't believe Susan because Penny hadn't ever said anything to me, nor had she ever said anything about it to her mother.'

'Yes, it's true,' Clare told him. 'She told me she had a miscarriage at the end of July, because of the anxiety caused by Susan's continuous attention towards you. Penny knew the game Susan was playing.'

'Did Penny tell you why she never told me?'

'She said that at the time she wasn't sure if you were having an affair. She wanted you to be with her because you loved her, not because you felt sorry for her losing the baby or because you thought you might lose your career if she said something. She feared you might think you had to stay with her because it was the honourable thing to do, not because you wanted to. She didn't want that.'

Duncan shook his head in disbelief and told Clare, 'I would never have left her. There was never any question of leaving her. It was never an option for me. Do you think she knew that?'

'Later on, yes,' Clare replied. 'For a time she was scared of losing you but she wanted you to love her the way she loved you. Her letters to me in the Gulf were much happier after New Year, and I think she knew you were trying to get out of the relationship with Susan.'

Duncan now knew for sure, for the first time, that Penny had been pregnant and had suffered a miscarriage. And she had borne it all alone, without telling him. Now he could do nothing but mull over what his life could have been with Penny, try to come to terms with his terrible sense of guilt, and wait for Christie's trial for murder.

It would prove a long wait.

Christie in the Dock

★ ★ ★

Susan Christie looked pale and drawn as she walked nervously into the dock at Downpatrick Crown Court on Monday 1 June 1992, flanked by a prison officer and a female warder.

Only an inch over five feet tall and wearing no make-up or lipstick, Christie seemed much younger than her twenty-three years. With her head bowed, her hair covering her forehead, shielding her eyes, she appeared timid and vulnerable, even coy. And she was visibly trembling. The intelligent, confident young army private, always so positive, self-assured and friendly, had all but disappeared. In the dock the jury saw a subdued, insecure, disorientated young woman.

She had dressed smartly in a pink blouse and a dark navy-blue suit, and appeared well scrubbed, with clean hair. But her hands, the nails bitten, betrayed her nervousness.

When asked how she pleaded, Christie replied in a trembling voice: 'Not guilty to murder, but guilty to manslaughter.'

Crown Prosecutor John Creaney, QC, outlined the case for the jury, claiming that Christie had murdered her lover's wife and then stabbed herself, sparking a huge manhunt after she told the police that they had been attacked by a mystery assailant. He explained how Penny McAllister was found dead with a stab wound in her neck at a remote part of Drumkeeragh Forest near Ballynahinch, where she had gone walking with Christie and her two pet dogs.

Mr Creaney told how Penny and Captain Duncan McAllister had been living in married quarters at an army base in Armagh while Christie, a full-time private with the Portadown-based 11th Battalion of the Ulster Defence Regiment, lived at home with her father in Lisburn.

He explained how Christie had joined a sub-aqua club where she first met Captain McAllister and, later, his wife Penny. He told how Christie had flirted, then fallen in love with McAllister and, after some time, agreed to have an affair with him, despite the fact that she was still a virgin at the time.

And he told how Christie and Captain

McAllister regularly had sex together without Mrs McAllister's knowledge.

Emphsizing his words, Mr Creaney said: 'When the evidence is analysed it can only lend itself to the interpretation that, having become embroiled with Captain McAllister and having reached a stage in that relationship where she regarded his wife as an obstacle, she determined to remove that obstacle.

'It had gone to the extent of seeking out a remote and infrequently visited forest area, going to that place and looking for a place which would suit such an attack.

'She had gone to the extent of inviting Mrs McAllister to come with her to that remote place and had gone to the extent of making sure they were in a part that was lonely, before she launched her attack with this knife upon her unsuspecting victim from behind.

And he told how, having murdered Mrs McAllister, Christie had then mutilated her own body and cut her clothes in a bid to back up her story that Mrs McAllister had been murdered by a mystery man, who had also attacked her.

Mr Creaney said that one week after the murder the accused had told police that she must have killed Mrs McAllister. And that Christie also told police she had become pregnant by Captain McAllister and had had a miscarriage. But Mr Creaney added: 'I do not believe this to be true.'

He stated: 'If ever there was a case where there

was evidence of premeditation and planning, this is it.'

And he read out details of an interview conducted by police with Christie shortly after the alleged murder, in which she said: 'I must have done it, but I do not remember it. There was no one else there. Oh God, I could not kill Penny. I have just blacked it out, I do not want to remember anything.'

Mr Joseph Corr, a senior scientific officer at the Northern Ireland Forensic Science Laboratory, went to the murder scene only a few hours after the attack and was shown the body of Penny McAllister. He was later shown a knife that had been found by police 260 yards from the body.

He told the court: 'I described the knife as a boning knife, usually used in a meat plant for boning sides of beef or large joints. It had a single-edge stainless-steel hollow ground blade and black moulded handle with a contoured grip.'

Mr Corr told how he discovered, from examination, that after being purchased the blade had been honed, so that it had an extremely keen edge. The knife was 25.5 centimetres long (10 inches), the blade being 12 centimetres (5 inches) long, which tapered from a maximum width of 2.5 centimetres at the hilt through the cutting edge to a point.

Mr Corr explained that Sarah Christie's blood was type B and Penny McAllister had group O. And that blood found on the right cuff of Susan Chustie's blue waxed cotton jacket had come from group O, Penny's blood grouping.

Summing up his evidence, Mr Corr told the jury: 'I would be of the opinion that Penelope McAllister had been attacked by surprise from behind. It would look like she had been grabbed by the coat and hair because her left ear-ring had been pulled off and the spring clip broken off and her head pulled back, exposing her throat, which was then sliced open in one swift movement.

'She probably went into an immediate state of unconsciousness as there is no evidence of a struggle or fight and no defence wounds were present on the hands. A considerable quantity of blood spurted from the body before it was laid down on the pine needles. She had been let down gently by her assailant, first to a sitting position and then laid down. Her arms had been arranged in position by the killer before leaving.'

Dr Patrick McGrath told the court how he had been called to a house in Ballynahinch, where he had seen Susan Christie lying on the floor in a doorway between the kitchen and a utility room, a blanket across the lower part of her body.

He said: 'She was very distressed, crying uncontrollably, sobbing, and she appeared shocked. She was wearing a blue waxed cotton coat and a grey sweat shirt, heavily stained with blood. She was also wearing black leather-type gloves, dark-coloured tracksuit trousers and trainers.'

Susan Christie complained of a pain in her neck and shoulders and a pain in her left leg. And she told the doctor she had been attacked and stabbed by a man in Drumkeeragh Forest. She took down her tracksuit trousers, revealing a small wound on her left thigh.

Dr McGrath also noticed that her underpants had been ripped apart and were slightly bloodstained. He then told how he had cleaned and dressed the abrasions and scratches on her left thigh. He also noted that when Susan removed her gloves, both hands were covered in blood. He searched for injuries to the hands but found none.

Susan had complained of neck and back pains, but Dr McGrath could again find no obvious injuries, save for a soft-tissue injury of her neck. An X-ray examination at Down Hospital, Downpatrick, later that night found no fractures, but she was supplied with a cervical collar.

As a result of a further examination of Susan Christie three days later, Dr McGrath came to the conclusion that scratches on her left thigh had been self-inflicted.

The next professional witness would be Dr Jack Crane, a pathologist, whose gruesome detailed description of the killing would cause Susan Christie all but to collapse in the dock.

Dr Crane, the Northern Ireland State Pathologist and a lecturer in forensic medicine at Queen's University, Belfast, told the court: 'There was an incision crossing the front and right side of Penny McAllister's neck. It was ten centimetres (four inches) and gaped open up to three centimetres; it crossed the front of the neck curving upwards and to the right and ended one centimetre in front of the ear. Underlying muscles, blood vessels, the larynx and the jugular vein were all severed.'

He said: 'A sharp-bladed instrument had been drawn across the front and right side of the neck, causing a deep gaping incision about four inches in length ...'

A noise from the dock drew the attention of the jury and others in court, for Susan Christie was trying to stop herself crying. Her hunched shoulders heaved and sank as she continued to sob. Dr Crane looked over and then continued his evidence. 'The voice box and the upper part of the gullet had been partially incised and the right main artery and jugular vein divided.'

Asked how quickly death had occurred, Dr Crane said: 'Death would not have been immediate. In my opinion it probably would have taken several minutes. She would probably have lost consciousness within a minute.'

As the pathologist finished speaking, Susan Christie slumped forward and the two female prison officers had to hold her to prevent her falling to the floor. She was sobbing uncontrollably. Judge Kelly suspended the hearing for fifteen minutes so that Christie could leave the courtroom to compose herself. Susan had difficulty in walking and had to be supported out of the courtroom. In a side room she all but collapsed again and could not stop sobbing and crying, having to catch her breath as the tears streamed down her face. A doctor was called and Susan was examined. But the sobbing and the anguish continued.

The doctor left the room while others tended Susan Christie and the judge was informed by court clerks that Christie could not control her emotions and that the doctor advised the hearing should be adjourned for the day.

Fifteen minutes after the interruption, Judge Kelly told the jury of eight men and four women that a doctor had advised that Christie was 'medically unfit to continue'. He would therefore adjourn the case until the next day.

On the morning of Wednesday 3 June, Susan Christie's lover, Captain Duncan McAllister, would begin his evidence as his young mistress sat in the dock, tearful and shaking, sometimes openly crying when he spoke of the intimate details of their passionate love affair. McAllister stood stiffly to attention as he took the oath and barely glanced at Susan Christie sitting in the dock. In turn, however, she would occasionally look, though only briefly, at the man whom she had loved with an intensity she had never known before in her life.

She listened as the two barristers openly discussed with her lover all the most intimate aspects of their love for each other, often in embarrassing sexual detail. Susan Christie hated the idea of the court, the press, the public in the gallery hearing all about the love that for nine months she had kept secret from the world.

Duncan told the jury that he was a captain in the Royal Signals, serving in Northern Ireland and living in married quarters in Armagh City. He said he and Penny had married in 1985 but had no children. McAllister told how one of his favourite hobbies was sub-aqua diving and that in February 1990 he had formed a club, and that Penny became the secretary though she hardly ever dived herself. He became the sub-aqua diving supervisor.

And he told of the first time he met Susan Christie in March 1990: 'We held open nights at the diving club where people who were interested in taking up the sport would come along and we would discuss with them the organization of the club and the training entailed. They would then decide if they wanted to join. Susan Christie was introduced by an army friend, Annette Gascoigne.'

McAllister revealed that Susan Christie soon became an enthusiastic member, buying all the necessary equipment, including an aqualung. Captain McAllister said that at the very beginning of their sexual relationship, in July 1990, he had made it clear that there was no intention to continue their relationship once he had left Northern Ireland: 'I told her that our affair would never lead me to leave my wife or affect my marriage.'

He told of the ill-fated diving expedition to the Ascension Islands in October 1990 when both Penny and Susan Christie, along with other members of the club, went diving for ten days off the islands. And McAllister told the court of the sexual activities Susan and he indulged in during the trip. He also hinted of Susan's jealousy at that time. 'Susan Christie sometimes made statements of fact that she felt that I did not pay her enough attention if Penny was around, or that she could get upset if I would not do things because I said I could not do them in case it aroused suspicions in my wife. And I think she resented that in some ways.'

Susan Christie became distressed in the dock as prosecuting counsel quizzed McAllister about the time Christie told him at the end of October that she had become pregnant. The court could hear Christie sobbing quietly as McAllister gave his evidence of the pregnancy, saying, 'Obviously Susan Christie was very distraught that she was pregnant and it came as a bit of a surprise because she said she was on the pill. I talked her through it and I obviously said there were certain options that could be taken, but at the end of the day it was her choice.'

And he outlined his alternatives to the court. 'They were obviously that she could have the child and name me the father; or that she could have the child and I would pay for the maintenance but not actually accept the child as my own; or, thirdly, she would have to accept that an abortion would be required.'

Counsel asked McAllister: 'Did you say

anything about what you intended to do so far as your wife was concerned despite the pregnancy?'

He replied: 'I made it very clear that I would not leave my wife despite the pregnancy.'

Captain McAllister did not once look at his former mistress when he told the court of the miscarriage Susan Christie had suffered in early December. She had phoned him, saying she had felt unwell while on duty, had visited a hospital and stayed overnight when informed by doctors she had had a miscarriage.

Prosecuting counsel asked McAllister: 'Did your relationship, that is your sexual relationship, further continue after this matter of her pregnancy?'

McAllister replied: 'It did, but not to the intensity that it had done prior to that, my lord.'

But he admitted that they continued to have intercourse together.

McAllister was then asked whether he had spoken to Christie after the murder of his wife. He told the court they had met and talked about Penny's death the day after. He said: 'Following a long conversation I asked Susan if she had been involved in any way whatsoever ... She went hysterical and said, "No, no, how could you believe such a thing?" I just told her that I had to be sure.'

Captain McAllister admitted that during the discussions they decided they would not disclose the fact that he and Christie were having an affair. And he told the jury of the final meeting he had with Christie, when they had agreed, once again, not to reveal to police they were lovers.

Under cross-examination by Mr Peter Smyth, Christie's lawyer, McAllister was asked what the army's attitude was to officers having sexual relationships with female soldiers who were not commissioned. He replied: 'The situation is that it is not recommended and there are obviously guidelines for what action should be taken should an affair be found out or should surface.'

Asked what the guidelines were, McAllister replied, 'Different actions can be taken, but the officer can be asked to resign his commission or disciplinary action can be taken. There are two types of action, administrative and disciplinary.'

Mr Smyth pressed the point and McAllister appeared annoyed. In answer to further questions, McAllister agreed that the army 'would take a dim view indeed' of a sexual relationship between a married officer and a female private soldier. Captain McAllister also accepted there was a disparity, a social disparity, between Susan Christie's background and his own because Christie's father was a non-commissioned officer.

McAllister was then asked about the start of his love affair with Susan Christie, when they both realized they were attracted to each other. He said a discussion had taken place in which he outlined the 'negative aspects' of such an affair, telling her: 'It came down to the fact that within an affair with a married man there would most probably be no outcome because I was not willing to leave my wife.

'Other aspects were our rank differences; that we would not associate in the same places; that I could not be seen with her in public places. That the way our relationship would work would be that there would be no phone calls to my home. I would never write to her or communicate by letter or anything of that sort.'

To those in court, McAllister's words sounded cold and very calculating.

McAllister told the court that when they began their affair he had not asked Christie about any other relationships she may have experienced and did not know she was a virgin. He found that out only later.

McAllister was asked: 'Did you consider the possibility that she might fall in love with you?' He replied, 'At that stage, no.'

Several women in court drew in their breath sharply as McAllister said that he had not bothered to consider the possibility of Susan falling in love with him because he had made it obvious theirs would not be a lasting relationship. He agreed, however, that three months after they first had sex together — at the end of October 1990 — he realized she was in love with him.

'And did you tell her that you loved her?' Mr Smyth demanded. 'Yes I did,' was the answer.

'And did you love her?' he queried. McAllister replied: 'I loved her in what could be termed a

253

friendship way or as a friend, my lord.'

For several minutes Mr Smyth continued his line of questioning and McAllister looked uneasy as defence counsel probed his description of his love for his mistress.

'When you were having intercourse with Susan Christie, did you tell her that you loved her?' he was asked. McAllister replied firmly: 'No, my lord.'

Smyth pressed him: 'You never told her that you loved her when you were having intercourse with her?' McAllister backed down slightly: 'Not as far as I can recall, no.'

Smyth pressed harder: 'When you were being affectionate with each other did you tell her that you loved her?' This time McAllister answered: 'I may well have done.'

McAllister claimed that whenever he told Susan Christie that he loved her he would qualify the statement by adding: 'I love you, but not in the same way I love Penny.' Some in the public gallery looked at each other and frowned when they heard the captain's reply. In the dock Susan Christie could be heard sobbing.

Under further cross-examination, however, McAllister accepted there would probably have been occasions when he told Susan that he loved her and that he did not qualify it.

Captain McAllister was then questioned about the expedition to the Ascension Islands when he was accompanied by both Penny and Susan. Mr Smyth asked him: 'You were enthusiastic about Susan Christie at this time?' McAllister replied 'No,' but admitted he was then very fond of her.

'And keen to have sex with her?' McAllister answered, 'No. Basically because my wife was in Ascension with us.'

'But your wife had been in Northern Ireland with you?' he was asked. 'Yes,' he agreed, 'but you are not all living in the same building. At that time I was trying to play down our relationship.'

Asked whether he had sex in Ascension with Susan Christie, McAllister replied, 'Yes, we did have sex there.' And he agreed it was on a number of occasions during the ten-day expedition.

And he was cross-examined over little drawings in Christie's diving log — pictures of the sun with a smiling face — which McAllister drew, a code signalling their love for each other. But McAllister denied that, claiming it did not mean love but only a reassurance about their relationship.

He was asked categorically: 'And although you did not love her you encouraged her in her love because you wanted to continue to have intercourse with her?' McAllister did not deny that, but replied: 'I have never said I did not love her.'

McAllister was then asked why he had later put double gold stars under his signature in Christie's log. 'I put it there because during this dive Susan Christie and myself had sexual intercourse under water, my lord.'

Judge Kelly intervened, asking: 'What did the gold star mean?' And McAllister answered: 'I actually cannot remember why I put that down.'

'And the double gold star meant that you had sex under water?' he was asked. 'No, that is not what I meant,' he replied. 'I am just saying that in that dive that is what happened and why I put those double gold stars there I cannot remember.'

'It is a very strange thing to put in a diving log?' McAllister agreed and added: 'Most probably it was because the dive that day on the China wreck was a very, very good dive with lots of fish life.'

McAllister was asked about a later dive at White Rock with Susan Christie, after which she wrote in her log: 'Sunny day, really sunny day.' Mr Smyth claimed that was a reminder from Susan to McAllister of her love for him. McAllister thought it was a reminder of what happened on the dive because they had exchanged intimate caresses. He explained: 'There was no sexual intercourse but in the dive there was like swimming upside down and messing around in the water and things like that. It was very much a fun dive.'

Asked who wrote 'Mickey the Moray' in the log, McAllister answered: 'Well, I wrote "Mickey the Moray".' And he explained: 'Mickey the Moray' was a name that Susan Christie had given to a certain part of my body. We adopted that phrase because of what Susan told me she had decided to call a certain appendage of my body, a reference to my penis.'

It was the only time that day when tension in the court lifted, as laughter rippled around the public gallery whenever reference was made to 'Mickey the Moray'.

The following day, 4 June, defence counsel Peter Smyth continued his cross-examination of Captain McAllister and began by asking him of Susan Christie's pregnancy.

Asked whether her pregnancy must have been a matter of considerable concern to him, McAllister replied: 'Yes,' agreeing that it greatly heightened the risk of exposing him as Susan Christie's lover. He acknowledged that Susan would come under pressure from her parents and possibly superior officers to indicate the father's identity.

As questions concerning the pregnancy, possible abortion and the miscarriage were being discussed in court, Susan Christie sat in the dock, holding her handkerchief, and often openly weeping, her eyes reddened by tears.

Three times under cross-examination McAllister denied that he had given Susan Christie three options of dealing with the pregnancy, but he later accepted that in his preliminary statement to police he had said, 'I told Sue she had three options.' Those in the public gallery looked at each other and some nodded as McAllister finally accepted, saying: 'If that is what I said then I must stand by what I said.'

Mr Smyth was making McAllister squirm. He had caught him out and would not let Susan Christie's lover off the hook: 'Not only have you agreed that these were your words used on a previous occasion but you have gone further than that and you have now adopted these words although these words were directly at variance with the evidence that you gave earlier under oath in the witness box.'

Asked to state the three options he gave Susan Christie, McAllister told the court: 'Firstly that she could continue with the pregnancy, have the child and say who the father was. The second one would have been obviously to have the child and then not divulge the identity of the father; and the third one would have been to have an abortion.'

Mr Smyth asked McAllister: 'If Susan Christie had opted for the first option, that she would have the child and say who the father was, that would have ruined your career and possibly ruined your marriage?' He replied: 'I think it would have ruined both our careers.'

Captain McAllister told the jury that at no time did he tell Susan Christie which option he preferred, but said that some days later she phoned and said she was going to have an abortion.'

Then Mr Smyth read out a statement McAllister had made to the police on 5 April 1991, eight days after Penny's murder: 'I told Sue that she had three options: One. An abortion, and I explained to her that was my preferred option. Two. She could have the baby, create a fictitious father and I would quietly support her. Three. Tell the truth and I would face the music but I would not leave Penny. Sue said she would think about it.'

Smyth then put it to McAllister: 'Do you accept that this is totally at variance with what you are saying this morning in that you have indicated to his lordship and members of the jury that you only indicated that the abortion was your preferred option after Susan Christie made her own decision?' McAllister looked embarrassed as he replied: 'I would agree with you that there seems to be a variance.' But he added: 'I would not agree it is fundamentally different to what I said today.'

McAllister denied that he had given Susan Christie a telephone number so she could phone and arrange an abortion. Mr Smyth continued: 'I suggest to you that her position was that she did not want an abortion; that she wanted to have the child; that she made it clear to you she wanted to have your child?'

McAllister replied, 'No. She said that she was faced with a decision; that she did not like the idea of having an abortion; but that she would actually make a decision based on what she thought was correct at the time.'

And Mr Smyth told the jury that Susan Christie would give evidence that there were not three options but only two; one was an abortion and the other one was that she could have the child and that McAllister would deny everything. McAllister said: 'Then our evidence would be in conflict, my lord.' Captain McAllister told the court that he did not know Susan

Christie was miscarrying until after she had lost the baby. He claimed she had phoned him only after she had miscarried.

Asked if he accepted that after the pregnancy and the miscarriage Susan Christie was emotionally stressed, McAllister replied: 'I think initially straight away, the first twenty-four hours, perhaps forty-eight hours, yes she was. But I think after that it could have been a relief.'

Mr Smyth asked rather incredulously: 'You do not perceive her or understand her to have any emotional needs after the first twenty-four hours?' He replied: 'After the first twenty-four hours I would not really say that she particularly spoke about it or was emotionally upset about it.'

Pointedly, Mr Smyth asked: 'I have to suggest to you that that is just arrant nonsense, that Susan Christie repeatedly brought up her distress about losing your child?' He replied: 'No, she did not, my lord.'

Smyth continued: 'I suggest to you that Susan Christie tried to bring up with you time and time again her feelings about the loss of the child and that you were more or less pushing her aside with: "Don't spoil it. We have got very little time together. Do not spoil it by bringing up these emotional issues"; something which you did not want to address, Captain McAllister?' In a detached voice, McAllister answered: 'I am afraid that that is not the case, no, my lord.'

But Mr Smyth would not be side-tracked. He went on: 'I want to suggest to you that you wanted to go on having sex with her; that you did not love her; that as you have indicated to the members of the jury that you only loved her as a friend; that you found her emotional admissions at this time after the pregnancy tiresome and that you just pushed them aside.'

McAllister replied: 'No, I would disagree, my lord. First of all I have not said that I did not love her. I did love her. I was very fond of her but not in the same way as I loved my wife. I did not find her tiresome. I realized that obviously because of the supposed miscarriage that she would be under stress. It would have been very easy for me at that stage to have ended everything. I did not do so because I felt that she needed support at that time.'

McAllister told the court that after the initial conversation with Christie after her miscarriage he never discussed the matter with her again, and never raised the matter in conversation.

Mr Smyth asked him: 'So it came to this. You never raised specifically the pregnancy or the question of the miscarriage with her in the week after it happened and you can never remember her raising it with you?'

He replied simply, 'No.'

Mr Smyth suggested that Captain McAllister continued his relationship with Christie because he knew they only had a few weeks and months together before she would leave Northern Ireland to go on an officers' training course. He asked him, 'There was a need for secrecy so far as your wife was concerned, Captain McAllister, and there was a need for secrecy so far as the army was concerned?' McAllister agreed.

He made another suggestion to Captain McAllister: that McAllister was the only person Susan Christie could talk to and he was turning his back on her; that he was prepared to have sex with her, prepared to meet her, but not prepared to address any of the emotional overtones of the relationship. McAllister replied coolly, 'That is not what happened, my lord.'

Duncan McAllister told the court that at no stage from the beginning of December 1990 until the end of March 1991 could he recollect any significant emotional conversations about his affair with Susan Christie, claiming that their meetings lasted only an hour or so and there was no time for in-depth conversations.

He admitted sending Susan flowers on St Valentine's Day, despite the fact that he was away in Germany with his wife at that time. 'I sent the flowers to Susan the day before I went away,' he said. But he did agree that he had phoned Susan on St Valentine's Day when away on holiday with his wife.

McAllister claimed that Susan Christie knew there was no long-term hope in their relationship, despite receiving flowers and phone calls. He said: 'I stated at all times and I qualified it at all times that there was not any future for us.' He claimed that

Susan was fully aware what was going to happen, commenting, 'At no time did she ever indicate that she thought that the relationship would ever go beyond Northern Ireland.'

He claimed that he had made it quite clear he was going to walk away from the affair despite the fact he was telling her that he loved her and Susan was telling him that she loved him. He added: 'I made it quite clear that I was not going to leave my wife and that I did not love her in the same way as I loved my wife.'

Mr Smyth suggested to McAllister: 'What you did was to turn your face away from Susan Christie. She became tiresome to you and the emotional side of the matter became tiresome to you and you did not want to listen to her problems and you wanted to pretend to yourself that she was going to be able to walk away and you were intending to walk away?'

McAllister replied: 'What I had decided was that the relationship was going to end but what she decided, I cannot say, my lord.'

There was a stillness in court and Susan Christie stemmed her tears as Mr Smyth began questioning Captain McAllister about the circumstances surrounding the murder of his wife, Penny.

'In March 1991 it is obvious that your wife and Susan Christie appeared to be on reasonable terms,' Mr Smyth asked. 'They were on speaking terms,' McAllister corrected him.

'Susan Christie would say that they were on

reasonable terms and will say that your wife had mentioned that she suspected that something was going on to you and that you reassured your wife.' Sternly, McAllister replied, 'No, she did not.'

'That never happened?'

McAllister answered, 'No, my wife never mentioned that to me.'

'She never expressed any suspicions?'

McAllister replied, 'No, my lord.'

'Or never expressed any doubts?'

Again McAllister replied, 'No, my lord.'

'She noticed nothing?'

Again, he replied, 'No.'

Mr Smyth cross-examined McAllister about the last weekend he and Susan Christie spent together, a weekend in March when Penny went to visit a friend in Dublin. Susan took leave so she could spend the time at Captain McAllister's home in Armagh City. Susan Christie would be going to Beaconsfield on 2 April for three months and Captain McAllister would be leaving Northern Ireland to take up duties in Germany in the summer of 1991.

Captain McAllister was asked to tell the jury what the atmosphere was like during the course of that weekend. He replied: 'I would say that on the Friday night it was just a normal night. I think we just sat watching a video. It was just a very ordinary evening. We then went diving on the Saturday as per normal. We were out all day and it was quite sunny and we drove down to the dive and afterwards we came back. It was quite a pleasant evening. Later we had a discussion about Susan going away in which Susan said she would miss me.'

Under cross-examination McAllister admitted that during the weekend Susan told him she loved him and he told her that he loved her.

'Was she distressed in anyway?'

McAllister replied, 'Yes, I believe she had a tear in her eye.'

In an incredulous voice, Mr Smyth said, 'A tear in her eye?'

'Yes.'

'You perceived a tear in her eye?'

Again he said, 'Yes.'

'That was about the height of it, was it?'

'Yes.'

Mockingly, Mr Smyth continued: 'Did the tear trickle down her cheek?' McAllister said he could not remember.

He was asked whether Susan Christie had any tissues out, and after prevaricating, McAllister eventually said, 'Yes.'

Mr Smyth suggested that Susan Christie was in tears for most of that weekend. McAllister disagreed. But he did agree that Susan was telling him that she was in love with him and he told her he also loved her. But he added: 'Again qualifying.'

Captain McAllister maintained that when Susan asked about returning to Northern Ireland to visit him, he stressed that their relationship would have to be a platonic one.

'And did she just accept that?'

McAllister replied, 'Yes, she seemed to accept it.'

'And you thought that the affair had been neatly brought to an end?'

'I thought,' McAllister replied, 'that it was a good time for reflection and that maybe the affair would not continue, yes.'

'And you are saying with equanimity she seemed to be walking away from you, the relationship being virtually over?'

He replied: 'Well, she did not come out with any of the classic lines which you would expect her to say if she was not going to accept that that was the way things were going to be.'

'And on the Sunday she is accepting it and she is quiet and calm and composed?'

'Yes, she was, actually,' McAllister replied.

'And on Wednesday she kills your wife?'

McAllister replied calmly, 'Well, that is what the accusation is.'

Mr Smyth continued: 'You see, I suggest to you that the juxtaposition of those two events is so bizarre that the first is just not so, that she was distressed at the weekend and that you know perfectly well that she was distressed?'

He answered, 'No, she was not distressed, my lord.'

'And you are denying this because you wish to distance yourself from any moral responsibility for what happened?'

He replied: 'No, I am not, my lord.'

'I put it to you, Captain McAllister, that she was frustrated and angry with your attitude over that weekend?'

He replied, 'No, she was not.'

Captain McAllister told the court that following his wife's murder he had had several conversations with Susan Christie and they agreed that their affair should be kept secret from the police. He knew Susan Christie would see the police the following morning, Saturday 30 March, and he knew she would have no time to see her friend Sandra Gordon, to warn her to keep their affair secret.

As Captain McAllister left the witness box he seemed to have lost much of the confidence that he had exuded when he began his evidence the previous day.

Susan Christie watched as her former lover left the box, a handkerchief to her face, her eyes still red from the tears she had shed as she listened to his account of their love affair.

The Killing Revisited

★ ★ ★

Susan Christie appeared hesitant as she left the dock at Down Crown Court and walked across the floor of the courtroom to the witness box. She seemed smaller than the young woman who had sat for a week in the dock and listened to the prosecution case urging the jury to convict her of murdering Penny McAllister.
She had said to other inmates in prison that she realized the next few days in the witness box would determine whether she would spend only a few years behind bars or most of her life.

Often, during that first week of testimony, Susan Christie had been unable to control her emotions. She found herself sobbing, weeping unashamedly and sometimes near to fainting as she listened to the sickening evidence of the horrific killing she knew she had carried out.

For the two days when her lover Duncan had given evidence Susan had been unable to tell how she felt towards the man she would have gladly given her life for. She had told friends how she had looked at him in the witness box and could not believe the things he said about their love affair, an affair that had totally consumed her. 'Some of the time I believe I am listening to a different person, a stranger,' she had told friends back at the jail after those days in court. 'It wasn't Duncan speaking, it couldn't have been.'

Now it was her turn to tell the judge and the jury what she felt had really gone on in those months when she had fallen in love with Duncan, of their affair and of her relationship with Penny, a woman whom she had counted as a rival and later claimed was a friend. Determined to put the record straight, she now wanted the world to know the truth of her love for Duncan and, more importantly, the real extent of his love for her.

Her counsel, Peter Smyth, had taken her gently through her life from her date of birth, 6 August 1968, her schooling, and her life as a Greenfinch, a private with the Ulster Defence Regiment. He led her through the time she joined the Drumadd Divers Sub-Aqua Diving Club in February 1990, a military club run by a British Army officer stationed in Ulster,

Captain Duncan McAllister. She told how in the early months of joining the club she found Captain McAllister to be jolly, and perfect at everything he did. 'I mean he could do nothing wrong,' she explained. 'He was good at everything. I really liked him. And he seemed to like me as well. We got on very well and we had a lot in common.'

She told how she had met Penny McAllister, also a member of the club, and of Penny's attitude to her.

'Duncan told me once that Penny was jealous of me,' she said.

In a quiet, sometimes inaudible voice Susan told of falling in love with Duncan McAllister, and, although a virgin at the time, agreeing to have an affair with him. And she told of their love. Her voice would become more confident when she spoke of their affair, as though gaining confidence from the relationship which had ended in tragedy.

Asked what her attitude to Captain McAllister would have been in August and September 1990, after they became lovers, Susan said: 'I was very much in love with him. I mean he was all I ever thought about.' She went on, her voice dropping, 'Well, at the time I thought he was in love with me, my lord.' Asked whether he ever said anything to her, she replied, 'He told me that he was in love with me.'

Mr Smyth asked: 'Captain McAllister has told the court that he loved you as a friend, that he would make it clear to you that it was not the same sort of love as between a man and a woman. What do you say to that?' She replied adamantly, 'He never said that to me, no. He told me that he loved me.' Barely audibly, she added, 'And I believed him.' Susan agreed, however, that McAllister also told her that he was in love with his wife, Penny.

Mr Smyth then asked: 'Miss Christie, did he ever say to you that his love was of a different quality or that it was of a different type than the love he felt for his wife?'

She replied, 'No, my lord.'

Susan Christie was asked about the diving expedition to the Ascension Islands in October 1990 when she and Penny were the only young women among a group of a dozen army personnel taking part. She commented, 'I was very much in love with him, but due to Penny coming along I felt very uncomfortable.'

Mr Smyth probed: 'And what about his attitude to you?' She replied, 'Duncan said he still loved me but that he could not express it as well as he did before because we were so closely living together and Penny would be there all the time.' But Susan Christie admitted she had behaved badly to Penny during the trip, saying, 'I was very cool to her.' She added, 'Later, because Penny and I were the only two females there, we became close and we more or less became friends.' Asked whether Penny had ever accused her of having an affair with her husband, Susan told the court, 'No, Penny approached Duncan. She never once accused me, my lord.'

Mr Smyth asked, 'Did she ever say anything to you or suggest to you or raise this matter with you?' She replied, 'No. She told me that she was jealous of me and of my friendship with Duncan because of the way we acted around each other.'

In answer to a question, Susan Christie claimed that Duncan had told her that Penny had asked him if he was having an affair with her. Mr Smyth continued, 'And did he tell you on one occasion or more than one occasion?' She replied, 'Oh, on several occasions he talked about it. And he told me that he denied to Penny having an affair with me.'

Asked whether Penny was aware of anything between Duncan and Susan, she replied, 'If Penny was, then she never showed it to me. She was not that sort of person.'

Later, during her evidence, Susan Christie broke down weeping when asked about her pregnancy and miscarriage.

Asked whom she told when she discovered she had become pregnant, Susan replied, 'I told Duncan McAllister. He was alarmed at first and then became more worried about me, that I might run and tell my family.' Asked to explain further, Susan went on, 'He did not want me to go and tell my mum and dad that I was pregnant before we had talked things through, my lord.'

Mr Smyth asked, 'And what was his attitude?' Tears welled in Susan Christie's eyes and she struggled to answer, fighting back tears. 'Duncan said that I could either have an abortion and he would support me emotionally afterwards, or, that I could keep the baby but that if I did so I would have to leave the diving club and never talk to him again, and, that if I said that he was the father he would deny it. He also told me that he would be shipping out immediately from Ulster and that I would never see him again.'

After sipping from a glass of water and wiping the tears from her eyes, she listened as Mr Smyth went on, 'Captain McAllister has said in evidence there were three options.' Christie said, more crisply, 'No, he is lying.' She went on: 'He told me that if I said he was the father he would deny it and he would never leave Penny for me.'

Asked directly whether she wanted the baby, Susan Christie replied, 'I wanted the baby.'

'And what was Captain McAllister's attitude?' She answered, 'He wanted me to have an abortion.'

Again Susan Christie looked close to breaking down. She began to cry as she added, speaking in a whisper, 'He wanted to give me some telephone numbers that he found in the *Belfast Telegraph*, but I would not take them.'

Mr Smyth asked, 'Captain McAllister has said that you had spoken to your doctor, but that he told you it was too early for an abortion?' Susan Christie replied, 'I told him that because I did not want an abortion. He wanted one but I didn't.'

'So that wasn't true?' She replied, 'No, that was a lie. I thought that in time he would accept the baby.'

Asked about McAllister's attitude to her at that time, Susan replied, 'He kept telling me that if I loved him I would have an abortion.'

Tears began to course down her cheeks again as she told the court of the miscarriage she suffered in early December. Sobbing as she spoke, Susan Christie told how she had phoned Captain McAllister, telling him she believed she was suffering a miscarriage. He had replied, 'Don't let your parents find out. Don't let anybody find out.'

Asked what support Captain McAllister offered after the miscarriage, Susan Christie replied through her tears, 'He held me while I cried, my lord.'

'And did you talk to him about your feelings?' She answered, 'No, I just could not stop crying.' She went on, 'I wanted to talk to him about my feelings but he kept saying that it was all over, that I had to forget it.'

Susan Christie then told the court how she had not seen much of Captain McAllister throughout December because he was working long hours. They would communicate by phone. When they began seeing more of each other in January 1991 the atmosphere became strained because she could not stop crying.

Asked why, she replied, 'Because I wanted our baby.' She went on, 'Every time I brought up the subject he kept saying, "It's over. You have got to forget it. You are over-emotional. It's nothing. You have to put it behind you."'

Asked whether she did manage to put the matter behind her, Susan Christie said, 'No, I could not. But he kept telling me, "You are going for a commission and you are going to be an officer. You do not show your feelings." '

Mr Smyth asked, 'And what were your feelings towards McAllister at this time?' She replied, 'I was angry that he would not listen to me. He was the only one who knew about everything. I still needed him and he was the only one that I knew, and I needed him. He told me that he loved me and that he wanted it to go back to the way that it had been.'

Susan Christie told the court the effect the miscarriage had on her as she prepared to go to Beaconsfield for the three-month course preparing her for officer training at Sandhurst. She explained, 'I could not motivate myself. I was losing a lot of weight. I felt constantly faint, very tired and sleepy. I even had to get smaller clothes and change my uniform from a size twelve to a size ten. I could not even bother talking to friends or going out. Some of my friends were complaining, thinking I had become a snob because I was to take a commission and I did not want to bother with any of them any more.'

Susan Christie was asked about her relationship with Captain McAllister when notified she would be going to Beaconsfield on 2 April 1991 for her course. She said, 'While I was away we planned to keep in touch with each other, by writing to each other. That I would ring him and hopefully see him at weekends when I returned home.'

And asked what the effect would be on their relationship when McAllister took up his new posting in Germany, Christie replied, 'When we started our affair he said that we would always stay in touch with each other no matter what and that we would always be friends, my lord.' She added, 'I was living in the hope that maybe he would leave Penny for me, but I was not really sure.'

'Did he ever indicate that he was prepared to do that in fact, Miss Christie?' She replied, 'Before I was pregnant we would talk about it.'

'And after that?' In a whisper, she answered, 'No.'

Susan Christie told how she resumed the relationship with Captain McAllister after he returned from the skiing holiday with Penny in February 1991, though they did not meet so often. But they did continue to have sex together. However, she confessed to being being unhappy most of the time. 'I was crying a lot. I was very moody.'

She told the court that she tried to talk to McAllister about their future from when he returned from skiing until the killing of Penny. But whenever they met he kept saying, 'Look, can we not talk about it later?' She said, 'Every time I tried to talk about our affair and where it was going I used to cry and he used to sort of draw away from me and say, "Look, I am not coming near you until you get control of yourself. Calm down."'

She said that McAllister continued to tell her that he loved her, but only after she pressurized him.

Susan Christie told the court of the time she believed Penny McAllister tried to kill her during a sub-aqua dive just eleven days before Penny's murder. She explained what happened: 'Penny was in the boat and I was diving with my friend Annette Gascoigne. I was scared because it was my first deep dive in dark waters. The only other time I had gone down deep was in the Ascension Islands where the water is far clearer.

'Duncan wanted us to dive to thirty metres but I did not want to go down that far. I was scared. I had to be very careful that I did not go down away past the diving tables. I only went as far as 19.1 metres.'

Susan Christie went on: 'When I came up and hit the surface I was screaming a lot at Annette and Penny shouted over to me to shut up and to start finning, swimming towards the boat with my feet.'

In answer to further questions she said, 'I was taking in a lot of water and we were going nowhere and I gave a distress signal. Penny was taking a long time to come to us and it crossed my mind that she was trying to kill me.'

Mr Smyth asked, 'Well, is there any substance whatsoever in that?' Susan replied, 'No. No, I mean she was not. I just felt at the time that she was trying to kill me.'

Christie said that after they clambered into the boat there was some talk about the incident, but it was quickly dropped.

Susan Christie was then asked about the long weekend she spent with Captain McAllister in his army married quarters just days before Penny was murdered. Penny had gone to Dublin for the weekend and McAllister invited Susan to stay.

Asked what the atmosphere had been like during the weekend, Susan replied, 'Well, it was good in the sense of the love-making aspect of it but, as for talking, not so good. I had planned to ask what was going to happen with our future but every time I brought it up, Duncan would say, "Look, let us not spoil the weekend. Let us have a nice time and we will discuss it later." '

She told how they had gone for a walk on the Sunday and Duncan had again said, 'We have had a wonderful weekend. Do not spoil it now.'

Mr Smyth asked: 'And what was your feeling when he adopted this attitude?' She replied, 'I was angry at him. I wanted to know where we stood and he would not tell me.'

She recalled that she had to pressurize McAllister into saying that he loved her but for her part she told the jury, 'I told him that I loved him and that I needed him.'

Mr Smyth asked her, 'In his evidence Captain McAllister said that during that last weekend together he made it clear that the affair was all over. Is that true?' Susan replied adamantly, 'No, he never. Duncan kept saying, "We will talk about it before you go to

Beaconsfield."' She went on: 'When the weekend was over I was angry at Duncan and I was upset. For me, that was to have been the weekend where I would know where I stood but I was none the wiser on the Monday, my lord.'

Speaking slowly, Mr Smyth asked Christie, 'You have said that you did tell him that weekend that you loved him and that you did love him even though you were angry at him. Was your emotional commitment to him in any way reduced by the time that you left him and for the succeeding two days?' She replied, 'No, I loved him. He was hurting me, but my love was so strong it was like a drug that you cannot do without.'

Susan Christie admitted that she phoned McAllister the next day to thank him for the weekend. Mr Smyth asked her: 'If the weekend was so unsatisfactory, in the sense that you were angry with him, why did you phone to thank him?' She replied, 'Because there was still the closeness between us. It was more like trying to grab hold of him and saying, "Look, I am still in love with you here."'

And then Susan Christie's counsel led her to the killing of Penny McAllister.

She admitted that it was her idea to take Penny and her dogs for a walk in Drumkeeragh Forest, though it was thirty miles from Armagh. She told how they had met at 11.30 on the morning of Wednesday 27 March; how they drove in convoy to the forest; parked their cars next to each other and set off, walking in a clockwise direction.

Susan Christie continued: 'We talked about diving, about what I intended to do in my army career, what Penny planned to do with her future and about the weekend she had just spent in Dublin.'

Asked about any argument they might have had, Christie replied, 'No, except for the diving incident of 16 March. We certainly talked about that.'

'Now Miss Christie,' Mr Smyth asked, 'what do you say about the allegation that you killed Mrs Penny McAllister in that forest on that afternoon?' She replied quietly, 'I accept it.'

'Do you remember anything about it?'

'I remember parts of it.'

'Do you remember having a knife?'

'No.'

'Do you remember anything about the knife at all?'

'No.'

'Do you remember anything about the actual killing of Mrs McAllister?'

'No.'

'Have you tried to remember?'

'Yes.'

'What was the last thing you can remember before you were aware that Mrs McAllister had been fatally injured?'

'I remember that we were walking along and Penny walked on ahead. I followed on and then she was lying on the ground and there was blood on her neck and I tried to stop the blood coming out.'

'And could you?'

'No. Then I ran. I ran. I ran and I left her all alone.' The court was silent for nearly a minute, everyone in the room looking at the diminutive, shaking figure of Susan Christie as she recounted how she had fled the killing scene, leaving Penny McAllister dying on the forest path.

Speaking slowly, Mr Smyth asked her quietly, 'Do you remember any part of the attack on Mrs McAllister?' Without looking up, Susan Christie, barely audible, replied, 'No.'

She was asked about the man she told police had attacked both her and Penny, but her voice could not be heard by the court as floods of tears streamed down her face. She said between tears, 'I was running from the forest ... my leg was sore ... when I left that forest I honestly believed ... we had been attacked and I did not believe it was me.' She remembered, however, preparing a photofit of her alleged attacker, drawing a picture for the police and giving a description of the man. And yet she could not remember inflicting injuries on herself. Asked about them, she said, 'No, all I can remember is them being there. I do not remember doing it.'

She told the court that Captain McAllister had visited her at her home in Lisburn on the Thursday evening, thirty-six hours after Penny's murder. She said, 'Duncan asked me not to tell the police of our affair. He said it was for the sake of Penny's memory not to tell the police.'

She recalled that the following day she saw McAllister again, this time in his house: 'He said that the police had asked him outright whether we were having an affair and he said to me that he had denied it and asked what I had told them. I said that they had not asked me and I had not told them. He told me, "Well don't, don't tell them anything." '

During further questioning Susan Christie revealed that she had told Duncan McAllister that the only person who knew of their affair was her close friend Sandra Gordon. She went on: 'Duncan asked, "Did you ever tell her my name?" and I replied that she knew who he was. He then asked me whether she would keep her mouth shut and I replied that I didn't know. Duncan then told me to go and ring her and find out.'

Susan Christie explained that she could not phone from McAllister's house because he feared his phone was bugged, so together they went to public phone box and rang Sandra and Susan made an arrangement to meet her the following morning, Saturday. She also phoned her father to tell him she would be home late. He informed her that the police had said they were coming to see her earlier than planned, at nine in the morning rather than eleven. She told McAllister.

Mr Smyth asked her: 'When you parted that evening did you know that Duncan McAllister was going to tell the police of your affair?'

'No, my lord.'

Susan Christie had been examined by her counsel for nearly six hours. Now she would face the sternest of tests, cross-examination by the prosecuting counsel, Mr Creaney.

After a few minutes, Mr Creaney asked, 'Would you agree that for four days you told the police a tissue of lies?' Christie replied quietly, 'Yes.'

He went on, 'When you walked the route with the police; when you went for that walk; when you helped the artist draw the impression; when you helped to make the photofit; was that all an act on your part?' Christie told him, 'No. At that time I believed that I had been attacked.'

'When do you say that you first believed that you killed Mrs McAllister?'

'I never accepted the fact until several weeks ago, my lord.'

'Is that the truth?'

'I have never fully accepted that I killed her.'

'You now accept that you killed her?'

'Yes, my lord.'

'Do you know why you killed her?'

'No.'

'Well have you thought about it?'

'I have thought about it.'

'Well, what are your conclusions, Miss Christie?'

'I would say now that I killed her for Duncan.'

'What do you mean when you say that you killed her for Duncan?'

'I mean to get Duncan.'

'For yourself?'

'Yes.'

'What do you regard that as? How do you describe that motive for killing?'

'That I was in love with him. I would have done anything.'

'Did you kill this unfortunate woman out of jealousy?'

'I would say that jealousy had a part in it, yes.'

'Was jealousy not the sole reason?'

'In my opinion, no. It was not solely jealousy.'

'Was it selfishness; a selfish jealousy to remove her as an obstacle in your plans for yourself and Captain McAllister?'

'I never saw Penny as an obstacle.'

'What did you see her as?'

'I saw Penny as almost a victim because of my affair with Duncan. Penny never deserved it. She was never hostile towards me or anything. She was always so nice to me.'

'She did not deserve to get killed, did she?'

'No, she never.'

'She never did anything at all to hurt you?'

'No.'

'She never provoked you?'

'No.'

'She never showed any animosity towards you?'

'No, my lord.'

Then, dropping his voice so people in the public

gallery leaned forward to catch his every word, Mr Creaney asked, 'Are you sorry that you killed her?'

'Yes, I am my lord,' she said in a quiet voice, almost a whisper so that the official shorthand writer had to lean towards her to hear her words.

Within a split second the mood in the court had changed as Mr Creaney asked: 'When you have been crying in this court have you been crying because of the sorrow in relation to Penny or sorrow for yourself?' Christie replied, 'When I talk about my baby I cry first for myself, for my loss. When I talk about what happened in that forest it is for her, what I did to her.'

'You see, I suggest to you that you have no remorse?'

'You are wrong, you are wrong, sir.'

He went on: 'If I suggest to you that your talk about your baby is simply an attempt to excuse yourself, is that not the case?'

'Sir, I have no excuse for what happened.'

Speaking more forcefully, Mr Creaney asked, 'Did you kill Penny because time was running out and she would be off with her husband to Germany and you would have lost him?'

'I was scared of losing Duncan, yes.'

'And the opportunities to get her were rapidly disappearing, were they not?'

'They were because I did not know where they stood.'

'Wednesday 27 March was your last opportunity

to get her on her own, is that not so?'

'It would have been, yes.'

Susan Christie flinched visibly as Mr Creaney asked, 'When you tell this jury that you forgot about this killing is that because it was a very messy business and that it shocked you? Is that the truth of it?'

'I have no explanation myself as to why I could not remember. All I know is that I cannot say.'

And then under cross-examination Susan Christie became entangled in her shoelaces, the laces she remembered stopping to tie in the darkest part of the forest just seconds before killing Penny.

Mr Creaney asked, 'Do you recollect mentioning that you bent down to tie your shoelaces?'

'Yes.'

'Of course that was a device, was it not? Your shoelace was not undone?'

'No, it was undone.'

'It was undone?'

'Yes, I think so.'

'You think it was undone?'

'Yes.'

'It was not undone?'

'I am not sure. I think it was undone but for what-ever reason Penny went on ahead.'

Mr Creaney suggested that Susan Christie's shoelace was not undone, that it was simply a device, a ploy so that Penny would be persuaded to go on, giving Christie time to get out her knife. 'Is that not right?' he asked.

'I do not remember it now,' she replied.

'But you do remember now bending down or pretending to bend down to tie your shoelaces?'

Ignoring the question, Christie replied, 'I remember Penny going on ahead.'

'Is there anything else that you remember now that I have prompted you about this?'

'As I say, Penny went on ahead and the next thing was she was lying on the floor.'

'Do you remember laying her down on the path?'

'No, she was lying on the floor.'

'She did not get on the floor on her own, did she?'

'Well, when I saw her she was lying on the floor, my lord.'

'Or is it that you do not want to tell the members of the jury how you lowered her to the ground after cutting her throat?'

Looking startled, Susan Christie said, 'I do not remember that.'

Changing tack, Mr Creaney asked: 'When do you say that you first realized you had cut your knickers?'

'I don't,' she replied.

'You don't?'

'No.'

'Do you remember cutting your own body?'

'No, my lord.'

'Do you remember pretending that you were injured about the leg?'

'No, I remember that my leg was very sore.'

He asked her, pointedly, 'Did you pull your tracksuit bottoms down a little bit, cut your knickers, and then put these small incisions on your flank and stab yourself on three occasions in the upper part of your thigh? Did you do that?'

'I have no other explanation but to say yes that I did do it.'

'Yes, and you remember doing it, don't you?'

'No, I don't,' she replied quietly.

'Or do you just choose not to remember doing it?'

In a voice barely audible, she said, 'I have tried to remember but I cannot remember it, my lord.'

'And do you remember where you threw the knife?'

'I don't know. I do not remember the knife.'

'Do you feel that if you saw the knife today, having seen it in court, that you might remember where you had got it?'

'Yes, I will look at it.'

While a court clerk collected the knife and brought it back into court, Mr Creaney asked, 'Do you remember holding such a knife and honing such a knife?'

Susan Christie replied, 'No, my lord.'

'Do you accept that you brought such a knife with you to that forest?'

But Susan Christie stuck to her story. 'I do not believe I brought a knife with me, no. I do not remember bringing a knife with me, no.'

Then the knife that killed Penny McAllister was brought into court and handed to the prosecuting counsel. Everyone looked at Susan Christie as the boning knife, with the black plastic handle, was shown to her. They wondered how she would react.

She was asked, 'Now just have a look at this knife for a moment please.'

There was silence as Susan Christie looked at the knife. The expression on her face did not change. Then she looked away.

'Now do you have any recollection of purchasing that knife?'

Quietly, Christie said, 'No, my lord.'

She was asked when she purchased the knife, and replied, 'I am sure I never bought any knife.'

'You are sure that you did not buy any knife?'

'As far as I am aware I did not buy any knife.'

'The fact of the matter is that you do not want to remember buying any knife.'

Susan Christie repeated her answer: 'I do not remember buying any knife.'

'But you could have bought the knife?'

'I could have. I had opportunities to buy a knife but I do not remember going out and buying one.'

The knife was taken away and Mr Creaney changed the point of his questioning. 'Miss Christie, you lived a lie or you told lies to a number of people for quite some time before Penny was murdered, and you persisted in that after she was murdered, is that not so?'

She agreed. 'I lied about the affair,' she said.

'You did that deliberately?'

'Yes.'

'You slept in her house with her husband?'

'Yes, I did, my lord.'

'You abused that house?'

'Yes, I did.'

'Whatever would happen you had determined from the summer of 1990 to continue your affair with Captain McAllister?'

'I was in love with Mr McAllister, yes. But I did not realize at that time how desperate I was and to what lengths I would go to keep him.'

'To the lengths of killing your opponent, Miss Christie?'

'Yes.'

'Or killing your rival.'

'Yes.'

'And you pretended, particularly to his wife, that your relationship with Captain McAllister was innocent, possibly a mere flirtation, is that right?'

'Yes, I did.'

'And you did it successfully, did you not?'

'No, Penny suspected.'

'Well you seem to have pulled the wool over her eyes.'

'Duncan always denied it and Penny believed

him.'

'Even on Ascension Island you tell us that she and you became friends? She did not know the antics that you were up to with McAllister, did she?'

'No.'

He asked, 'Did you get a certain pleasure, as it were, out of that?'

'I felt guilty.'

Mr Creaney took Susan Christie through the succession of accidents she had been involved in, as well as illnesses, during the years she had been with the UDA. And he asked her to tell the jury of the accidents, the scares and the dangers she had been exposed to when diving with the sub-aqua club.

Pointedly, he asked her, 'You enjoy being the centre of attraction, don't you?' She replied, 'Yes. I do admit that I do like people making a fuss of me, but no, you are insinuating that I made things up when I was suffering sickness. I was not.'

He suggested to Susan Christie that the reason she detailed her various diving accidents and experiences had been to provide a reason for the killing of Penny McAllister. 'No, I am not blaming my diving. That is not why I killed Mrs McAllister. I am not trying to make that out. At the time of one dive I did feel resentment towards Mrs McAllister because I felt at the time that she was trying to kill me but, no, I did not blame her. She was not guilty in any way of trying to harm me.'

He asked, 'When you told the jury that you

thought that Mrs McAllister was trying to kill you on the March 16th dive, were you being serious?' She replied, 'What I am saying is that at that time when she took so long to reach me in the boat that was my initial feeling, that she was trying to kill me. But it was an initial reaction and I never dwelt on it.'

'When did you first think Penny McAllister had tried to kill you?'

'I was in the water and I was giving a distress signal. I thought I was drowning.'

Asked whether she had ever told anyone else that she thought Penny had been trying to kill her, Susan Christie replied, 'I don't know if I ever told anyone that. It was just my initial reaction. Then I forgot about it.'

He continued, 'Did you go to the forest on the 27th with it in your mind that Penny had tried to kill you on the 16th?'

'No, I put it behind me. I didn't think about it.'

'By the weekend of 16 March you were resentful of Penny, is that not so?'

'I was not resentful of Penny. Penny is not someone that you could resent. She was a likeable person.'

'But you resented her?'

'I was jealous but I never ... I could say that I was jealous of her.'

'Did you imagine that she was trying to murder you?'

'No. All I can tell you is what I felt at the time. It

was just that I had come to the surface and thought I was drowning. I was wrong but I did think at the time that she was taking too long to get to me ... I thought I was dying ... that she was trying to kill me. But I know that to be wrong. She would never have tried to kill me.'

Mr Creaney suggested that Christie's account of Penny's attempt to kill her was simply an invention because she had never mentioned it to anyone before the court hearing. He continued his cross-examination. 'You are now saying that Penny McAllister deliberately exposed you to danger. Is that right?'

'Yes, that is correct.'

He asked, 'That is the death threat?'

'Yes, that is correct.'

'The death threat was in not rescuing you after the dive? Is that what you are telling the jury?'

'Yes, that is correct. She had no control under the water. It was when I hit the surface.'

Dismissing the incident as a non-event, Mr Creaney suggested, 'This was simply another unusual but not very serious incident in the pattern of your diving career?' She replied in a spirited manner, 'To you, yes, it might have been an insignificant thing. But to me as the person to whom it happened it was a major thing.'

Susan Christie was also closely cross-examined about her pregnancy. 'Did you say that at a certain stage, when you say that you were pregnant, you were playing for time?' She replied, 'Yes. I was referring to the fact that I did not want an abortion. I was playing for time. I lied because I did not want an abortion.'

'Did you consciously decide to tell Captain McAllister a lie that your doctor had said it was too early to have an abortion?'

'No, Duncan kept pestering me. "Make up your mind now," he kept saying. I just told him that story because I did not want to make up my mind then. I wanted to have the baby.'

Then Mr Creaney asked, 'There does not seem to be anybody who can say medically whether you were ever pregnant?'

She agreed, 'No, there is not, my lord.'

And Susan Christie was cross-examined about why she had not taken her contraceptive pills during the expedition to the Ascension Islands. She maintained there were several reasons, the first being that the group's luggage was delayed a day. She also lost the pills for a day, forgot to take them on occasions and was constantly sick during the trip. But she added, 'There were four different reasons but they were not intentional if that's what you mean.'

He asked her, 'You were not trying to make yourself pregnant, were you?'

'No.'

'That did not occur to you?'

'No.'

Later, Mr Creaney asked her, 'You said you wanted Duncan's child and it was very significant to you emotionally, but you never went to a doctor to check whether you were pregnant?' Susan Christie told the court she knew she had become pregnant after taking a home pregnancy test which showed positive.

He then asked her, 'As far as you were concerned you then had something you could hang on Mr McAllister. What about that suggestion?'

'To say that I did not want Duncan to acknowledge that he was the father would be wrong. I did.'

He continued, 'If indeed you were pregnant it would have put you in a strong position to bargain with him; perhaps get him to leave his wife?' Susan Christie answered, 'When I found out I was pregnant it was a shock. I never planned to get pregnant. I went to Duncan and I asked him what he thought about it. I did not say that this would mean that he would leave his wife for me, no.'

Susan Christie became distressed in the witness box when Mr Creaney questioned her about the miscarriage. She was asked to describe in detail exactly what happened. She was in tears as Mr Creaney asked, 'There was no foetus, was there?'

'No, there was just heavy loss of blood.'

'A heavy period, let us put it?'

'There were severe cramps and heavy blood.'

'A heavy period is what you experienced, is that not right?'

'Yes. But all I know is that I was pregnant because the home pregnancy test had shown positive.

And then later I started to bleed.'

Then Mr Creaney moved on to the scene of Penny's murder. He asked Susan Christie why she had taken her dog, Sapper, for a walk in Drumkeeragh Forest the Sunday prior to Penny's murder, when there were other forests far closer to her home. She told him that the other forests had been busy that day, the car parks full, so she had decided on Drumkeeragh.

'Did you stay long enough to walk to the place where the trees are very dense? She replied, 'I never went up that path.'

'So that, although you were there you did not actually happen to make it to the place where ultimately Mrs McAllister was killed?'

'The only part I went to was where all the trees are cut down.'

'You know the suggestion that I am about to make is that you went down there on that Sunday to "suss" the place out?'

'No.'

'Are you sure about that?'

'Yes, I am sure. I never went to Drumkeeragh Forest to plan to kill Penny. I never ... What I am telling you is that on the Sunday I did not go there to plan to kill Penny. I went there to walk my dog.'

Susan Christie told the court under cross-examination that the first date she and Penny made to walk the dogs had been Monday 25 March, but Penny had phoned to postpone it. Penny knew they were to walk their dogs in Drumkeeragh Forest. Asked who had suggested Drumkeeragh, Susan Christie said, 'It was my suggestion. She did not know where it was.'

Christie told the court that she had spent most of Monday 25 March in bed, crying, unhappy and upset. Asked why she had become upset, she replied, 'I was upset about leaving for Beaconsfield on 2 April. I was also upset because that weekend I spent with Duncan I wanted to know where we stood but we had not discussed it.'

'Well, had you a happy feeling or a kind feeling for Duncan at that stage?'

'I was angry towards Duncan.'

'And what about Penny? What were your feelings towards her?'

'To Penny there were no feelings of hostility, my lord.'

Susan Christie claimed that she had tried to phone Penny on the morning of Wednesday 27 March to cancel the walk because she was not feeling well, but Penny had already left.

'Were you feeling not really up to it?'

'I had just started my period and I was not feeling up to it, no.'

And Mr Creaney led Susan Christie towards the moment of murder. She told how she and Penny heard noises in the bushes as they walked and Penny thought it might be a man. She thought Penny must have been paranoid for Susan thought it was probably animals in the undergrowth.

Then Mr Creaney asked her, 'Now you say that your memory stops when you bent down, and you do not know whether your shoelace was undone or not but you bent down. And the next thing you were conscious of was Penny lying on the ground and she was bleeding from her throat?'

Speaking very quietly, Susan Christie said, 'Yes, my lord.'

'And you attempted to help her?'

'Yes.'

'And then you tell us that you were attacked by a man?'

'No. No. I was wrong. At that time I believed that we had been attacked ... I did not believe that I had attacked Penny at that time. I did not. What I am saying is that when I left Penny I know now, I know now that when I left her I ran but when I left that forest I left believing that we had been attacked. I did not know that I had done it, my lord.'

'And you say that you believed that somebody attacked your body as well as attacking Penny's body?'

'Yes, my lord ... I believed that I had been attacked when I left the forest. I really believed that I had been attacked.'

Speaking in a quiet voice again, Susan Christie went on, 'All that I can say now is, yes, that I did kill Penny. It took me over a year to even accept that. I have never been able to say, "Yes, I did kill her" but I really believed that at that time, I never killed her. It was somebody else. Now if I saw a man there I may have used his description, yes. That is the only thing that I can think of, that I saw him and that I used his description and I put him in place of me. But before this time I always thought that I was innocent. But I am not.'

But Mr Creaney continued to press: 'What I am suggesting to you, Miss Christie, is that that was a plot that you had worked out in advance and that you were carrying it into effect, that you were telling this story to cover up at that stage for the truth; that is the way in which you killed this woman?'

'I don't know when I planned it. I don't know when I planned it.'

'Did you deliberately make up a story of a man to convince the police as to what happened?'

'I must have made it up, yes. I made it up but I believed it at that time.'

'And your story fitted the facts of the killing and also fitted, to some extent, with what the police could observe on your body; that is the knife wounds on your body and the torn pants?'

'I agree with you, yes.'

'And you gave a most accurate description of the man?'

'Yes, that is correct.'

'Despite the shock that you say that you had, you were not saying, "Look, this is too difficult for me. This is something which I really cannot remember in detail at the moment." Instead you went into the minutest of details, did you not?'

'Yes, I think I did, yes.'

'Do you remember saying about the man, and this is in addition to the details of what he was wearing that you gave earlier, that he had short, layered, brown hair just about collar length? It was parted just off centre. He had blue eyes. He seemed to have a bit of a stubble.'

'If I said that then, yes, I said it.'

'And later did you say, "He had a fresh complexion. I will never forget his face"?'

'I must have, yes.'

'You invented every word of what you told the police on the night of the killing and you continued to invent it further the next day. Isn't that right?'

'I agree with you, yes. I made it up but I did not know at the time I was making it up. It was in my mind and I was just relaying what was in my mind at that time.'

'And did you tell the police on the day after the killing in relation to Penny McAllister that in the beginning there was friction between you and that Penny was jealous of you because, as a new girl, the men paid attention to you instead of Penny?'

Quietly, Christie said, 'Yes.'

'Was that true?'

Speaking even more quietly, she replied, 'As far as I know it was, yes.'

Mr Creaney raised his voice and asked her again,

'Well, was it true?'

'Yes, that is what Duncan told me. That she was jealous of me.'

'And there were times that Penny liked you and at times she did not?'

'I would say that as far as I know Penny was always friendly towards me to my face but, behind my back, I don't know.'

The following day, Wednesday 10 June, Susan Christie returned to the witness box to continue her evidence. It was her third day. She looked pale and under some strain. She gave evidence that after the killing, as she ran from the scene, she saw the boys riding their bicycles and later related to the police, in detail, how she had seen the Rice family in their red motor car, as they sat enjoying a picnic in the forest.

Mr Creaney asked her, 'So that despite your shock you were able to switch on your memory again when it came to events after the killing?'

'Yes. But why should I kill Penny, I can't explain.'

'The only thing that you wanted to avoid describing again was how you must have crept up on this woman, pulled her head back, cut her throat and laid her on the ground. Now that is the only event I suggest to you with which you were not prepared to go. Is that not so?'

Looking pale and shaken, Susan Christie replied, 'As to why I cannot remember I have no explanation.' She also denied being able to remember purchasing the knife, honing the knife or using it as well as being unable to remember ever planning the murder. She said, 'Well, I accept that there must have been a plan but what I am telling you is that I cannot remember planning it. I do not remember a knife.'

At the end of his cross-examination Mr Creaney asked Susan Christie about the principal ambitions in her life in March 1991 and, in particular, on 27 March of that year.

'I was torn between my career and Duncan.'

'Did you tell the police that your career took precedence?'

'No. If I could explain. I kept this affair secret for over a year ... and all of a sudden I had people telling me ... and I believed at that time that Duncan really loved me ... and I had policemen telling me, "No Sue, he did not love you. He was using you for sex. You meant nothing to him." Now when somebody tells you that, then you hurt inside and your pride takes over.'

'Did your pride take over?'

'I did not want them to see how hurt I was. I believed Duncan McAllister loved me as much as I loved him. But to have people turning around and saying, "No, he has told us that he was just using you for sex, you meant nothing to him." That hurts you.'

A few minutes later Susan Christie left the witness box. She appeared shaken, uncertain of herself as she walked back to the dock, her shoulders drooping. At that moment she feared she could well be convicted of murder.

Susan Christie's Mind

★ ★ ★

Susan Christie was her bright, confident, positive self on the morning of Friday 12 June, the final day of evidence in her two-week-long trial. She had slept well, woke early and ate a good breakfast. She joked and chatted with other prisoners, and she flashed a beaming smile as some of her mates shouted 'Good luck' to her as warders led her away from the remand centre for the short journey to Downpatrick Crown Court.

Her ebullient good humour would last throughout the fifteen-minute journey, and she hardly stopped chattering.

Ever since Norma Squire had known that it was a young woman who had butchered her daughter she had been curious, even anxious, to come face to face with her daughter's killer, to see what sort of person could bring herself to slit the throat of such a lovely person as her beloved daughter. Norma had asked herself a thousand times, while lying awake at night unable to sleep, what Susan Christie would look like in the flesh. She had conjured up so many images in her mind during the fifteen months since Penny's death. She felt she would be unable to cope with seeing her for the first time in court. She needed to prepare herself for the shock of seeing her daughter's killer, a young woman only a few years younger than Penny.

As Norma made her way to the court building that Friday morning she was trembling with anticipation and nervousness, knowing that finally she would come face to face with the girl she knew in her heart had deliberately and cold-bloodedly murdered Penny. There was no doubt in Norma's mind that Susan Christie had planned and executed Penny's awful, awful murder simply because she was an obstacle to her own obsessive love for Duncan.

She felt the shock of seeing Christie, as she always called her, step into the dock might be too much to bear. She wanted to have the opportunity of seeing her in the flesh before seeing her in court, so she asked a police officer if it would be possible to see the defendant before the day's proceedings in court began that day.

Norma said later, 'I didn't want it to be too much of a shock, because I didn't know how I would cope with seeing this woman face to face. The policeman took me to a window overlooking the courtyard where the vans bringing prisoners to the court parked and the defendants alighted. I watched the vehicle arrive and stop outside. I saw the van door open and then I saw Christie. She was laughing and chatting with her guards as she jumped out of the van and walked confidently towards the court entrance.'

Unbelievingly, her voice filled with scepticism and not a little anger, Norma commented: 'In those few seconds that I saw her in the courtyard Christie portrayed a totally different person to the timid, cowed little creature I saw later in the dock.'

The two weeks of Susan Christie's trial had also become a trial for both Penny's parents, Norma and Desmond. They had not attended the first nine days of the trial because they knew they would have been unable to take the strain, or the trauma of listening to the horrific evidence of Penny's murder. They knew they could not face the ordeal of sitting for days on end listening to the evidence, the witnesses detailing the killing of the daughter they had loved so much, the legal arguments and the psychiatric experts brought in to give their professional views of the state of mind of Susan Christie at the time she killed Penny.

Norma described how she attempted to strengthen her nerves when she knew she was about to face Christie and how she felt physically sick. She said. 'I was forty-five. Penny and I looked alike, so after Christie had sat down in the dock that day I stared at her. I wanted her to see Penny in me. I wanted her to see what Penny would have looked like if she had been allowed to live.'

Norma Squire could not take her eyes away from Christie's hands. She seemed mesmerized as she sat staring at the small, plump hands with bitten nails that had killed her daughter with such ferocity. She said: 'I looked at Christie's hands for a long, long time, the hands that had drawn that butcher's knife across my daughter's throat, and I felt there were dark forces in this world.'

Speaking in hushed tones, Norma went on: 'I felt evil in that courtroom. Christie looked at me, twice, then looked away. I made a big effort not to lose my dignity for Penny's sake. And I didn't. I just looked straight into her eyes and made her look away.'

Throughout the day's hearing they sat in the public gallery beside their son-in-law, Duncan McAllister, and hardly exchanged a word or a glance as they listened intently to the evidence and watched Christie in the dock.

Consultant psychiatrist Dr William Anderson Norris, with more than thirty years' experience in forensic psychiatric cases, told how he had examined Christie twice during her remand in Maghaberry Prison after reading notes on her family background and her medical history. He explained that he asked Christie to try and assess what sort of person she had become, evaluating her own personality.

'She described herself as being somewhat shy,' he said, 'despite the fact that other people saw her as over-confident and cocky. That was her word: "cocky". She said that at times she would feel nervous and yet she had an ability to compose herself and felt she was good at hiding her feelings. She described herself as a private type of person who was disinclined to talk to others about her problems and who found it difficult to share emotions and feelings. She told how she tended not to confide in people.

'She also spoke of her tendency to be a perfectionist with high standards and a desire to do well. She also had high expectations of herself. She knew she was ambitious and pushed herself to attain or achieve her ambitions.'

Dr Norris also gave evidence of Christie's sexual development, saying her periods had started when she was fourteen. She explained how each month, prior to her period, she would have swelling around the breasts, signs of fullness in the abdomen and would become somewhat irritable. Asked to explain her irritability, Christie had said that she would give short answers to her mother and when working on the army radio would sometimes give short replies to questions.

Dr Norris had also probed Christie's sex life. He told the court: 'She told me she had a boyfriend for a period of four to five months but that had not involved sexual intercourse. She had not been sexually intimate with anyone until she met Mr Duncan McAllister.'

Dr Norris had also examined Christie's medical history. He told how she had been struck and knocked unconscious by an army Land Rover in 1987, injuring her back. As a result she had been on sick leave for a month and had been on painkillers for her back injury for some months. It also included her admission to Ards Hospital with a ruptured ovarian cyst, which had not needed surgical treatment. On that occasion she was off work for a week.

Some weeks later, when on duty in Berlin, she was admitted to a military hospital with similar symptoms but after a few days' observation had returned immediately to her army duties. She had told Dr Norris of the diving incident in September 1991 when she had been admitted to Craigavon Area Hospital suffering from the bends after diving with the sub-aqua club.

He had also probed her personal habits and interests. Christie had told him she was a non-smoker and did not drink on a regular basis, probably drinking only a couple of times a year. He added: 'On these occasions she would tend to drink to excess.'

She also told him she had taken a contraceptive pill from July 1990 until April 1991 on medical advice, because doctors considered the pill might help prevent the recurrence of ovarian cysts.

The court was silent, those in the public gallery straining to listen to every word as Dr Norris gave evidence of Christie's relationships with both Penny and Duncan McAllister. As he gave his evidence Norma Squire never seemed to take her eyes off Christie, who sat in the dock, her eyes on the floor in front of her.

Crown Prosecutor John Creaney, QC, asked: 'Did you develop the history of her relationship with Duncan McAllister?'

'Yes, that is correct, my lord,' Dr Norris replied.

'And what did she say about that, please?' Creaney asked.

Norris replied: 'She said that she met him in March 1990 when she was aged twenty-one and that was at the sub-aqua club to which she had been introduced by a friend, Annette Gascoigne. She had become very attracted to him and saw quite a lot of him since the club met on Tuesday, Wednesday and Friday and they went diving at the weekend.'

'Did she say anything about his wife?' Creaney asked.

'Yes. She said his wife Penny was also a member of the sub-aqua club but at the beginning after Miss Christie joined the club Penny did not attend.'

'And what did she say to you about the situation, if anything?'

Dr Norris told the court, 'Miss Christie said she was attracted to McAllister and she used to flirt with him. Shortly afterwards they started an affair. Prior to starting the affair, however, McAllister was said to have told Miss Christie that his wife was jealous of her because of her popularity in the club and Penny felt out of it.'

He went on: 'Miss Christie also told me that McAllister had told her Penny wanted her out of the club because there tended to be friction between Penny and Miss Christie. Christie tended to be offhand with Penny and was generally unpleasant to her. Christie was flattered by McAllister's interest in her, particularly since he had such a beautiful wife.'

Dr Norris explained: 'At the outset of the affair McAllister had told Miss Christie that he would not leave his wife. He indicated that they could not go out openly and that no one should know about the relationship. He also told her that he was not prepared to risk his marriage or his career. By that he meant by associating with someone of a junior rank.'

And Dr Norris outlined for the jury their affair. He said: 'In July of 1990 they met several times away from the sub-aqua club and they first became intimate on 25 July. Then, following his return from a course in Berlin, they were intimate frequently, sometimes at his house.'

Dr Norris also revealed Susan Christie's feelings, saying: 'She told me that she found that this new relationship was a very exciting experience and said that she was living two lives. On the one hand she had her regular work in the UDR and all that entailed, and at the same time was conducting an affair with a married man. She told me she felt guilty but felt the excitement outweighed the guilt, being deeply in love with McAllister.'

And Dr Norris told of the Ascension Island expedition, as a result of which Susan Christie believed she had a much better relationship with Penny, despite the fact that during the time on Ascension she had been intimate with McAllister on three separate occasions, including when they made love during a dive twenty metres below the surface.

Dr Norris expanded on the relationship between Susan and Penny, saying, 'My lord, I recall that at this time Miss Christie said that it was not on a best-friend basis or a best-friend-type of relationship. Penny is said to have admitted being jealous of her and Susan Christie apologized to her for her behaviour, that is being unpleasant to Penny. Susan Christie said that Penny had always been nice to her and felt this enhanced her feelings of guilt in the sense that Penny was a very likeable and nice person while she, Christie, was cheating and sleeping with her husband.'

But Dr Norris added: 'However, her love for McAllister still seemed to relieve this feeling of guilt.' Dr Norris also told the jury of the time Susan Christie became pregnant by McAllister in October 1990: 'She probably became pregnant during the expedition to the Ascension Islands. When I pressed her on this, Susan Christie was adamant that the pregnancy was an accident brought about by the omission of the contraceptive pill on two successive days. She made the diagnosis of pregnancy herself, using a pregnancy test kit.'

In the public gallery, Duncan McAllister looked concerned as Dr Norris went on: 'She told me that McAllister was alarmed when she told him that she was pregnant and he gave her two options. One was to obtain an abortion, and that if she did that then he would support her emotionally. Secondly, the other option was that she could continue with the pregnancy, leave the sub-aqua club, keep the baby and they would end their relationship. If she claimed that he was the father then he would deny it.

'Miss Christie told me that McAllister reminded her that his marriage would be at risk and that he would be at risk and that he would be posted out in Northern Ireland if it was to be known that he was responsible for the pregnancy.

'Miss Christie denied there was any third option. She made the point that he left the decision up to her but wished her to make it there and then. However, she delayed making the decision, feeling that she wanted to play for time. She still loved McAllister.'

After a pause, Dr Norris continued: 'However, a few weeks later she bled for about a week. She had lower abdominal cramps and said she had a miscarriage. She did not, however, visit her doctor or any other doctor. However, at the time, she believed that she was pregnant.'

Duncan McAllister appeared even more uncom-fortable as Dr Norris continued his evidence: 'In the reception area at Lagan Valley Hospital where Miss Christie went, she telephoned McAllister, who became quite alarmed and concerned that she might have spoken to her relatives or spoken to anyone else about the miscarriage.'

Mr Creaney asked: 'Did she then go on to say what the reaction was from McAllister?'

Dr Norris continued, 'She said that he became quite upset when she told him she was pregnant. She did not want an abortion. She did not believe in abortion. Then she felt that he used emotional blackmail, and I have here in quotations, "Have the abortion or else!"

'This was the turning point in the relationship. She felt very mixed up. There were a lot of conflicting feelings. As a result of Duncan's attitude she felt hurt. At the same time she could not let go and was very dependent on him. Duncan, she said, was the only person who had known about the pregnancy. And yet she was forbidden to confide in anyone else and when she attempted to talk through her feelings she was told that she had to put the miscarriage behind her.

'She had attempted to ventilate her feelings on numerous occasions but he always found some way to avoid discussing them and told her that she had to learn to be tougher in her emotions, particularly if she was going to be a commissioned officer. Showing her emotions, McAllister told her, was unbecoming to an officer.'

Susan Christie had told Dr Norris of all the

events she said she recalled when she and Penny went for a walk together in Drumkeeragh Forest around lunchtime on Wednesday 27 March.

Dr Norris said: 'She stated that she did not recall a man being there. She recalled Penny walking ahead of her and she remembers stopping to tie her shoelaces. Penny was out of sight. Her next recall is of seeing Penny lying on the ground bleeding. She, Christie, began to scream and tried to stop the flow of blood. She then goes on to say that her first statement, that is the statement that she gave to the police, cannot be correct. She didn't remember a man being there or being attacked.'

Dr Norris said that during one of his interviews with Susan Christie only a week before the trial, she had told him, 'During the past few weeks I have been feeling depressed and worried about having to come to terms with the whole thing and accept it. I have been in prison for over a year. I have never had a chance of getting over it. I have got to bring up my feelings, how I feel, my feelings about Duncan and how Penny was killed. I have not been given a chance to let go of the past. I am constantly reminded of the incident. Part of my head says I did not do it; the other part says there is the forensic evidence and the motive. I cannot say definitely I did or did not do it.'

Dr Norris told the jury that on the two occasions he had interviewed Miss Christie she had been neatly, tidily dressed, her hair combed, and she was very relaxed. He added: 'I found her an intelligent

and articulate young woman. She smiled appro-
priately and talked quite spontaneously and freely.
Her behaviour throughout the examination was
entirely appropriate to the situation and the matters
we discussed. She was not depressed or unduly
anxious. She did become tearful when relating how
upset she was when Captain McAllister refused to let
her discuss or talk through her feelings about her
pregnancy and miscarriage. I found her mental state
quite normal.'

Dr Norris explained in some detail the
symptoms that doctors seek when examining a person
they believe might have suffered a major depressive
episode. He explained that a person must reveal five
out of nine possible symptoms during the same two-
week period before a psychiatrist would accept the
person was indeed suffering from a depressive
episode. Two of the symptoms are a depressed mood
and a loss of interest in all, or almost all, activities
most of the day and nearly every day during a given
period of time. Other symptoms include a significant
weight loss or weight gain when a person is not
dieting which would entail a person losing or gaining
five per cent of their body weight in a month, or an
increase in appetite every day. Insomnia or hyper-
insomnia (sleeping a lot) nearly every day; acute
restlessness or the opposite, sitting doing nothing all
day; fatigue or loss of energy most of the time; a
feeling of worthlessness or excessive inappropriate
guilt. The other two symptoms are a diminished

ability to think or concentrate most of the time; recurring suicidal plans or a specific plan for committing suicide.

Dr Norris explained that there were three categories for a major depressive episode: mild, moderate and severe.

The court fell silent again as Mr Creaney, speaking quietly and slowly, asked Dr Norris, 'Taking into account your examinations and all that you have learned about the case, what is your diagnosis in relation to the state of the accused on 27 March 1991?' Judge Kelly, the twelve members of the jury, the witnesses, the solicitors and their clerks, the packed public gallery as well as members of the press in Downpatrick Crown Court that day fell silent and turned to Dr Norris for his answer. They all knew full well that his reply to that question would probably be the most vital in the entire two-week trial. It was central to the prosecution case. Most people in court knew the reply to that question would probably decide Susan Christie's fate. How Dr Norris replied would weigh heavily on the jury's decision either to find Susan Christie guilty or not guilty of murder.

Susan Christie sat motionless in the dock, her head bent forward looking at the floor. Many looked for an instant towards her, trying to see what was going on in her mind at that moment and then, quickly, they switched their eyes back to Dr Norris as he began his reply.

Slowly, deliberately, in measured tones, he began

in his Irish burr: 'I felt that she had been under very considerable stress pressure. She was very unhappy my lord, and — '

Suddenly, there was movement on the lawyers' benches as Christie's barrister jumped to his feet. He had been looking, not at Dr Norris, nor at Judge Kelly, but at members of the jury. Dr Norris stopped in mid-sentence and all eyes turned to Susan's lawyer who had chosen to interrupt one of the most dramatic moments of the trial, preventing the eminent psychiatrist giving his considered opinion on one of the vital questions the jury would have to consider before reaching their verdict.

Those used to the ways of criminal lawyers, those who had spent much of their lives attending courts, knew the reason for the intervention. Mr Smyth needed to diffuse the moment of drama, to reduce the tension in the court, just in case Dr Norris did not give the answer the defence needed to plead that Susan Christie should not, could not, be found guilty of murder. Mr Smyth said he wished to raise a legal point. Judge Kelly simply asked whether Mr Smyth wished to address him without the presence of the jury. He knew the answer before asking the question but the protocol the legal system is rigid. Politely, Judge Kelly asked the jury to retire.

Mr Smyth argued that the state of Christie's mind should not be a question for a psychiatrist, but left for the jury to decide: whether Christie's state of mind at the time of the killing in March 1991 impaired her responsibility.

Fifteen minutes later the jury returned and Dr Norris continued exactly where he had been stopped by the intervention. He spoke slowly. 'In the rating that we have referred to for major depressive syndrome I would put it in the category of mild.'

Judge Kelly said, 'Just to get that clear, it means in your opinion that she was suffering from a mild depressive episode. Is that right?'

Dr Norris replied, 'Yes.'

Prosecuting counsel Mr Creaney then began to question Susan Christie's claim that she could remember nothing of the killing, nor even of buying and honing the knife. He asked Dr Norris what 'confabulation' meant, after evidence given the day before that Susan was suffering from 'confabulation' at the time of the killing.

Dr Norris answered, 'The term confabulation is used to describe when a person is unable to recall events, when they have a lapse of memory. Then they confabulate or fabricate to fill in those memory gaps.' But he added, 'That condition occurs where there is a disease of the mind, a physical disease of the brain ... And the accused was not suffering from disease of the brain.'

Sitting in the dock, Susan Christie looked nervous when Dr Norris was asked about her loss of memory. He replied, 'Her amnesia is very selective. It relates to a very specific period of time and that is around the time of the murder of Penny McAllister.'

However, Dr Norris did accept that amnesia can be a self-protecting mechanism, protecting the mind from terrible events that have occurred.

Mr Creaney asked quietly and deliberately, 'And what about amnesia extending into such matters as the purchase of a knife the honing of a knife?' Dr Norris replied, 'I do not think it would extend to that.'

Susan Christie momentarily pursed her lips, and continued to look at the floor.

Cross-examining, Susan's lawyer pressed Dr Norris on Susan Christie's depressed mental state prior to the killing and the fact that one of the reasons for her stressful state was the secret, illicit affair with a married man.

Dr Norris explained, 'The stress depends on the individual. I have indicated that Miss Christie was an intelligent young woman, a resourceful young woman. Her abilities had been recognized at the very early age of eighteen when it was thought she might go forward for a commission in the army.'

He also agreed that the miscarriage Christie suffered would be distressing and that she felt pressure building up because she was due to go to Beaconsfield in April 1991 on an officers' training course.

Try as he might, Mr Smyth was unable to persuade Dr Norris that Christie's depressive state was ever more than mild or that she was incapable of exercising control and judgement at the time of the killing. Dr Norris said, 'I feel that she had the ability to exercise control and exercise judgement as to the rightness or otherwise of her actions.'

Mr Smyth asked, 'One hundred per cent?'

Dr Norris stated, 'Yes.'

Pressed by Mr Smyth over the question of Christie's amnesia, Dr Norris told the court, 'My feeling is that she is pretending she does not remember what happened.'

Susan Christie passed an anxious weekend in Maghaberry Women's Prison in Lisburn only a few miles from where she had spent most of her teenage years. Outwardly, she remained the same self-confident young woman who had bounced around the prison ever since her arrest fourteen months earlier. In her heart, however, Christie would remain anxious until the jury had announced their verdict.

She knew full well that Judge Kelly's summing-up to the jury the following Monday morning would, more than likely, decide how many years she would languish in jail. To Susan Christie, Judge Kelly had appeared kind and considerate throughout the two-week trial, showing no animosity whatsoever towards her and, seemingly, supporting her counsel rather than the prosecution. She had always known there would be a jail sentence imposed, for she had pleaded guilty to manslaughter. She had no idea, however, whether Judge Kelly or members of the jury would believe her testimony that she could remember nothing of the actual killing because she was suffering from mental abnormality that substantially impaired her mental responsibility.

The court was almost silent as Judge Kelly began his summing-up: 'The events of this case, members of the jury, are a series of tragedies. The paramount tragedy, of course, was the vicious and gruesome killing of Mrs Penny McAllister. She was by all accounts a beautiful young woman, popular and happy, and above all innocent of any wrongdoing whatsoever. But from that paramount tragedy other tragedies flow which have brought misery and unhappiness to many — to her husband, to her parents, of course, and to his, and no doubt to her many friends.

'But there is also the tragedy of the young woman in the dock, Susan Christie, who is now twenty-three years old. Only two years ago she was virginal, chaste. and unsophisticated in many ways, with her career in the army as her solitary interest. She had never committed a criminal offence and now she has to acknowledge before you the guilt of a serious crime, the crime of manslaughter. And now she faces the most serious charge in the criminal calendar, which is the charge of murder ...'

He continued, 'One may plan a murder, one may premeditate a murder, one may prepare for a murder, but still at the time of that planning, that premeditation and that preparation be mentally abnormal. And that is something that you must not forget ...

'The ultimate question is, is it more likely than

not that Susan Christie was suffering from mental abnormality at the time that she planned and premeditated and executed the act of killing? That is what this case is all about, nothing more than that. At the end of the day it comes back to this question: is it more likely than not that Susan Christie was suffering from the mental condition of diminished responsibility?'

As the court rose for the lunch break those closely watching Susan Christie noticed a look of relief flash across her face as she was led from the court.

When he resumed, Judge Kelly spent some time examining the psychiatrists' evidence on the state of Susan Christie's mind and the Acts of Parliament covering abnormality of the mind induced by disease. He said, 'The two diseases put forward in this case by the defence are listed as diseases. Major depressive episode is a disease. Major stress is a disease and there is no dispute between the prosecution and the defence that either of these conditions is not a disease. And the conflict between the psychiatrists is that the accused was suffering from neither condition, according to Dr Norris, whereas the two psychiatrists for the defence say she was.'

Judge Kelly continued, 'The accused had never been to a psychiatrist before; she had never been treated for a psychiatric illness before, but it is not necessary in establishing this defence to show a history going back over the years to any psychiatric abnormality.'

He went on, 'The defence submit that quite apart from the psychiatric evidence, that using your own common sense and looking at this young woman, can it possibly be said that she was, to use the layman's phrase, in her right mind in planning and doing this; can you conceive of a girl of her background going out to buy a knife, sharpening it and carrying out this vicious murder, this vicious act of killing, if she had not taken leave of her senses?'

Susan Christie appeared worried as Judge Kelly went on, 'There is no doubt that the accused bought or got hold of a knife, honed it and sharpened it and attacked her victim from behind and sliced her throat. There is no doubt either that for three days she invented a lying story about a man with a knife and kept up that lie to a series of people for three days afterwards. If there were no other evidence in the case but that, that would be clearly murder, an act done with an intent to kill or cause grievous bodily harm.'

He paused for a moment or two and then went on, 'But there is other evidence ... What is central to this case, you may think, and in particular to the defence, was her affair with Captain McAllister. Both the psychiatrists cast it as one of the major factors, if not the major factor, in bringing about the mental abnormality that she experienced, and which was finally triggered off and exploded in the forest.

'These psychiatrists have said in effect that there was the passionate intensity of her love for him at twenty-one years; the sexual relationship it gave her, until then a virgin; the secrecy and sense of guilt it brought to her; the pregnancy and miscarriage that followed; his lack of support in her situation and the future uncertainty in the relationship; all these they said, with other stresses, which were minor, induced the condition of a major depressive episode or acute reaction to stress.'

Judge Kelly outlined the facts of the case in some considerable detail, giving examples of both Captain McAllister's evidence as well as Susan Christie's and showing where the evidence differed and where it dovetailed. He also examined Susan Christie's tendency to form intense dependent relationships:

'She had such with her father, but much more was such a relationship in 1990 with Captain McAllister. Dr Brown pointed out that the difficulty with such a relationship — that is an intense dependent relationship — was that the more intense and dependent it was, the more intense a depression is brought about if it was damaged or let down ...

'Now Dr Brown said that her intense dependency in her relationship with the captain and the fear of failure of her army ambitions and the miscarriage and the lack of support from Captain McAllister and the lack of other support that she could turn to all led to his opinion that her condition was consistent with a major depressive episode.

'He found this was confirmed with a pattern of symptoms which are typical of this mental abnormality; that is depression, loss of interest, tiredness, excessive sleeping, poor concentration, weight loss and contemplation of suicide.'

And the judge went on to elaborate on the concept of amnesia. 'The condition of amnesia has not been invented by Susan Christie. It is a condition which has been canvassed in very many criminal trials for scores of years. It is a condition in which the person commits the crime but does not genuinely remember the horrific parts of it.

'In a study of amnesia published in 1984 the authors looked at thirty-four people charged with killings. Of the thirty-four cases, nine of them suffered from genuine amnesia of the offence and all nine were found to be suffering from depression.'

Judge Kelly went on to discuss whether the killing had been carried out when Susan Christie was in a state of emotional turmoil, because 'the crime would have been readily discoverable and the accused, an intelligent woman trained in searching places and in the use of forensic evidence, would have known the crime to be easily discoverable'.

Speaking even more slowly, Judge Kelly concluded, 'Now, members of the jury, it seems to me that if you accept the evidence of the defence psychiatrists you will find this girl properly guilty of manslaughter. If you accept the prosecution evidence on its own you may think that the proper verdict is one of murder.

'But I want you to reach a verdict on all of the

evidence and all of the circumstances, including the medical evidence, using your common sense, considering this girl and her background, the enormity of the offence she committed.

'Do you really think she was in her right mind when she went out to buy a knife and to sharpen it and plan this dreadful act? If your conclusion is that she has failed to make out the defence of diminished responsibility, then your verdict will be one of murder. On the other hand, if you conclude that it is more likely that she was suffering from diminished responsibility, the proper verdict is one of manslaughter.'

With little or no expression on her face Susan Christie looked at the jury of eight men and four women as they filed out to consider their verdict. There was no knowing what was going through her mind. Then she too was taken below to await their decision. It would prove a long wait.

After three and a half hours the jury returned to tell Lord Justice Kelly they had failed to reach a unanimous verdict. So he told them he would accept a majority verdict, whatever it may be, murder or manslaughter. In less than thirty minutes the jury returned their majority verdict: not guilty to the charge of murder. As the jury returned their verdict, Susan Christie looked down so that no one could see her face. When she looked up again there was a calm about her face, giving away nothing that might reveal her inner thoughts. Then she was asked to stand.

Judge Kelly told her: 'Susan Christie, you have been found guilty of manslaughter, a cruel and vicious killing that has revolted and bewildered a community. It is one that has brought long-term misery to the relatives and friends of the young woman who was your victim. What you did, monstrous though it was, was an irrational act of killing. The jury have found that at the time and for a time beforehand, presumably as the culmination of a passionate and unhappy love affair, you were not in your normal mind and that your responsibility for it was substantially impaired.

'I must say that there was considerable medical evidence and other evidence in the case to lead the jury to that verdict.

'I believe the facts revealed in court during the course of this trial have brought home to you, perhaps for the first time, the enormity of what you did. I believe that you will carry that burden for a long time to come.

'In passing sentence I take into account in the first place that there is no evidence that you will repeat acts of violence. Indeed, the evidence is all the other way, that the crime that you committed was entirely linked to a set of circumstances that are unlikely to occur again. Therefore a long term of imprisonment is not appropriate. Nor is there evidence to indicate that you need psychiatric or other treatment and, accordingly, a hospital order is not appropriate in your case.

'However, it is my duty to reflect the public

concern for the sanctity of human life and in terms of the unhappiness that your crime has caused to so many. So a degree of punishment must be imposed and, in determining what the proper sentence is, I take into account all the mitigating factors which have been brought to my attention during the course of the trial.

'The length of sentence I impose means that you will still be a young woman when you are released from prison. It will enable you to start a fresh life, although you will not be free from the burden of the awful crime which you have committed. I hope that you will be able to find some degree of happiness, which so far has eluded you. I sentence you to five years' imprisonment.'

Judge Kelly's final words brought screams from Penny's mother sitting in the public gallery and she collapsed into the arms of Duncan McAllister.

Susan Christie looked quickly at Penny's mother and father and at her lover Duncan before she was led away by the warders. Her face betrayed no emotion, but she knew she had been very, very lucky. For Susan Christie not only believed she would be sentenced to ten years' jail but also believed she deserved a ten-year sentence.

Desmond Squire's eyes swelled with tears as he stood outside the court and tried to answer the welter of reporters' questions. Shaking his head as though unable to believe the short sentence imposed, he said, 'If this had been medieval times she would have been burned as a witch.'

His wife, Norma, hardly able to control her anger and her deep sorrow, said between tears, 'My daughter was a young woman with wonderful prospects. She would probably have had a child by now. I have never been vindictive in my life, but I wish a lot of evil to that woman.'

★ ★ ★

The trial of Susan Christie left a bad taste in the mouths of most people who had in any way been associated with the case. Those people included the police, the army, many witnesses and of course the family and friends of Penny McAllister.

Christie's trial appeared a remarkably one-sided affair which seemed to take its cue from the behaviour of the judge, Mr Justice Kelly, who, throughout the two-week trial, appeared to treat Christie as a young woman who could do little wrong.

He referred to Christie quite frequently as 'this young woman'. He would show her remarkable courtesies, more akin to the behaviour judges reserved for distressed witnesses than a defendant in a murder trial who had already pleaded guilty to the slaying of an innocent victim.

Judge Kelly appeared to go out of his way throughout the trial to ensure Christie's well-being, seemingly worried by any distress or discomfort she appeared to be suffering. He would ask her, 'Are you feeling well enough to continue?' or 'Could you please speak up a little so that everyone can hear?' At other times, he would ask Christie whether she was feeling all right or whether she wanted some water.

It seemed to many in that Downpatrick Crown Court that Mr Justice Kelly was speaking to his daughter rather than a woman on a murder charge, a defendant who had accepted that she had in fact killed an innocent young woman in a most brutal manner.

The character and personality of the Susan Christie who emerged during her two-week trial was barely recognizable compared with the Susan Christie known to the soldiers she had worked alongside her throughout her time in the army. Nor did those members of the Drumadd Diving Club recognize the miserable, tearful, out-of-sorts young woman presented throughout the court hearing. The Susan Christie they had known was a bubbly, fun-loving extrovert who showed great determination and an ambition to reach the top.

Throughout the trial Christie was portrayed as a young woman who had been under severe stress and strain due to various influences, but chiefly through her nine-month involvement with Captain McAllister and her alleged diving experiences, alleged pregnancy and alleged miscarriage.

Those who knew her well, however, including her army friend Annette Gascoigne, Corporal Jock Grey, who was close to Susan in the diving club, and Sergeant Davey Hudson who worked with her in the operations room, saw no change in Susan's demeanour or behaviour throughout the nine months she and Duncan were having an affair.

To many who have studied the case there was also some surprise at the witnesses who were not called to give evidence, because the evidence they could have provided would have shown the jury a more accurate picture of Christie's character and demeanour during the months leading up to the murder.

Major Clare Harrill, Penny's best friend, would have given evidence that Penny knew that her husband was having an affair with Susan Christie. She would also have stated that Penny found that she herself was expecting a child and suffered a miscarriage at the time Duncan and Susan began their affair.

Corporal Jock Grey, twenty-four, a slim 5 foot 11 inch jovial character, was closer to Susan Christie than anyone, save Duncan McAllister, in those last nine months. They spoke most days on the phone, they were both keen members of the diving club and in the three months prior to the murder they would go out together. Yet he was never called to give evidence.

Jock Grey would have said that he noticed no change in Christie throughout that time. He would have stated that he was always attracted to her, wanted to date her, become her boyfriend. They would talk about it, but every time he brought up the subject Susan would say 'No'. She wanted them to be friends, and go out together, but not to date. In the last three months, however, Christie and Jock did go out together, but only on a platonic basis. During those last three months, when Christie stated in evidence that she was feeling depressed, Jock would have said that that was far from the case. He was someone who was interested in her, who noted her moods, her behaviour, who wanted to be close to her, and so would have been aware of a change, particularly a dramatic change, in her moods and behaviour. But he noticed nothing.

He would also have disagreed with her father, Mr Robert Christie, who told the court of his daughter's 'odd' behaviour before the killing, suggesting she was not her usual self.

Jock Grey maintains that the only time he saw a change in Christie was on the Sunday, three days before she killed Penny. She seemed sullen and withdrawn on that day. He noted it because he had never seen her like that before. And yet he was not called to give evidence.

There was also Corporal Christopher May of the Royal Corps of Transport, one of the diving team on Ascension. Throughout that two-week expedition Christie, Jock and Christopher were always in each other's company. Chris May had given a statement to police about Christie's behaviour on Ascension, and drew their attention to Christie's attention-seeking antics during the expedition. He would have stated how he saw Christie, sometimes in a sullen, miserable mood, at other times enjoying the fun of the expedition and entering into all the club activities with enthusiasm. He also told police how Christie made life hard for everyone on Ascension, refusing to pull her weight and making meals particularly heavy going for everyone by her refusal to eat any food cooked by Penny.

And yet Christie told the court, unchallenged, that her time in Ascension had been wonderful and that she had found herself more deeply in love with Duncan than ever before. But Corporal May was not called to give evidence.

Major Paul Stevenson of the UDR was the patrol commander in charge at the scene of an explosion when a gunman was blown up. Christie claimed in evidence that she had been at the scene at the time and had seen the mutilated body, which had greatly affected her. However, Major Stevenson would have told the court that Christie never saw the body, because, when she arrived on the scene, it had already been placed in a body bag and was in the ambulance on the way to the morgue. But he was not called to give evidence.

Another witness who could have revealed Christie's aversion to the truth was Captain Anne McNabrne of the UDR, who had been Christie's commanding officer during most of her five years in the army. She would have been an excellent character witness, revealing Christie's progress through the army, and detailing her career as well as her attitude to work and her relationships with other soldiers. She would also have been able to refute Christie's claim, that she had personally been under direct threat from the IRA. This was not so. Captain McNabnie would have told the court that Christie was under no more or no less of a threat than any other member of the UDR. Yet she too was not called to give evidence.

Dr Galway, who had treated Christie for her alleged decompression sickness was able to give accurate evidence concerning his opinion of that alleged incident. He was not called.

Christie's frequent visits to hospital for one alleged ailment or another during those nine months were put forward in the trial to show the pressures she had been under. However, none of the doctors who were concerned with treating Christie during her various hospital visits was called to give evidence. They would have been able to reveal that on no occasion had they ever been able to find anything actually wrong with Christie and had only admitted her for observation based on her descriptions of various symptoms.

And then there was one of the highlights of Christie's story, when the jury heard of her alleged miscarriage in November 1990. Many would have believed the court should have examined the evidence of her alleged miscarriage far more closely. Extraordinarily, Christie claimed that the only reason she did not seek medical attention when she went to Lagan Valley Hospital at the time of her miscarriage was that she had apparently seen someone she knew and become embarrassed. That mystery person was never called to give evidence although Christie alleged she spoke to the person at the time. As a result, Christie alleged, she suffered the most traumatic event in her entire life, the loss of the baby she desperately wanted, alone at home, never seeking medical attention, never seeking medical help, never seeking medical advice.

And yet, ironically, all evidence showed that Christie would seek medical advice, and hospital treatment, for the slightest ailment. Throughout the nine-month-long affair with Duncan McAllister, from July 1990 to March 1991, Christie went to hospital on no fewer than four separate occasions. Virtually nothing was ever found to be wrong with her.

And yet, when Christie discovered she was pregnant, as she admitted to the court, she never went to a doctor or a maternity clinic at any time. She took no advice. Nor did she ever seek confirmation she was pregnant from any doctor or medical source. Weeks later, when she allegedly suffered a miscarriage, she again sought no medical attention. If indeed she had been pregnant it seems extraordinary that Christie never sought medical advice and she would have known that a miscarriage can produce harmful effects and even serious internal damage to a woman's reproductive organs as a result. Yet for some unknown reason she never sought advice or attention.

Annette Gascoigne, Christie's close friend during those nine months, was called to give evidence. And yet the evidence she was invited to give proved purely peripheral to the case. Later, Annette would say, 'I could have provided the court with so much more evidence about Susan Christie: her state of mind throughout that time, her affair with Duncan McAllister, and the discussions I had, on a number of occasions, with her. As a result I felt I did not give members of the jury information they should have known about her. I felt totally underused. Since that day I have always wondered why I was not invited to provide the court with more evidence.'

Another army witness, Sergeant Davey Hudson of the UDR, believes he too could have provided far more valuable evidence than he was invited to give. Sergeant Hudson had been Christie's supervising operations room sergeant from October 1990 to the time of the murder, working closely with her throughout that period. They worked together, at least twice a week, sometimes for a twenty-four-hour stretch at a time.

The Portadown operations room of 11 UDR was the focal point of all the incidents in that area of Northern Ireland. Hardly a day would pass without some form of terrorist activity. Those who worked in the operations room had to be responsible, intelligent and diligent. They also had to be monitored closely, for a mistake on their part could have ended in a life-threatening situation. Called by the prosecution, Sergeant Hudson gave evidence to rebut certain evidence put forward by Christie in the witness box. He told the court that Christie had been a good competent soldier who showed attention to detail and was most reliable.

He gave evidence concerning the incident in early March 1991, when Christie alleged that she had made a serious error through lack of concentration. She told the court she had ordered a vehicle patrol to enter an out-of-bounds area, thereby putting the patrol at risk. Christie, of course, should never have made such a decision, but referred the matter to higher authority for a decision. Sergeant Hudson informed the court that Christie had been mistaken in her evidence. She had never sent the patrol into the area at that time or given any such order. On that day he had made the decision and told the troops to leave their vehicle and go into the area on foot. He categorically denied that Christie ever gave an order without his permission. The jury was left in little doubt that on this occasion Christie had lied to the court.

Sergeant Hudson was also asked about Christie's behaviour during the critical twenty-four-hour period before Penny's murder, when Christie was on duty working her long shift. Throughout that time Sergeant Hudson was her superior officer, in charge of the operations room. The shift ended only five hours before Christie went for a walk in Drumkeeragh Forest.

Mr Justice Kelly spoke to the jury of Christie's state of mind and alleged mental abnormality at the time of the murder after her long, arduous shift. Christie had told the court she was feeling tired and unwell at the end of her shift because she had no sleep whatsoever during the night. However, Sergeant Hudson would have told the jury that during her shift Christie slept in an easy chair from midnight to 4 a.m. and then went to bed and a total of nearly eight hours' sleep. But he was never asked.

He could have further told the court that at no time during that long shift did Christie tell anyone in the operations room that she felt tired or unwell, nor did she say anything about tiredness to her friend Annette Gascoigne during their phone conversation.

Later, Sergeant Hudson commented, 'I told the court that Christie appeared out of sorts and with-drawn during the early part of her shift. However, I could have told the court about Christie's antics in the ops room that night. She laughed and joked with all the team and wasn't in the least depressed. She made phone calls in the evening which seemed quite boisterous and chatty. In fact she appeared in good form. However, I was only asked about her appearing withdrawn during the early part of her shift, giving a totally false impression of her state of mind throughout the entire twenty-four hours.' There were a number of other questions which were not raised throughout Christie's trial as well as other matters which, it is clear in retrospect, were not fully investigated during the two-week-long hearing.

It appeared odd, some would say extraordinary, that from all the evidence put forward by witnesses who had ever known Christie, including those she worked closely with in her army career, members of the Drumadd Diving Club who met two or three times a week, and friends who had known Christie during that nine-month period, only one witness corroborated her evidence: her father.

A number of vital questions that arose as a result of Christie's evidence were, surprisingly, hardly touched on by Mr Justice Kelly in his summing-up, and much of Christie's evidence was never put under substantial sceptical analysis. Perhaps if her evidence had been more closely examined and if more witnesses had been called, the jury might well have reached a verdict of murder, rather than of manslaughter.

In his summing-up Judge Kelly put great emphasis on the alleged various accidents and incidents which ended in Christie being admitted to a number of hospitals during the nine months of her affair with Captain McAllister.

First, in June 1990, Christie suffered a ruptured eardrum while diving in a swimming pool. Splintering an eardrum is considered by divers to be a minor injury, though initially painful, which only time can heal. As a result, it meant Christie was unable to dive for the eight weeks the eardrum took to repair itself.

Second, on 18 July 1990, following a dive offshore, Christie collapsed, complaining of pains in her lower abdomen. She was taken by ambulance to Ards Hospital. Doctors who examined Christie could find nothing wrong and told her the likely cause of the pain could have been a rumbling ovarian cyst. She was detained for observation for thirty-six hours and then discharged.

As a result, doctors advised to start taking the contraceptive pill, because research had found the pill could help an ovarian cyst. However, those diving with Christie that day believe her 'abdominal pains' were in fact simply a ruse to gain attention, and that there was nothing wrong with her at all.

Third, in early August 1990, there was the Berlin incident when Christie claimed she had been kicked in the stomach by senior NCOs during an army exercise. She was taken to a British Army hospital in Berlin, but doctors could find nothing wrong with her. Once again she was detained for observation for thirty-six hours and discharged. It seems from all the evidence, including the evidence of witnesses, that Christie fabricated the Berlin incident and that she never suffered a kick to her stomach or any other part of her body.

Fourth, on 8 September 1990, Christie maintained that she suffered from decompression sickness as a result of a dive on that day. In his summing-up Judge Kelly quoted a psychiatrist, who stated that the incident of the bends and other diving experiences in 1991 were 'the most frightening'. He then added, 'Now that for some reason has been challenged by the prosecution. Well, it is a matter entirely for you, the jury. I would have thought that that was a frightening experience to have this condition known as the bends which required treatment by a specialist in a recompression chamber ... This girl was going down many metres into the water, sometimes in difficult conditions.'

In other words, Judge Kelly had accepted Christie's evidence that she suffered from decompression sickness on 8 September. However, further investigation, or the calling of more witnesses, would have revealed that it would have been very difficult for Christie to have suffered a bend during that dive. All the independent evidence and the great majority of the statistical evidence points to the fact that Christie did not, in fact, suffer from decompression sickness that day.

In evidence, Christie stated that immediately after the dive she had felt itchiness around her neck, which she knew to be a sign of decompression sickness. She said the soreness in her legs so affected the drive home she twice had to stop; she developed a severe headache; she later lost control of her left leg; became dizzy and nauseous. And yet Christie did not get in touch with any member of the diving club or seek any medical attention until thirty-six hours later. All divers are told that as soon as they feel the slightest possibility that they are suffering from decompression sickness it is imperative they get immediate medical aid because the bend only gets progressively worse. It cannot get better without recompression. And Christie, along with every other member of the diving club, attended the three-hour lecture on decompression sickness. She was fully aware of the symptoms as well as the consequences of not obtaining immediate medical attention.

Christie told the court that she had contacted Duncan McAllister on the Sunday and he had driven her to hospital. That was a lie. Duncan had offered to come to her house and drive her to hospital, but she had refused his invitation. Despite her alleged condition she had driven herself to the hospital. More importantly, after arriving and parking her car at the hospital, she had then walked, on her own, without any assistance, into the hospital. And this despite the fact she had told the court she was allegedly suffering from severe pains in her ankle and knee joints.

Moreover, Duncan McAllister was Christie's dive partner that day. And he did not suffer any symptoms whatsoever, though they dived to the same depth and came up together, in stages, according to dive tables. It would be virtually impossible for Christie to suffer a bend without McAllister also doing so. And statistically, taking into consideration the depth they dived to that day and the stops on the way up, it would have been all but impossible for Christie to have suffered a bend.

The court heard from Christie that she felt the minor bend she suffered was a 'terrifying experiece'. And yet, only days later, Christie was telling her friend Annette Gascoigne about the recompression chamber and laughing and joking about the incident. She never suggested to Annette the incident had been terrifying. And despite the incident, Christie was keen to dive immediately she was able to do so, diving to below the twenty-one-metre depth she had been ordered not to exceed. These did not seem like the actions of a diver who had only recently suffered a terrifying incident.

And then there was the all-important question of Christie's alleged pregnancy and subsequent miscarriage. She had told the court that she discovered she was pregnant after allegedly missing a period, but never sought medical advice; that she confirmed her pregnancy after conducting a home pregnancy test; and that she suffered a miscarriage on 4 December.

This series of events was challenged by the prosecution. Judge Kelly told the jury, 'The prosecution suggest she was not pregnant and that she did not have a miscarriage. But where is the evidence about that? Those are bold suggestions by the prosecution, but where is the evidence?'

These questions seem extraordinary in light of the fact that, in reply to questions while in the witness box, Susan Christie admitted that when she miscarried there had been no foetus, agreeing that what she had suffered was nothing more than a heavy period. In other words, she could not have been pregnant.

Much of Christie's evidence had been taken up by what happened on Ascension and her alleged pregnancy. Most of the evidence she gave was never corroborated by anyone. Indeed, members of the diving club who were on that expedition with Christie dispute virtually all evidence she gave in court.

She told the court she had suffered from the effects of paint fumes from cans of paint stacked in the corner of her sleeping quarters. This was impossible: not one can had ever been opened.

She told the court she was suffering from constant sickness and diarrhoea throughout the expedition. She never complained to anyone during the expedition. Furthermore, the divers were away from base most days and Christie was never 'caught short'.

She told the court the heat on Ascension was stifling and that she suffered from too much sun. During the time that Christie and the club members were on Ascension the weather was not that hot. In the evenings members had to wear warm clothing and although there was air conditioning in the living quarters it was never switched on because it was never hot enough to warrant it.

But no member of the diving expedition was asked to give evidence to support or deny her claims.

At no time did Christie ever seek medical attention or advice over the pregnancy despite the fact that the instructions on every home pregnancy test tell the woman she must seek medical attention if the reading is positive. Christie apparently ignored these instructions.

Christie alleged that she became 'totally distraught' as a result of the alleged miscarriage. However, she took no time off work and never visited a doctor. More than that, within days she was diving again in a swimming pool, instructing novice divers. Even her father saw no change in her at that time.

Perhaps one of the most unfathomable facts of the case was not Christie's alleged pregnancy and miscarriage but that of the victim, Penny McAllister. For what possible reason would Penny tell Susan Christie that she had once been pregnant and had suffered a miscarriage? The two young women were not friends. In fact they did not get on at all. They saw each other as rivals for Duncan's love and attention. And yet for some reason Penny did tell Christie. It seems extraordinary that she did so when she never told her husband Duncan, nor did she tell her mother, and she loved both of them.

The only person who knew of the relationship between Penny McAllister and Christie, from Christie's viewpoint, was Christie's friend from her school days, Sandra Gordon. In evidence, Sandra Gordon revealed that Christie had told her that Duncan's wife was 'a nice-looking girl, who had a good figure and had nice long, blonde hair'. She formed the impression Christie was jealous of her.

Sandra Gordon told the court, 'On Ascension one or two of the divers had told Penny that Susan was having an affair with her husband, Duncan. As a result Penny had tackled Susan about having the affair but Susan denied it, saying that she and Duncan were only good friends and that there was nothing else to it. Susan told Penny not to believe the rumours.'

Under cross-examination Sandra Gordon was pressed to agree that she may have been mistaken or may have misheard Christie, but Sandra Gordon was adamant: Christie had told her that Penny had tackled her about the affair.

As April approached, Christie knew that she would be away from Northern Ireland, away from Duncan McAllister from the very beginning of the month. She knew she would be away for three months, attending the Beaconsfield educational course, returning to the province at the end of June. More importantly, Christie also knew that Duncan and Penny would leave Northern Ireland at the beginning of June.

She knew Duncan had made the decision to move to Germany. He had been offered a staff posting in Northern Ireland, but had elected instead to serve in Germany. Christie would have had no idea if or when she would see her lover again. But this point was never mentioned in court. This fact could have been one of the influences which might have persuaded the jury to convict Christie of murder, rather than accept her plea of guilty to manslaughter. There do, however, appear to have been other facts which could have persuaded the jury that Christie's actions immediately prior to her attack on Penny McAllister pointed to premeditated murder.

Eight days before Penny's murder, Christie suggested to her victim that they should take their dogs for a good, long walk. Penny's Gordon Setters certainly needed constant long walks to keep them fit and healthy. And Christie's young dog, Sapper, only twelve months old, also needed plenty of exercise.

On Sunday 24 March, just three days before the murder, Christie took Sapper to Drumkeeragh Forest. It would be suggested in court that she went there on that day for the specific purpose of making a recce of the forest for the murder she planned.

At some time during the week before the murder it was also suggested in court that she went out, bought a boning knife and then arranged for the knife to be honed, making it razor-sharp. To police and to the court Christie maintained that she could not remember buying the knife that she used to kill Penny; nor could she remember honing the knife or asking someone to sharpen it. And of course Christie maintained that she could not recall killing Penny.

Christie lured Penny McAllister to the murder

scene by pretending they were just taking their dogs for a walk; she left her dog Sapper at home, allegedly because he was not feeling well; she put a knife in her pocket; she wore a pair of gloves on a warm day; she walked around the forest with her intended victim for more than an hour; she carried out the killing expertly; she gently laid Penny's body to the ground; she inflicted wounds on her own body either before or after the killing; and then she made up a detailed story of an attacker in a bid to deceive the police.

And yet, apparently, Christie did all this when she was allegedly depressed, allegedly suffering from acute stress and allegedly suffering anxiety attacks. At the same time, according to psychiatrists, Christie was showing signs of depression, revealed by a loss of interest in life, tiredness, sleeping excessively, poor concentration, weight loss; a pattern of symptoms typical of mental abnormality. She had allegedly even contemplated suicide. And more. It was suggested that she was also suffering a major depressive episode.

All these matters were referred to in some detail by Mr Justice Kelly in his speech to the jury. But he would go further. Having explained the pattern in some detail, Judge Kelly then added, 'One psychiatrist said that the disease of a major depressive episode can significantly impair the mental responsibility of a person. Significant means important, notable, and you may consider that it is the equivalent to substantial.'

And there was the question of Christie's alleged amnesia, which many people in the court considered to be, at the very least, most convenient.

Christie could apparently remember everything about the facts leading up to the actual killing. Everything, that is, except one matter and only one matter: anything to do with the knife. She could not remember buying it, seeing it, putting it in her pocket or using it. She stated categorically that no such knife had ever been used in her home but she could not remember where or when she had purchased the knife, where or when it was honed or where it had come from. She maintained she simply could not remember.

It should be pointed out that if Christie had been able to remember purchasing the knife, and sharpening it, then of course it would have been very difficult, if not impossible, for the defence to argue in court that Penny's murder had not been premeditated. And that would almost certainly have resulted in the jury finding Christie guilty of murder.

In his summing-up Judge Kelly quoted Dr Hugh Alexander Lyons, a psychiatrist called to give evidence by the defence, who said he believed Christie's amnesia to be genuine. Judge Kelly added, 'So Dr Lyons's clear opinion is that the amnesia, the forgetting of the act is, in his opinion, genuine.'

There were two other matters where amnesia allegedly prevented Christie from remembering what happened. The first was the actual killing of Penny, the second was the inflicting of the wounds on her own thigh.

Judge Kelly briefly touched on those lapses of memory by quoting Dr Lyons again: 'Anything to do with the knife or anything to do with the actual killing has been wiped from her memory ... Amnesia is self-protective to the self because of the horrific memory that the person cannot bring themselves or herself to remember because it is so unpleasant.'

If Christie had remembered killing Penny, then the defence would also have had grave problems in persuading the jury Christie was not guilty. If she had remembered wounding herself that would have suggested most strongly that the murder had been premeditated because it made it likely that Christie had planned the murder and the cover-up story of a mystery attacker.

According to the Right Honourable Lord Justice Kelly the entire crux of the defence's case rested on the mental state of Susan Christie. The jury had to decide whether at the time of the murder Christie was suffering from a mental abnormality arising from either depression or acute reaction to stress, both of those mental diseases, or neither.

The main question for the jury was whether Christie was depressed and therefore not totally responsible for her actions at the time of the murder, or whether she was simply being extremely cunning and manipulative and actively misleading the court with the evidence that she gave in the witness box.

At the end of his summing-up, Judge Kelly appeared to cast doubt on the possibility that Susan

Christie could be guilty of murder. He asked them, 'I want you to reach a verdict on all of the evidence in the case and all the circumstances including the medical evidence, using your common sense, considering this girl and her background, the enormity of the offence she committed. Do you really think she was in her right mind when it was committed? Do you really think she was in her right mind when she went out to buy a knife and sharpen it and plan this dreadful act?'

He went on, 'If your conclusion is that she has failed to make out the defence of diminished responsibility then your verdict will be one of murder.' The final words of his summing-up to the jury were spoken slowly. He emphasized, 'On the other hand, if you conclude that it is more likely than not that she was suffering from diminished responsibility the proper verdict is one of manslaughter.'

After Mr Justice Kelly had heard the jury's majority verdict of not guilty to murder, he then sentenced Christie to a five-year jail term, saying, 'I hope that you will be able to find some degree of happiness, which so far has eluded you.'

The question which no one has been able to answer is why Mr Justice Kelly, an able, highly intelligent, experienced judge, should have seemingly conducted the hearing in a way which those in court felt had been biased towards the defendant, a young woman who had already pleaded guilty to manslaughter, and, in so doing, had therefore admitted to killing a totally innocent woman in the most dreadful circumstances.

But Mr Justice Kelly's professional abilities would be subjected to higher authority. And he would be found wanting.

The Question of Guilt

★ ★ ★

Lord Justice Kelly's decision to sentence Susan Christie to only five years in jail caused a storm of protest throughout Britain, and especially in Northern Ireland. It would have meant Christie would leave jail just eighteen months after the trial.

As the *Sunday Life* newspaper wrote at the time, 'If it is the case that a young and attractive woman can lose her life so brutally through absolutely no fault of her own, and that her killer can be freed in so short a time as Susan Christie, then we are entitled to ask: does the punishment fit the crime?'

It concluded, 'People are deeply perturbed that a

young woman had her life so brutally ended while the killer can walk free from jail in a year or so. There appears a deep gulf between the public perception of the Susan Christie case and the judge's verdict.'

As a result, the Attorney General's office did examine the case and asked the Northern Ireland Court of Appeal to look again at the case and the length of sentence imposed. Five months later, in November 1992, three appeal judges gave their verdict. The most senior appeal judge, Lord Chief Justice Hutton, argued that despite the evidence of the psychiatrists he considered there were a number of features in Christie's history, prior to 27 March 1991, which indicated that her residual mental responsibility was considerable.

He said, 'She had never sought medical help for her depression or stress, and she was not taking any anti-depressant drugs or sedatives. It was never suggested at the trial that she was suffering from any form of mental illness which would justify or require a hospital order requiring her to be detained in a mental hospital.

'Christie was able to continue at all times with her work in the UDR and never took time off because she was suffering from depression or stress.'

Judge Hutton continued, 'In my opinion there was a second and more important group of factors which pointed to the conclusion that, notwithstanding the substantial impairment of mental responsibility found by the jury, Christie had a very considerable degree of residual responsibility for the killing which made a sentence of five years unduly lenient.'

He went on, 'These factors were that the evidence established that the killing was premeditated and planned and, moreover, that Christie, immediately after the killing and for a number of days thereafter, took determined and deliberate steps to mislead the police and to try to conceal the fact that she had killed Mrs McAllister and to suggest that the killing had been carried out by a man who had attacked both Mrs McAllister and herself.'

Mr Justice Hutton then turned to the actual killing. He said, 'The following matters relating to the killing are not in doubt, and I consider that they establish a very considerable degree of residual mental responsibility on the part of Christie. She brought with her to Drumkeeragh Forest a boning knife 25.5 centimetres in overall length with a blade 12 centimetres long, and the edge of the blade had been honed and was very sharp. Therefore it is clear that when she set out for the walk with Mrs McAllister, Christie planned to kill Mrs McAllister and bought the knife with the very sharp blade with her for that purpose.'

Judge Hutton then discussed the state of Christie's mind immediately after the killing, saying, 'There is no suggestion that the state of Christie's mind suddenly changed after she had killed Mrs McAllister. Therefore I consider that her determined efforts to seek to evade detection for the killing by suggesting that a male attacker had killed Mrs McAllister are a very clear indication that at the time of the killing and during the earlier part of that day her residual mental responsibility was very considerable.'

In conclusion, Judge Hutton said, 'I am of the opinion that the range of sentences appropriate for the offence committed by Christie was a range of between seven to ten years, and that a sentence below this could not reasonably be considered appropriate. Therefore I consider that the sentence of five years was unduly lenient.'

He continued, 'Notwithstanding the previous unblemished record and character of Christie, I consider that the appropriate sentence in the Crown Court would have been ten years. However, the authorities indicate that the Court of Appeal can take into account the strain and burden which the second hearing imposes on the offender. Therefore I would quash the sentence of five years' imprisonment and in place of it pass a sentence of nine years' imprisonment.'

The second appeal judge, Lord Justice Murray, argued that the question of whether Christie's five-year-jail term was too lenient must be approached on the basis that Christie knew the nature of the act which she did when she killed Penny and knew it to be morally wrong.

He went on to examine pointers to Christie's residual responsibility for her crime, including the extent of her preparation and premeditation of the crime: the acquisition and sharpening of the knife; her elaborate cover-up of the crime; the obvious advantages to herself of removing her rival from Duncan McAllister's affections; the complete absence of any mental illness; and her clear admission of jealousy.

He continued, 'To my mind, the killing of young Mrs McAllister by Susan Christie was an indescribably wicked and evil deed prompted not by any grievance, real or imaginary, which she felt against her victim, nor by any hatred towards or even dislike of her victim, but by the jealousy which she allowed to find entrance to her heart and mind.

'In the result I assess as really considerable her residual responsibility for her appalling crime, a crime which cut down in its prime a young, happy and vigorous life, caused deep and lasting pain to those who have been bereaved and, I believe shocked to the core the whole community.

'It is my judgement, therefore, that Susan Christie must be severely punished.'

He too believed Judge Kelly's punishment unduly lenient and agreed that a nine-year term would be appropriate.

The third appeal judge, Mr Justice MacDermott, however, disagreed with the other two judges, defending the decision of Judge Kelly to sentence Christie to five years' jail. He did not believe Judge Kelly had been 'unduly lenient'. He added, 'He may have been lenient, he may have been merciful, but of themselves neither leniency nor mercy is a fault.'

To Susan Christie, however, the Court of Appeal review meant her sentence would be increased from five to nine years' imprisonment. In reality, with remission for good behaviour, Christie would be released in the autumn of 1995, having served four and a half years' imprisonment.

Susan Christie has never, as yet, publicly uttered a single word of sorrow or remorse for the killing of Penny McAllister.

ALREADY AVAILABLE FROM

BLAKE'S TRUE CRIME LIBRARY

DEADLIER THAN THE MALE
Ten true stories of women who kill
Wensley Clarkson

NATURAL BORN KILLERS
Britain's eight deadliest murderers tell their own true stories
Kate Kray

IN THE COMPANY OF KILLERS
True-life stories from a two-time murderer
Norman Parker

THE SPANISH CONNECTION
How I smashed an international drugs cartel
John Lightfoot

DOCTORS WHO KILL
Terrifying true stories of the world's most sinister doctors
Wensley Clarkson

VIGILANTE!
One man's war against major crime on Britain's streets
Ron Farebrother and Martin Short

THE FEMALE OF THE SPECIES
True stories of women who kill
Wensley Clarkson

WOMEN IN CHAINS
True stories of women trapped in lives of genuine slavery
Wensley Clarkson

THE MURDER OF RACHEL NICKELL
The truth about the tragic murder on Wimbledon Common
Mike Fielder

CAGED HEAT
What really goes on behinds the bars of women's prisons
Wensley Clarkson

YOU COULD WIN THE AMAZING
SLEUTH'S SILVER DAGGER!

The first twelve titles in Blake's True Crime Library series each contain a question relating to the book. Collect the numbered editions of Blake's True Crime Library, and when you have the answers to all the questions, fill in the form which you will find at the back of the twelfth book and send it to Blake Publishing to be entered into a prize draw.

HERE IS THE FIFTH QUESTION
What was the name of the judge at Susan Christie's trial?
The winner will receive the exclusive sleuth's silver dagger and five runners-up will receive three free copies of Blake's True Crime Library titles.

How To Enter
Fill in the answer form contained in the twelfth book in the series and post it to us. If you have won, we will notify you. Whether you are a winner or not, you will still be eligible for a *FREE* True Crime newsletter!

Competition Rules
1.   The 'How to Enter' instructions form part of the rules.
2.   These competitions are not open to any members of Blake Publishing or their families, or Blake Publishing's advertising agents, printers or distributors.
3.   The prizes will be awarded in order of their value, to the senders of the first winning entries after the closing date.
4.   Entries must be on the entry coupon supplied and will not be accepted after the closing date.
5.   No claim is necesary, winners will be notified.
6.   In cases where a manufacturer discontinues a product which has been specified as a prize, Blake Publishing Ltd will substitute the nearest equivalent model of similar or higher value.
7.   The Editor's decision is final, and no correspondence can be entered into.

BEAT THE RUSH!
ORDER YOUR COPIES OF FORTHCOMING TRUE CRIME TITLES DIRECTLY.

Simply fill in the form below, and we will send you your books as they become available.

Name: ....

Address: ....

....

....

Daytime tel.: ....

Card (please tick as appropriate)

Visa ❏ Mastercard ❏

Access ❏ Switch ❏

Card number: ....

Expiry date: ....

For Switch cards only

Issue date .... Issue number ....

Please send me *(tick as appropriate)*

❏ Deadlier than the Male
Wensley Clarkson

❏ Natural Born Killers
Kate Kray

❏ In the Company of Killers
Norman Parker

❏ The Spanish Connection
John Lightfoot

❏ Doctors who Kill
Wensley Clarkson

❏ Vigilante!
Ron Farebrother

❏ The Female of the Species
Wensley Clarkson

❏ Women in Chains
Wensley Clarkson

❏ The Murder of Rachel Nickell
Mike Fielder

❏ Caged Heat
Wensley Clarkson

All titles are £4.99. Postage and packing are free. No money will be deducted from your card until the books become available.